Of Irish Ways

Of Irish Ways

Mary Murray Delaney

Illustrated by Richard Rein

KILKENNY PRESS
New York

In memory of
Michael and Ellen Murray
and my brother
William Eugene Murray

This 1985 edition is published by Kilkenny Press,
distributed by Crown Publishers, Inc.,
by arrangement with Dillon Press, Inc.

Printed and Bound in the United States of America

Library of Congress Cataloging-in-Publication Data
Delaney, Mary Murray, 1912-
   Of Irish ways.
   Bibliography: p.
   Includes index.
   1. Ireland—Social life and customs—20th century.
2. Ireland—Description and travel—1951-1980.
3. Ireland—History. I. Title.
DA959.1.D45   1985   941.5082   85-24177
ISBN: 0-517-490080
   h g f e d c b a

CONTENTS

FOREWORD

There are many Irelands, though it is a miracle there should be even one.

There is the Ireland of the American pseudo-intellectual: a priest-ridden, impoverished country of a clever-talking peasantry who may live in an unspoiled natural paradise but who are, for all that, a charmingly impractical people.

There is the Ireland of the Irish-American-in-the-street: a country of ideal values realized, a land where religion truly tempers the daily norm, where love, peace, and simplicity keep the stress of life in check.

There is the Ireland of the warrior-for-justice: that symbol of tenacious devotion to human freedom represented by the dream of an 800-year-old struggle of the Irish to keep their neighbor to the East honest.

Such is the complexity of Ireland that all of these are true, each in its own way, yet each so highly qualified by the others that, by itself, each is totally false. But so great is the lure of Ireland, so impenetrable its magic, so much resembling the Mystery of Woman, that every reader and every writer finds the journey a form of the Quest. What other country so persistently dominates — or unsettles? — the Western mind?

A fraction of the size of almost any of our states, Ireland has acted a part in history out of all proportion to her size or material resources. Bieler, Toynbee, and other historians have found Ireland to have been the saviour of Western civilization after the collapse of Rome. Americans are startled to learn that more signers of the Declaration of Independence were born in Ireland than in any other country abroad — and that during the Revolution a "hyper" member of England's House of Lords laid the war itself at the door of the trouble-making Irish in America. And in our own century this same little Ireland has taken home four Nobel prizes, though it remains, otherwise, almost low man on the European Economic Community totem pole (an awkward metaphor: one can think of Ireland only in feminine terms).

If you, Irish American or otherwise, have not resolved for yourself the enigma of Ireland, why not do it here? You will, in time, form an Ireland as the morning star in your life. We can thank Mary Delaney for her moving vision of *la belle dame* and for inducting us along that path to self-understanding which all men must walk.

Long ago Terence taught us that every man is enriched by the history of others: no man *is* an island. In that sense Mary Delaney's book will reward every reader, but in a very special and important sense it will help complete the Irish American; must we not understand our fathers to know ourselves?

EOIN MCKIERNAN
President, Irish American Cultural Institute

PREFACE

WHEN I WAS FIVE years old, Eamon de Valera kissed me. President of Sein Fein at the time, and leader of the Irish Resistance Movement, Mr. de Valera had stopped in our town during one of his fund-raising drives in America. It was when I presented him with a bouquet of roses that he rewarded me with the kiss.

The excitement over my having been chosen to present the roses is what I recall most vividly about the incident. Nuns clapped their hands with joy. Uncles reached out to touch the spot where the patriot from their mother country had planted the kiss. An aunt exclaimed, "Look — he's left the mark of the blarney on her cheek," and in truth, there was a strange, pale mark on my face that had never been apparent in the past.

Blarney or not, the event marked the beginning of an insatiable curiosity on my part concerning my Irish heritage. The close relationship I enjoyed with my grandparents caused the curiosity to become even more pronounced as time went on.

When I first knew my grandmother, she gave the impression of having always been a woman of great wealth, for she had an awesomely aristocratic bearing. I can see her now standing on the porch of her white frame house, the inevitable cameo brooch perched on the collar of her black silk frock. She had, I remember, a beautiful, if somewhat imperious, way of speaking, and there were times when, kneeling beside her in the parish church, I would hide my head, trying desperately to render myself invisible as she intoned the last prayers of the Mass.

" . . . and Holy Michael, the archangel!" In that conspicuously dramatic voice she prayed to be delivered from the evils of the devil, while I, kneeling beside her, prayed for my own particular kind of deliverance. Now, I can appreciate how spirited she was. How absolutely smashing to be able to pray in tones like Sara Allgood emoting on the stage of the Abbey Theatre, and yet, with such undeniable faith and sincerity.

In the years following my grandfather's death, I lived with my grandmother from time to time. But I never really knew her. It was only after she was gone that I learned about the lean hard times. There was the portrait of my great-grandparents hanging in her parlor, which I was to find had been given to her by her parents so that she would be sure to always remember them, when she left Ireland as a young girl to come to America. I learned, too, about the way she had labored side by side with my grandfather on the farm they purchased when they first settled in Wisconsin. How she birthed and raised seven sons and two daughters, and the sacrifices she made in order that her family might have a proper education before she could achieve her dream of building the fine house in town.

Somehow, I sense the cameo was linked with her pride, for she never once spoke to me of those early struggles. I suspect she did not wish me to know about them. But I forgive the small deception, and can only bless both her and my grandfather for having managed to pass on to me some shreds of their extraordinary tenacity, a necessary ingredient for accomplishing the task of completing even the most humble piece of literature.

During those growing-up years when Grandmother was no longer around to answer my questions, I was puzzled by the fact that we had nothing of Irish history in our schools, and wondered, too, why it was virtually impossible to find books about Ireland in our public library. Even today there is not much material on Irish life and history available, which may explain, at least to some degree, why Irish Americans generally are not well informed in regard to their cultural heritage.

It is to be hoped that *Of Irish Ways* will help bridge the gap between past and present, and, in the process, honor the memory of those noble and heroic ancestors, many of whom, under the most difficult circumstances imaginable, were able to make such magnificent contributions to the development of their adopted country. If the book also serves to create within the reader a thirst for further knowledge on the subject of Ireland, it will have served a worthwhile purpose.

ACKNOWLEDGMENTS

The author gratefully acknowledges permission to include the following selections:

"Cradle Song," "The Drover," and "A Poor Scholar" by Padraic Colum, from *Collected Poems of Padraic Colum;* "The Hedge Schoolmasters" by Seumas MacManus, from *The Story of the Irish Race*. Reprinted by permission of The Devin Adair Company.

"A Christmas Childhood" by Patrick Kavanagh. Reprinted by permission of Mrs. Katherine B. Kavanagh and The Devin Adair Company.

Excerpt from *Drums under the Window* by Sean O'Casey. Reprinted by permission of Macmillan, London and Basingstoke, and Macmillan, New York.

Excerpts from *Twenty Years A-Growing* by Maurice O'Sullivan. Reprinted by permission of Chatto & Windus Ltd., London.

Thanks are due the following people who helped with the loan of books or responded so generously to the author's request for additional information on Ireland:

Joseph Flood, Mr. V. A. Fitzpatrick, Olive Grady McAndrews, Comdt. C. B. O'Donaghue of Co. Cork, Nora Ryan of Ardfinnan, Co. Tipperary, Mrs. John Byrne, Mrs. Alice Rogers, Mrs. Harry Blackmun, Margaret Moser, Sister Maria Clotilde, Kathleen Leet, Dr. William Neville, Ethel Tigue, George Heeren, Adalade Hennessey, Hugh Walton of Lufthansa Airlines, Father Peter Quinn, Columbian Fathers, Father Farrell Sheridan, C.S.SP., Holy Ghost Missionary College, Kimmage, Dublin;

Bord Failte Eireann, Dublin and Chicago, especially Maurice Dunne and Christine Miller of Chicago; Maria White of *Failte romhat go h-Eirinn* (Ireland of the Welcomes), Dublin; and Bridget Higgins of Coras Iompair Eireann, Chicago;

Bryan (Walter) Guinness (Moyne, Baron of Bury St. Edmunds), Vice-Chairman, A. Guinness & Co., Dublin;

Dr. Patrick J. Dowling, Secretary of the Irish Literary Society, London, and author of *The Hedge Schools of Ireland;*

Dr. Eoin McKiernan of the Irish American Cultural Institute, for contributing a condensed list of significant dates in Irish history;

The Honorable John Lynch, then Prime Minister of Ireland, who made it possible for me to receive the Eire-Ireland Bulletin of the Department of Foreign Affairs from the Press and Information Counsellor, Embassy of Ireland, Washington, D. C.;

The Honorable Eamon de Valera, then President of Ireland, who so kindly granted me an interview June 23, 1971.

And finally, my thanks go to Ida Weinblatt and Ebel Girard for the diligence and patience displayed while typing the first draft of the manuscript; and to Delaney, Joyce & O'Dell Travel for allowing me the necessary time to research and complete *Of Irish Ways*.

ULSTER

DONEGAL

Derry

DERRY

ANTRIM

Donegal

TYRONE

Belfast

CONNACHT

Sligo

SLIGO

FERMANAGH

MONAGHAN

Armagh

DOWN

MAYO

LEITRIM

CAVAN

ARMAGH

Dundalk

ROSCOMMON

LONGFORD

LOUTH

GALWAY

WESTMEATH

MEATH

Galway

Athlone

Dublin

DUBLIN

OFFALY

KILDARE

Kildare

WICKLOW

Wicklow

LAOIS

CLARE

Kilkenny

Carlow

CARLOW

Limerick

TIPPERARY

KILKENNY

LIMERICK

Cashel

WEXFORD

Clonmel

Wexford

Tralee

Waterford

WATERFORD

LEINSTER

KERRY

CORK

Cork

MUNSTER

IRELAND

CHAPTER 1

THE EMERALD ISLE

IRELAND IS AN old woman who has managed to keep her beauty without the aid of cosmetics. Gifted with an extraordinary quality of magnetism, symbol of man's eternal quest for freedom, she seems to hold forever captive her far-off sons and daughters.

"Eternal is the fact that the human being born in Ireland and brought up in its air is Irish," said George Bernard Shaw.

Mary Blake, longing for the green-robed splendor of her motherland, expressed a similar thought when she penned these lines more than a hundred years ago:

If I had never heard the name of thy sorrow and
strength divine,
Or felt in my pulses the flame of fire they had
caught from thine;
I would know by this rapture alone which sweeps
through me now like a flood,
That the Irish skies were my own, and my blood
was the Irish blood.

There is a uniqueness about the Emerald Isle that is difficult to define. Sometimes, standing in the wet weird light of the Atlantic, one is almost inclined to believe in the existence of the "little people." Even the most sophisti-

cated skeptic would probably agree that if there were such
a thing as the "little people" they would certainly be found
in Ireland!

Even the shape of the country is unusual. At first glance
it resembles some prehistoric animal like a dragon, which
is appropriate enough when one stops to consider the
ancient beginnings of this country. Notice the beak-like
mouth above Dublin, the ears attached at Donegal, the
Mayo and Galway wings, and to the southwest, the forked
tails of Clare, Kerry, and Cork. Turn the map sideways
and you will see the shape of a Scottish terrier. Viewed
from a plane window, just before landing in Shannon, the
island blurs and seems to dissolve in the strange, misty
light, like a ghost rising up from the sea.

Ireland is an island of 32,424 square miles, its greatest
length 302 miles, its greatest width, 189 miles. Because of
the winding, changing coastline, especially from Donegal
to Cork, there is no part of the country that is more than
seventy miles from the sea.

Completely surrounded by the sea, Ireland has eight
hundred lakes and rivers, and is ringed with mountains.
The highest of these is Carrantuohill at 3,414 feet, near
Killarney in County Kerry.

The climate, like the people, is gentle. The average
temperature in Feburary, the coldest month, is forty-two
degrees, while in the warmest months of July and August,
temperatures hover in the seventies. As for snow, if it comes
at all, it is inclined to disappear like the dew at dawn. The
Irish insist there is no such thing as rain in Ireland, merely
soft weather, a drift of silvery mist coming down off the
mountains, carrying a scent of sea and heather.

Because of early geological conditions, Ireland became
an island before Britain. This is why certain plants such
as the strawberry tree and the flowered butterwort are

found in Ireland, but not in Britain. This early severing of the land between the two countries also accounts for the difference in fauna distribution. For example, there are only two kinds of mice in Ireland, while there are four in Britain. The little freshwater sponge found in Irish lakes are not found in Britain. And for the benefit of those who doubt, there are no snakes in Ireland!

In parts of Ireland the effects of glacial times are still in evidence, particularly in Kerry and Wicklow where there are still traces of glacial sand and transported boulders. Much of the beauty of Ireland's mountain lakes and corries is due to the effects of the Ice Age.

A glance at the map would suggest Ireland is small enough for a visitor to see everything in two or three weeks, but be assured it is virtually impossible to see everything worthwhile in that amount of time. Should anyone suggest that a certain route around the island might be uninteresting, pay no heed. There is not a single route in Ireland lacking in interest!

The visitor, whether searching for leprechauns or merely seeking to find the secret of Erin's enchantment, should allow himself a generous amount of time in which to complete his journey. In spite of the fact that Ireland occupies less space than the average state in America, it takes much longer to travel from one place to another. This is not so much due to the condition of the roads, which despite the rising hills and hairpin turns are fairly good, but rather with the leisurely pace of the people.

Ask a countryman how to get to Ballyshannon and he is apt to converse with you at great length. You will want to prolong the chat, and as you learn more about the Irish you will find yourself wanting to adopt their ways. It is essential that you shed the "hurry, hurry, the sky is falling" philosophy; otherwise, you will miss many of the unexpected treasures that pop up in your path through Ireland.

For example, the old man sitting at the side of the road chewing on a wisp of straw may be one of the last of the old Gaelic storytellers. He will charm you with his wit, spin tales for you, and since he is apt to toss off a bit of blarney now and then, you might as well know the meaning of the word: Blarney is the truth as only an Irishman can tell it!

The country is divided into four provinces, often called Ireland's "Four Green Fields" in song and legend. Each province is made up of several counties:

Connacht	Leinster	Munster	Ulster
Galway	Carlow	Clare	*Antrim
Leitrim	Dublin	Cork	*Armagh
Mayo	Kildare	Kerry	Cavan
Roscommon	Kilkenny	Limerick	*Derry
Sligo	Laois	Tipperary	Donegal
	Longford	Waterford	*Down
	Louth		*Fermanagh
	Meath		Monaghan
	Offaly		*Tyrone
	Westmeath		
	Wexford		
	Wicklow		

The counties marked by an asterisk belong to Northern Ireland and are controlled by a Parliament of Belfast, which is subordinate to the British Parliament. A glance at the map of Ireland will show, however, why it can be confusing to refer to the six separated counties as Northern Ireland, since County Donegal, belonging to the Republic, is actually the northernmost county. It is equally misleading to think of Northern Ireland and Ulster as synonymous, since Cavan, Donegal, and Monaghan, though a part of the province of Ulster, belong to the Irish Republic.

The tie that binds sons and daughters to the county of their ancestors is exceedingly strong, so it is important to make a brief mention of each of them. Since the six separated counties will be discussed in a subsequent chapter, we shall confine our present explorations to those counties that make up the Republic of Ireland.

Donegal, with its fjords and glens and towering mountains, is one of the most beautiful parts of Ireland, and although it is the most northerly county, it is nevertheless a favorite vacation spot. The people are hardworking, patient, and skilled at weaving tweed by hand. Donegal is a great place to cycle or walk. Its foundations are made up of all sorts of interesting rocks which add extraordinary form and color to the scenery. The popular seaside resort of Bundoran has a long, sandy beach, and on either side of the beach is a range of cliffs which the waves have managed to carve into fantastic lavender-blue shapes.

Near the town of Mountcharles in Donegal, an impressive Celtic cross marks the grave of Ireland's beloved Queen of Song, Ethna Carbery. There, in the words of one of her last poems, ". . . the purple mountains guard her, the valleys fold her in."

The county of Donegal is blessed with many lakes where trout is abundant. Lough Derg ("Red Lake"), surrounded by moors and hills sprinkled with heather, is where St. Patrick is said to have spent forty days of prayer and fasting in one of the mysterious caverns on an island in the middle of the lake.

Just outside the town of Donegal, and still protected by the sea wall, is the remains of a Franciscan friary. Here at Donegal Abbey the writing of the Annals of the Four Masters was completed. This impressive compilation, written by the great O'Clerys and Fearfasa O'Mulconry, covers early Irish history up to A.D. 1616. The two bound volumes

that make up the work are housed in the library of the
Royal Irish Academy.

Ballyshannon, the largest town in south Donegal, is built
on the rising banks of the Erne River. To the northwest of
Ballyshannon, on the Kilbarron road, is the site of the
Abbey of Assaroe (Eas Aedha Ruadh, "the Falls of Red
Hugh"), named after an early king who was drowned in
the falls. Founded in 1178, little is left of the abbey except
for some fragmentary walls and the graveyard where bees
hum a requiem over the tomb of the O'Clerys.

Across the bay is Sligo, a picturesque town in the county
of Sligo with a population of approximately fourteen
thousand. Sligo, on the main trade route between Donegal
and the west, is an important depot for Galway homespuns
and Donegal tweeds. The Irish name for Sligo is Sligeach,
or "Shelly River." Guarded on one side by the Knocknarea
Mountains and on the other side by Benbulben, the town
looks northward to wooded green, brown, and grey hills.
Behind them rise the rocky heights that keep the black
wind from blowing in off the Atlantic.

Under bare Benbulben in Drumcliff the poet Yeats is
laid to rest. "Cast a cold eye on life, on death. Horseman,
pass by," reads the epitaph written by the poet himself. And
although William Butler Yeats was born at Sandymount
near Dublin and died in the south of France, he will be
forever associated with Sligo and the tiny island of Inishfree
which he immortalized in his lovely lyric, *The Lake Isle
of Innisfree.*

Because of the centuries of trade with Spain, Galway
exhibits many features of Spanish influence, both in its
architecture and in the dress and manners of its people.
The western portion of the county, called Connemara, lies
between Lough Corrib and the Atlantic. Like Mayo,
Connemara is sometimes bleak and then again, a place

of unbelievable scenic grandeur. Dominated by the rocky mountain range known as the Twelve Bens, and holding within its area a great many Irish-speaking people, one has the feeling he has stepped into another age. Indeed, this remote part of Ireland is a place where native wit and courtesy have remained unspoiled. In many areas, only a few crows and seagulls fly up over desolate and lonesome lands, but further out toward the Atlantic there are rock-fringed inlets and brown-shawled women moving among white thatched cottages. Here and there fern and heather struggle to clothe the naked rocks and then give up, as if sensing the washed cliffs have a beauty of their own.

In the tiny village of Kinvara, Dunguaire Castle, with its excellent cuisine, awaits its onslaught of guests. Like Bunratty Castle, Dunguaire holds a nightly medieval banquet. Fifty miles from Shannon airport, the castle turns a pale luminous pink in the glow of sunset, a sharp contrast to the gray waters of Galway Bay. King Guaire, a hospitable man who reigned over the whole province of Connacht, occupied the castle in the seventh century. In more recent times, James Joyce's friend, Oliver St. John Gogarty, owned it.

Three miles out of Liscannor in County Clare, the Cliffs of Moher rise in breathtaking majesty above the sea nearly seven hundred feet and extend for five miles along the Atlantic Coast. This impressive precipice is especially interesting in the nesting season for the quantity and variety of strange sea birds it attracts.

County Mayo, God help us! Mayo does indeed contain some of the bleakest country in Ireland. Nevertheless, it also contains some of Ireland's loveliest scenery, boasting a magnificent coastline as well as cliffs, islands, and sandy beaches. Here Ireland's holy mountain, Croagh Patrick, rises up more than twenty-five hundred feet from the shore of Clew Bay. Beyond it lies Achill, the largest island off the Irish coast. The people in County Mayo, if somewhat austere, are pleasant, intelligent, and have a profound sense of responsibility. They also seem to live to a ripe old age; it is not uncommon to find a man of eighty — a stage of life he is apt to refer to as "the youth of old age" — contemplating the purchase of a new motorbike.

In the northern part of the county there is a place called Pontoon, one of Mayo's many famous angling resorts. Situated between Lough Conn and Lough Cullen, it takes its name from a single-arched bridge that spans the stream. On the bridge, one can stand for hours gazing at the beautiful, black, and terrible waters where waves leap up in gray frozen sheets, seeming to seek warmth from a sky that holds no sun.

To watch the waves leaping up on Lough Cullen in the morning and see the moon go down on Galway Bay that night is a vivid contrast in mood. The city of Galway has existed near the head of Galway Bay from the earliest times. According to the Annals of the Four Masters, a fort was erected here by the Connachtmen in A.D. 1124. When Richard de Burgo took the city in 1232, Galway became an Anglo-Norman colony with families among its settlers whose descendants were later known as the Tribes of Galway. Thumbing their noses at the native Irish, these settlers in 1518 enacted a bylaw that stated, "Neither O nor Mac shall strutte ne swagger thro' the streets of Galway." Following a number of successful raids, however, the natives inscribed on the West Gate of the city this plea to the diety: "From the fury of the O'Flahertys, good Lord deliver us."

On the other side of the Shannon is County Limerick. Limerick City is the third largest city in Ireland. Famous for bacon-curing and butter-making, it is also the center for tobacco-making in the South. The women of Limerick, well-known for the guipure lace they make at the Convent of the Good Shepherd, also have a reputation for beauty.

Each May, Croom holds a Limerick Festival to commemorate County Limerick as the birthplace of the limerick. An amusing story told about the limerick concerns one of the fathers of the modern limerick, Sean O'Tuomy. He was once forced to go into the service of Mrs. Windham Quin of Adare, and being no fonder of his wattle (cane)-carrying mistress than he was of the task of caring for her hens, was driven to describing her thus:

> 'Tis very well known I have always shunned
> Contention, clamour and jawing,
> And never much liked the chance of getting
> A barbarous clapper-clawing;
> I always passed on the other side
> When I heard a hag's tongue rattle,
> Until I happened to stumble on you,
> Oh! dame of the slender wattle!

With a complete change of mood, we leave Limerick and follow the Shannon to County Kerry. Coming down from the north counties where mountains are so bare and bleak and startlingly beautiful, one is struck by the contrast of the southern mountains, soft and lovely and drowsing under lavender heather quilts.

Killarney is still unspoiled and seems to defy the painter or poet to succeed in capturing its infinite variety of shape and color, or come close to describing the beauty of its many lakes and glens. Like the Gaelic storytellers of old, Killarney men in jaunting carts will delight you with their tales as they drive you past Kate Kearney's Cottage and along narrow roads where lambs crouch on mountain rocks like little white clouds. Resting for awhile at the Gap of

Dunloe, one can gaze up at the head of the gap, 795 feet above sea level, and listen to echoes reverberate among the rocks and hills in an eerie fashion.

A trip around the Kerry Ring reveals quite a different pattern of shapes and colors. This broad peninsula stretches southwest from the Killarney region for nearly thirty-six miles and has an average width of fifteen miles. Kerry has many quiet little resort towns, such as Ballyheigue, where amethysts and Kerry diamonds may be found in the cliffs and rocks. On the road that takes you around Kerry Head, you will come on other unexpected treasures: an old church-yard, a round tower, or a tiny cemetery beside a farmhouse where a child, shy as a leprechaun, will draw you in to look at the place where her uncle, the bishop, is buried.

Although the River Lee is associated with the county of Cork, so too is Blarney. Not far from gay Cork city is Blarney Castle. Climbing to the top and leaning back over a battlement eighty feet up, you may kiss the stone that is guaranteed to bestow on you the gift of eloquence.

Approaching Cork by way of the harbor at Cobh is comparable to standing at the top of Pike's Peak and knowing for one awesome moment that there truly is a place called Heaven. Mist, ignited by the morning sun, rises up over the city where houses are stacked on terraced hills like toys, and as the forty-seven bells of St. Colman's Cathedral begin to chime, one feels he is indeed approaching the Gates of Heaven. Strangely enough, Cobh means "haven." Yet how ironic that it was from this "haven" emigrants embarked on their sad, perilous journeys during the years following the famine.

Around Bantry Bay and Glengarriff there are gardens with beds of brilliantly colored flowers that are almost tropical in their luxuriant growth. Glengarriff, warmed by the Gulf Stream, has an abundant growth of arbutus, fuchsia, yew, and holly. Bantry House in Bantry Bay has an almost jungle-like garden alive with masses of wisteria. Bantry House, one of the few family houses open to the public, is an elegant example of a sixteenth century mansion and of the way the gentry lived when English earls dominated the fortunes and politics of the Irish.

Before going on to Waterford, we stop at the interesting resort of Youghal, pronounced "Yah," meaning Yew Wood. This resort at the mouth of the Blackwater River is noted for tennis, fishing, and boating. Long ago, Sir Walter Raleigh was mayor of the town and his house, Myrtle Grove, still stands, a stately Elizabethan mansion.

The city of Waterford, located in the county of the same name, first gained importance as a settlement of Danish Vikings who occupied it as early as A.D. 853. The fourth largest town in south Ireland, Waterford is noted for several important industries, such as meat-processing, furniture-making, iron-founding, and footwear. Waterford's world-famous glass industry has been revived in recent years. In the county of Waterford are many seaside resorts and quiet market towns that lie beneath the slopes of the Knock-mealdown Mountains. Waterford's original name was Cuan-na-groith, "Haven of the Sun."

Continuing on up into County Wexford, which is about fifty miles long and twenty-four miles broad, we find a land that rolls and dips between winding hollows and road-side apple trees. Through its wide and fertile valley runs the River Slaney. Wexford ("the sea-washed town"), was besieged and taken by the Normans in 1169, and in 1649 Cromwell captured the town, butchering its inhabitants. The extreme south of Wexford was the first part of Ireland to be colonized from Great Britain. The country is noted for its excellent breed of horses, and fox-hunting is popular in the windswept hills.

In the neighboring county of Wicklow, great masses of domed granite mountains pierce the sky, and hill-encircled lakes decorate the countryside. A favorite holiday spot for Dubliners, it is easy to see why Wicklow is called the Garden of Ireland. Yet, in the seventeenth century, the town of Wicklow was the object of many attacks while the O'Tooles and O'Brynes contended with the English for its possession. Exploring the Wicklow Mountains, aware of the eerie whispers feathering the silence, we cannot but wonder if the unsubdued O'Tooles and O'Brynes who made the mountains their stronghold for centuries have come back to haunt the place.

Scattered around the lakes of Glendalough ("Glen of Two Lakes") are some of Ireland's most treasured ruins. It was here that St. Kevin came to seek solitude. Living for some years as a hermit, he often slept in the hollow of a tree. One of the most interesting remains associated with the saint is the Deer Stone, an artificially hollowed stone into which, legend says, St. Kevin used to milk a mysterious white doe to provide food for a child he found abandoned at his hermitage.

Pausing in Avoca, near Tom Moore's Tree, and contemplating the white petals of the wild cherry trees fanning out against the emerald hills, we recall the lines in which the poet describes the Vale of Avoca:

There is not in this wide world a valley so sweet
As that vale in whose bosom the bright waters meet
Oh! The last rays of feeling and life must depart
Ere the bloom of that valley shall fade from my heart.

In the Avoca district, just outside Woodenbridge, is a place where the goldsmiths of ancient Ireland obtained much of their material.

Although there are no gold mines in Dublin, there is a wealth of interest for the visitor in this small county: Dublin city, the Abbey Theatre, St. Stephen's Green, Joyce Tower (a tower that actually was occupied by Joyce's friend, Oliver St. John Gogarty), mold-scented bookstalls, swans floating, arched bridges, the River Liffey, Trinity College Library and the Book of Kells, Irish Georgian architecture, and streets where once lived Daniel O'Connell, Brendan Behan, Shaw and Swift, Goldsmith and Beckett and O'Casey, and Oscar Wilde.

Off now to Meath, a county once ruled by pagan and early Christian kings of Ireland. The Hill of Tara in Meath, once the seat of High Kings, was for centuries the religious, political, and cultural capital of Ireland.

Nearby Louth, a fertile county with a coastline of sandy bays, is Ireland's smallest county. Nevertheless, it has been historically important. Its principle town of Dundalk was a frontier town of the English Pale, a name given to that area of the country brought under English control by Henry II in the twelfth century. Dundalk is also associated with the famous warrior and hero of Irish legend, Cuchullain, leader of the Red Branch Knights, who lived around the time of Christ.

West of Louth is Monaghan, the county which for many years was the home of Sir Tyrone Guthrie. Monaghan also holds within its boundaries the village of Aughnakillagh, birthplace of James Connolly, one of the leaders of the 1916 Easter Rising; and Rockcorry, birthplace of John R. Gregg, the American immigrant who pioneered the Gregg system of shorthand.

On to Cavan — and up the southern slopes of Cuilcagh Mountain. Here is the Pot of Shannon where Ireland's largest river has its source. In County Cavan ("The Hollow"), near the little town of Virginia, is Cuilcagh House, where Jonathan Swift began writing *Gulliver's Travels*. The very northern section of Cavan is a wild district of bog and mountain.

One of the most celebrated of Ireland's holy places is found on the banks of the Shannon in County Offaly. This is the monastic city of Clonmacnois which flourished under the patronage of several early Irish kings, including Rory O'Connor, Ireland's last High King, who was buried at Clonmacnois in 1198. St. Kieran founded the first of the famous Seven Churches of Clonmacnois in A.D. 548, and although he died the following year, the abbey developed into a great center of piety and learning. The Festival of St. Kieran, held annually on September 9, brings hundreds of pilgrims into the area. Still standing among the ruins is the Great Cross of Clonmacnois, also called the Cross of the Seven Churches. It is said that anyone who is able to meet the tips of his fingers around the shaft of the cross possesses the power to save human life in certain circumstances.

County Laois is sometimes referred to as Dunne country, because the Dunnes in the sixteenth century fiercely resisted the English. Laois is also the birthplace of C. Day Lewis, the late Poet Laureate of England. Born in Ballintubbert, Lewis left Ireland when he was a small boy, but always returned to spend his Easter holidays and summer vacations at a small seaside resort in County Mayo. Only a few years ago he returned to Ireland to take part in commemorating the fiftieth anniversary of the 1916 Easter Rising. Standing in the courtyard of Dublin's Kilmainham Jail where the fourteen rebel leaders had been executed by a British firing squad, Lewis concluded his tribute to the martyrs with these words:

> They are gone as a tale that is told, the
> fourteen men. Let them be more than a legend:

Ghost voices of Kilmainham, claim your due —
this is not yet the Ireland we fought for.
You living, make our Easter dreams come true.

Naas, in County Kildare, was the seat of the kings of Leinster in early times. St. Patrick used to visit Naas, camping on the site of St. David's, the present Church of Ireland. In Kildare there has been a great devotion to St. Bridget, the "Mary of Ireland." In fact, the busy market town of Kildare was named from the oak under which she set up her cell.

The Curragh, an enclosed plain east of Kildare, is the headquarters of Irish racing. Many famous racehorses have been produced at Tully which lies two miles south of Kildare, and on these grounds are Japanese Gardens that portray, with splendid oriental symbolism, the triumphs and disasters of man's life.

Coming into Carlow we find ourselves in the second smallest of the Irish counties. Driving through the fertile limestone land of the Barrow Valley, we stop at Muine Bheag where salmon and trout and pike leap up in the River Barrow. Muine Bheag is a sportsman's paradise, for the Carlow Foxhounds and the Mount Loftus Harriers hunt the district.

The county's principal town, also called Carlow, is noted for its beet sugar industry and flour milling. The town was walled by the Duke of Clarence in 1361, taken and burned in 1405 by Art MacMurrough, and again by Rory Og O'Moore in 1577. Carlow was the scene of battle once more in 1798 when several hundred Irish insurgents were killed during a street battle. Over four hundred of them were buried in gravel pits outside of town, and in the market square at Tullow is a statue of Father John Murphy, a leader of the insurgents who was put to death there.

County Kilkenny, bordering on Carlow, is the Sliever-

dagh Hills and the Booley Hills and the rich Valley of the
Nore. At Castlecomer is Ireland's largest coal-mining area,
a district noted for its smokeless anthracite. Kilkenny, the
county's main city, is known as the Marble City because
of its fine limestone. The word Kilkenny is derived from
the sainted abbot, Canice, who founded its first church.
Though the Cathedral of St. Canice was severely damaged
by Cromwell's soldiers, it has been remarkably preserved,
holding within its walls many marvelous relics, including
a female effigy wearing an old Irish cloak and a twelfth
century font of black marble.

Tipperary, largest of Ireland's inland counties, has the
Galtee Mountains in the south as well as the Knockmeal-
downs. Flowing from north to south through the county is
the River Suir, so Tipperary offers fishing in addition to
hunting and mountain-climbing. There are interesting caves
to be explored at Mitchelstown, and, of course, no one
should miss the magnificent Rock of Cashel.

Clonmel ("Honey Meadow") is the chief town in Tipperary; it was here that Ireland's Horatio Alger got his
start. An Italian boy, Charles Bianconi, came over to Ireland at the age of sixteen to seek his fortune. Unable to
speak English, he managed to learn the magic words "buy"
and "one pen-nee." Walking sometimes as much as thirty
miles in a day, he peddled his stock of prints and pictures
and statues. In 1815, at a time when Ireland had no railroads, Bianconi started his first car for hire, a single-horse
jaunting cart that went from Clonmel to Cahir. Within a
few years he was running more than a hundred cars,
including mail coaches. The family home, Longfield House,
still stands in Cashel, and was recently presented to the
Irish Georgian Society by Bianconi's great-granddaughter.

Tipperary men are said to have hearts as strong as bulls.
Whether this is true or not I cannot say, but I can vouch

for the fact that they have the gallantry of a Sir Walter Raleigh. Having wandered into an old cemetery in Tipperary one day, I was wondering how on earth I might make my way back out through the tangle of meddlesome nettles. Before I could so much as take one step forward, a tall Tipperary man exclaimed, "It wouldn't do for you to be walking through the lot of them again," and picked me up in his big strong arms and carried me out of the cemetery. The county has many lovely wooded areas and beautiful hills slumbering beneath patchwork quilts made of many shades of green, ranging from pale turquoise to emerald.

Now, with the Irish rain whispering around us, we seek the pleasures of the poet's country, a part of which lies in Westmeath and a part in Longford. Here along the banks of the Inny River, Oliver Goldsmith and Leo Casey sought solitude. Was Goldsmith writing about an Irish village when he wrote *The Deserted Village*? It is possible, since part of his youth was spent in Longford and also in Roscommon. But while Goldsmith may indeed have been thinking of Ireland when he wrote of "that loveliest village of the plain," and of "the poor exiles and the tyrant's power," Leo Casey was considered by many Irishmen to be more truly an Irish poet. Casey was, after all, one of the Fenian Boys and a contributor to the *Irish Nation,* the newspaper that served as a mouthpiece of the Young Ireland movement. Born in Gorteen, County Longford, he is probably best known for his patriotic ballad, "The Rising of the Moon." Although Leo Casey only lived to be twenty-four, the spirit of the poet lives on in these prophetic lines from *The Missioner*:

> He trod the path of the yellow stars,
> Free from the earth and its slimy wars —
> Free! yet his spirit dwelt with those
> Who waged the strife with Freedom's foes.

Not far from Leo Casey's birthplace, on the banks of the
Shannon in County Westmeath, is Athlone. Marking the
boundary between Leinster and Connacht, and often re-
ferred to as the heart of Ireland, this historic town is the
Capital of the Midlands. Athlone was formerly known as
Ath Mor ("Great Ford"), and possession of the town was
disputed from the early part of the twelfth century until the
British gained control of it in the seventeenth century.

Just off Marydyke Street in Athlone is the house where
the famous Irish tenor, John McCormack, was born.
Admired by Yeats, envied by Joyce who in his early life
had wanted to be a singer, the eighteen-year-old McCormack won the first place Gold Medal at the 1902 Feis
Ceoil, the National Irish Festival in Dublin.

Continuing on through Longford, past the gleaming
River Inny, we recall Leo Casey writing in a more cheerful
vein, "In leafy Tang, the wild birds sang; The dew was
bright on the Derry heather." It is said of a Longford man
that he has a sharp eye — can see a speck at the top of
the hill.

One ought not to rush through the midlands. Here you
encounter the sort of warm, natural people that inhabited
the world of childhood, a place where you are greeted with
a "hundred thousand welcomes" and invitations to "sup with
us." The upper midland area is made up of quiet farmlands
and brown velvet bogs, but there is a splendid beauty about
the landscape where, in an unbelievable haze of gold and
blue and lilac, birds fly up out of pastures:

> One is for sorrow,
> Two is for joy,
> Three for a wedding,
> Four for a girl —
> And five for a boy.

County Leitrim, touching on Longford, is squeezed in between Sligo and Roscommon on one side, with Cavan, Fermanagh, and Donegal on the other. Divided into two parts by Lough Allen, Leitrim is a skinny index finger pointing to the Bay of Donegal. In Dromhair on the bank of the River Bonet there once stood Breffni Castle, stronghold of the O'Rourkes. Now the ruins, pregnant with memories of a ruined marriage, are all that remain to remind us that it was from Breffni Castle that Dervorgilla, wife of Tiernan O'Rourke, eloped with Dermot Mac-Murrough. Leitrim has the Slieveanierin Range with summits up to 1,922 feet, and the Bencroy and Slievanakilla, and many other charms still undiscovered by the traveler.

Now at the end of our journey, we arrive in County Roscommon. The Cistercian Abbey in Roscommon was founded in 1161. Clothed in ivy, the ruins of the abbey give evidence of past splendour with its cruciform church and lofty central tower. On an island in Lough Key are the ruins of the Abbey of Trinity where the Annals of Loch Ce were compiled.

At the southern end of the Arigna Mountains nestles the little village of Keadue. Suddenly, we are aware of another of the numerous links that bind our own land of the free to the land of the Emerald Isle. For here in Keadue was the home of Turlough O'Carolan, last and greatest of the Irish bards, and composer of the music to our national anthem, "The Star Spangled Banner."

CHAPTER 2

IRELAND'S OTHER ISLANDS

IF THE WORLD is full of weeping, many are the tears that must have fallen on those wild and beautiful islands where a courageous community of people managed to survive for so many centuries. Most Irish Americans know something of the Blaskets and the Aran Islands. But few of us are familiar with the Emerald Isle's sable side, the little-known islands of five hundred or more which, in the words of Dr. Eoin McKiernan, president of the Irish American Cultural Institute, "cut fin-like through the Irish seas, or, like a whale, hump slightly above the water's surface."

These islands, once a refuge for rebels from English law, often provided a sanctuary for the starved and evicted people of the interior during the nineteenth century. It is recorded that the population of the Blaskets doubled as a result of the Great Famine. Emigration to America eventually brought about a marked decrease in the island population so that we find most of them no longer inhabited today. Some of the island people own cows and sheep, but the main industry is fishing — lobster in the summer, and mackerel in the winter. Although making a living on such primitive patches of land is difficult, the islanders, a people who take great pride in being independent, do not always look with favor on the government's efforts to ease their hardship by resettling them on the mainland.

Inishmurray ("Murray's Island"), located just outside Sligo Bay, is so low-lying that during World War I a German submarine mistakenly took it for a ship and torpedoed it. Inishmurray takes its name from St. Muiredeach, a follower of St. Patrick. This lonely, mysterious island was inhabited until some twenty-odd years ago. Because it was an ecclesiastical citadel for a thousand years or more, the island contains an impressive array of monastic ruins. Outside the cashel — the impressive dry-stone wall enclosing the monastic ruins — is an ancient Irish sweat-house which, differing from the European saunas, uses dry heat only. Within the sacred grounds of the cashel only men are allowed to be buried; at least this has been the case for the last hundred years. Although the expectant mother was encouraged to go into the cashel, pray before the lichen-covered stone cross pillar, and thrust her fingers into its perforated face and sides, she was for some reason excluded from it after death. The women's graveyard lies outside the cashel wall.

The seventh century abbot of Inishmurray, St. Molaise, has been immortalized through a life-size oak figure, carved in the tradition of figures on the later High Crosses. Today the figure can be seen in the National Museum in Dublin. Because of the wars visited upon the Irish from the twelfth century on, and because of the perishable nature of the material, few early wood carvings and examples of religious wood sculpture remain.

Another St. Molaise who lived in the sixth century, and was also known as St. Laserian, is the patron saint of Devenish, an island on the River Erne in Northern Ireland. Not long ago, the island was bought by the British Israelites, an offshoot of a Christian sect who believe the island to be the burial place of the prophet Jeremiah. In truth, Devenish has from earliest times been associated with

holiness, and the graveyard of the ancient church was
held in such veneration that the dead were brought from
long distances to be buried there. St. Molaise himself is
supposed to have floated to the island in a stone coffin.
The coffin, still on display, promises salvation to anyone
who can make a complete turn-around while lying in it.

The coast southwest of Skibbereen in County Cork is
dotted with islands, described by an early Irish writer as
"Sea-girt isles, that like to rich and various gems, inlay the
unadorned bosom of the deep." One of the most famous of
these islands is Clear Island. In the ancient ecclesiastical
books it is called Insula Sancta Clara, and in the old Irish
manuscripts, Inish Damhy. On the northwest point of the
island is the ruin of the castle of Dún an Óir, the "Golden
Fort," formerly a stronghold of the O'Driscolls. Referred
to more often now as Oilean Cleire or Clear Island, it is
still a community of Irish-speaking people. With only forty
children in school and twenty-two adolescents in a drama
group, Oilean Cleire has done remarkably well in Munster
Drama Festivals, and further distinguished itself by capturing the Glor na nGael national award in 1967.

An island that floats gently in the marina of the Shannon
some twenty-five miles northeast of the Shannon airport
is called Inish Cealtra or "Holy Island." On this island is a
superb collection of ecclesiastical remains, including a
peculiarly constructed building called the Anchorite's Cell,
or Confessional, along with the ruins of a church called
Teampall na bhFear nGonta ("Chapel of the Wounded
Men").

Off to the north lies another of Ireland's outer islands,
Arranmore. Hilly, and with the typical stony pastures of
Ireland's northwest sea islands, it is not as isolated as
Inishmurray, and was described back in 1893 as the largest
and most fertile island on the coast of Donegal. Neverthe-

less, like many other islands, Arranmore's economy has declined over the years to such an extent that two primary schools have only one-third the number of children of a generation ago. Returning from a visit to the island in 1969, Dr. Eoin McKiernan regretfully reported that there were only 125 "smokes" or occupied houses remaining on the island, and that the last marriage had been celebrated in 1961.

Still further north and shaped like Cinderella's slipper is Tory Island, a place so cut off from the world during the early part of the nineteenth century that few of its five hundred inhabitants had ever so much as visited the mainland. On the island of Tory ruins of ecclesiastical structures abound, along with other structures from pre-Christian eras. Here we find places where sea kings entered and caves where Druids held their solemn rites.

It was on Tory Island that the holy children of the King of India were said to have come to see St. Colmcille; and who knows but what the legend concerning them may partially explain the tradition of burying men and women in separate places. So fatigued from their journey were the holy children of India that when they reached the island they fell down dead. St. Colmcille was summoned and he prayed for the restoration of their lives. However, as soon as he had brought them back to life, he was forced to tell the children — six brothers and one sister — that they could stay alive only long enough to go to confession and receive the last sacraments. All was completed and the children were buried with great ceremony. But something was wrong, for each night the body of the girl rose to the surface of the grave. Finally, St. Colmcille, exhibiting that innate sensitivity of the Irish, realized that because of her virginity she was offended at having been buried with six men, even though they were her brothers. After being buried in a solitary place, she was at last able to rest in peace.

Oddly enough, on these remote islands, the dead were often neither allowed to rest in peace nor even to remain in the confines of their graves. On Achill Island amongst the ruins of Burrishoole there is a recess containing the collected bones of monks. The bones and skulls, held in great veneration by the peasants, call our attention to an exceedingly strange custom which seems to have been practiced well into the nineteenth century. Whenever illness struck one of the islanders, the mother of the family made her way to Burrishoole. Borrowing the skull of a monk, she took it home and boiled milk in it, thereby providing an infallible remedy for the afflicted one. The vessel was subsequently and courteously returned to its proper niche.

Achill, located fourteen miles from Newport in County Mayo, is the largest island off the Irish coast. At one time it boasted close to six thousand inhabitants. It was in Achill that the term "boycott" originated in the year 1881 following the actions of Captain Boycott, a land agent who was ostracized by his tenants for charging unfair rents. In a speech to the Land League on February 26 of that same year, J. Dillon, M.P., firmly established the rules for dealing with such land grabbers:

> When a man has taken a farm from which a tenant has been evicted, or is a grabber, let everyone in the parish turn his back on him; have no communication with him; have no dealings with him. You need never say an unkind word to him; but never say anything at all to him. If you must meet him in fair, walk away from him silently. Do him no violence, but have no dealings with him. Let every man's door be closed against him; and make him feel himself a stranger and a castaway in his own neighborhood.

One of the most interesting ruins in Ireland is Achill's

Carrig-a-Holly, castle of Grace O'Malley. Grania Uaile
("Grace of the Islands") was actually quite remarkable in
her own right. Brave, beautiful, and possessed with all the
instincts of a natural rebel, she was the daughter of Owen
O'Malley and wife of O'Flaherty, Chieftain of Connacht.
After O'Flaherty's death, she married Sir Richard Bourke,
also known as MacWilliam Oughter. Widowed once more
in 1585, she sought to assuage her grief by returning to
her favorite pastime, that of smuggling.

The special esteem accorded this female sea pirate by
the Irish stems not only from her daring pranks but from
the fact that she is supposed to have resisted Saxon rule.
Of course, there are those who never did believe she showed
much resistance, and in truth, she did on occasion fight
right alongside the English. But it is known that when she
had an opportunity to be presented at court, she accepted
with no other purpose in mind than to ruffle Elizabeth I's
feathers. No bowing or scraping on Grania's part. No
indeed. She merely looked at the queen and then proceeded
to engage her in the sort of conversation she might have
indulged in with her nextdoor neighbor. Such impertinent
deportment could hardly endear Grania to the queen. It is
no wonder Elizabeth had so low an opinion of the Irish.

The Irish, on the other hand, thought enough of Grania
Uaile to make a point of preserving her skull. Tradition
has it that the skull formerly occupied a nook in the ruins
of Burrishoole until it was stolen in the night and carried
off to Scotland to be ground up with other pilfered bones
and used for fertilizer. Since the Irish regard any desecra-
tion of a graveyard with horror, the skull is believed to
have been miraculously rescued and returned to the abbey.
In the interest of accuracy, however, it seems only fair to
point out that there is some dispute regarding the final
resting place of Grania's skull. Some claim it to be on

Clare Island, which was, after all, the seat of the dominions of Grania Uaile. Clare and the hundreds of other islands studding the beautiful Bay of Clew are alive with legends concerning this sixteenth century female buccaneer whose castle guards the harbor's entrance.

Farther down the coast and located just off the mainland of Connemara is that tiny island of piety, Mac Dara's Island. Time was when local fishermen honored St. Mac Dara by dipping sails three times when passing the island, and even today's men of the sea keep a bottle of holy water strapped in the prow of their currachs, making the sign of the cross when they come in sight of the isle. Here is an area where patterns have survived, and where every year on July 16 people come to take part in a reverent pilgrimage. Patrick Pearse, leader of the 1916 Easter Rising, and a poet and teacher as well, gave special honor to the island by naming a favorite character after St. Mac Dara in his play, *The Singer*.

Happily, there is no dearth of singing on Ireland's other islands. Thousands of birds fly up over the dizzying cliffs, quicksilvering the air and flooding it with melodious sounds. There are plovers and blackbirds and skylarks, puffins, guillemots, penguins, oystercatchers, nightjars, wagtails, Irish dippers, Irish jays, and the cuckoo, who is only a summer visitor. In fact, there are at least one hundred different kinds of birds in Ireland and if they appear to be more colorful than those of other countries, it is because they are flying up over forty shades of green and as many tints of beige, pink, lavender, and blue.

In truth, the far-famed Saltees, those twin islands lying off the coast of Wexford, are considered to be one of the richest bird sanctuaries in Europe. No more does man occupy the Saltees, but on the summit of the larger island there stands a limestone chair giving proof of one man's need to indulge in dreams of grandeur. Erected by Prince Michael I, self-proclaimed ruler of the Saltees, an inscription carved on the throne by Michael himself, a man still living in Dublin, reads in part:

This chair is erected in the memory of my mother to whom I made a vow when I was ten years old that one day I would own the Saltee Islands and become first Prince of the Saltees.

Now, only birds fly out over Prince Michael's throne, and sometimes gannets pause to rest on the blue-gray stone chair before making their way west to the Skelligs.

The Skelligs, a group of small island rocks southwest of Dingle Bay, are classed among the curiosities of the Atlantic. Great Skellig consists of two peaks. Rising from the ocean in the shape of a sugar loaf and thrusting itself to a height of 710 feet, the larger peak has its beginnings in some thirty-four fathoms of ocean. Although no inscription is carved upon this awesome feat of nature, its various projections are covered with grasses of such sweetness that an early Irish poet once wrote of the island:

Islets so freshly fair
That never hath bird come nigh them,
But, from his course through air,
Hath been won downward by them.

Ireland's long western coastline supports great colonies of birds. A large proportion of the world population of the storm petrel, a sea bird whose song falls upon the ears like fairy music, breeds off the west and southwest coast. On Little Skellig there is a gannet colony of over fifteen thousand breeding pairs, the second largest gannet colony in the world.

Not much more than a century ago, Great Skellig was a sanctuary for penitents, many of whom made the stations of the cross in a singularly hazardous manner. To accomplish the ritual, the penitent, in his attempt to ascend to the top of the rock, had to squeeze through a hollow part resembling the shaft of a chimney, which is called the Needle's Eye. Climbing by way of holes and steps cut in the rock, the penitent needed to possess the skill of an acrobat if he expected to complete the mission. One especially perilous obstacle was called the Stone of Pain, a long narrow fragment of rock projecting from the summit of Skellig and extending several feet out over the sea. Anyone making this station had to straddle the rock fragment, edging slowly forward until he was close enough to touch the cross looming up over its furthermost tip.

Fortunately, the older and less adventurous pilgrim was content to accomplish his mission in a more conventional manner, merely praying before the crosses erected in front of the oratories or the Clochain. Many of these primitive "beehive" stone dwellings, built in the ancient Roman manner with stones closed and jointed without mortar, and with circular arches on top, are found on Skellig.

The islands of Aran, Inishmore, Inishmaan, and Inisheer resemble a small string of theatres — all of which offer a magnificent view of Galway Bay on the eastern side and look out to the Atlantic from the southwestern shoreline. The islands, consisting of almost twelve thousand acres, had a population of about 1,500 in 1967 as compared to 3,000 a hundred years ago. The islands are for the most part barren and stony, the soil made by the Aran people themselves from sand and seaweed. One of the most interesting characteristics of the landscape is the maze of dry-stone walls that separate the small holdings and enclose tiny fields of potatoes.

Still used for fishing and for transporting cattle to the islands is the currach, a primitive type of vessel said to be

as old as the history of Ireland itself. The currach was the
next advance in sea travel after the raft and the canoe.
Long ago, sinners were required to launch out in the frail
craft and let themselves drift at the mercy of God, and
saints employed them as a means of bringing the gospel to
heathens. When St. Brendan embarked on a search for
knowledge in the sixth century — with the warning words
of his foster mother Ita still ringing in his ears, "Study not
with women!" — he made the voyage in a currach large
enough to carry ten people and forty days' provisions. Some
say the Firbolgs, some of Ireland's first settlers, came to
Ireland in similar boats made of wattles or wickerwork
covered with animal hides. While this may be open to
dispute, it can be safely said that the Irish did use such
currachs in the invasions of Britain prior to the departure
of the Romans.

Nowadays the framework of the currachs is made of
wooden laths, and tarred canvas or calico is substituted for
animal skins. Currachs are never beached; they are lifted
up and carried by two or three men whose heads are hidden
in the lap of the boat. Though the crafts have a fragile
appearance, they are, in fact, extremely seaworthy. Back
in 1907 when the French windjammer *Leon XIII*, carrying
wheat to Limerick from Portland, Oregon, crashed into the
rocks near the mouth of the Shannon, it was the bravery
of the Quilty fishermen and the seaworthiness of the currachs that made it possible to effect a rescue. To show their
gratitude, the men of France collected a sum of money to
build a church at Quilty in memory of the men who saved
their lives.

Actually, the boats that rescued the crew of the *Leon
XIII* were of the old type, about twenty feet long and a
little over three feet wide, made no doubt by a man in
whose family the craft had been practiced for centuries.

Although the present-day currachs are well suited to lighter fishing, they can be somewhat dangerous since the least touch of a rock can tear a hole in the canvas, or worse still, puncture the wooden ribs. Maurice O'Sullivan in his autobiography, *Twenty Years A-Growing,* tells of the terror he felt on his first voyage to the Blasket Islands, when the currach, mounting the waves, rose and fell, sending bright jets of foam into the air.

The Blaskets, a group of seven small islands lying off the Dingle Peninsula, County Kerry, were once the home of a sturdy fishing community, an Irish-speaking people who managed to preserve many ancient traditions. For a long time the Blaskets were a favorite haunt for students of folklore and the Irish language. Due to successive bad fishing seasons, its inhabitants were moved to Dunquin on the mainland in 1953. In their new settlement, the islanders, striving to maintain their old traditions and customs, remain to this day an Irish-speaking community.

Inish Tuiscirt, one of the smaller islands, contains the ruins of an oratory of St. Brendan, the district's patron saint. And on the Great Blasket, which is four miles long and three-fourths of a mile wide, there once stood the castle of Piaras (Pierce) Ferriter, poet-leader of the Kerrymen Rising of 1641, and the last Irish chieftain to surrender to Cromwell.

Far to the north is Rathlin Island, shaped something like a boot but seeming more like a lost piece of a jigsaw puzzle that once belonged to nearby County Antrim. Because of its vulnerable position, Rathlin was the first place in Ireland to suffer from Danish invasions, and is also associated with Robert Bruce. Bruce, crowned King of Scotland at Scone in 1305, retreated to Ireland after being attacked by the English. One day when he was hiding out on Rathlin Island he noticed a spider trying to attach his

web to the ceiling beams. Six times the spider tried and
failed, and because Bruce had also known six failures, he
decided to let the spider teach him what he must do. After
the spider succeeded on his seventh effort Bruce left the
island. So successful were Robert Bruce's invasions in the
ensuing years that by 1309 he had made himself master
of almost all of Scotland.

Today, fewer than one percent of Ireland's other islands
are inhabited, though here and there one might find a
house, usually a refuge for lobster fishermen. Caves and
inlets which once served as hideaways for smugglers and
Irish rebels have been taken over by the seals.

The native Irish, who seem to have an explanation for
everything, offer an intriguing one relating to seals and
insomnia. If an individual should chance to complain of
not being able to sleep, likely as not an Irishman will tell
him that the only people who do not sleep are the people
of the sea. And who are these people of the sea? There are
some who say they are seals, because at one time seals
were thought to have been human beings in disguise, or
under spells. In olden times when people hunted seals so
they might use the soft white fur to trim cloaks and
dresses, they were ever alert for signs indicating that the
hunted one was under a spell of enchantment.

A man from Kerry once saw a group of seals take off
their skins and dance around in their human shapes. Being
a bold Irishman, he stole one of the skins and the lovely
young woman who belonged to it, leading her to his home
and taking her for his bride. Three children had they and all
was well until the day the youngest child found the seal-
skin tucked away in the loft. Upon seeing it, the mother,
remembering her people, felt such a rush of longing that
she slipped into her old skin and went back to sea. Never
again did the Kerryman see his enchanted wife, but some-

times on sunny days she swam up to the surface just off-shore and talked and sang to her children.

There is a sadness about these outer islands. The turbulent waters of the sea have been an ever-present threat to the man who took his living from its depths. So too was there a sense of loneliness, of an intensity that could not have been borne had it not been for the long night of the storyteller. And although no one is left on the Great Blasket but the seals, the island people of the past live on in the richness of a literature they have bequeathed to us. There is Tomas O'Crohan's *The Islandman,* Peig Sayer's *An Old Woman's Reflections,* and Maurice O'Sullivan's autobiography, described by E. M. Forster in his introductory note to the book as "the egg of a sea-bird — lovely, perfect, and laid this very morning."

"The like of us will never be again," Tomas O'Crohan predicted some forty-five years ago.

There is truth in his words. Even so, there is still the egg of the sea-bird, still the words of Maurice O'Sullivan's grandfather who, in the midst of telling about the olden times, is suddenly moved by a memory of old friends, "all on the way of the truth now."

"Did you never know how the life of man is divided," he asks looking out at the sea with the tears still in his eyes.

"No, I never heard that before," the boy answers.

"Twenty years a-growing," says the old man slowly. "Twenty years in blossom, twenty years a-stooping, and twenty years declining."

Then, in the way of the Irish who have a talent for making the journey from sadness to joviality in less time than it takes to fling a fish line into the sea, the grandfather says briskly, "Indeed, it is many things you have never heard before. But go on with you now. Be happy when you can."

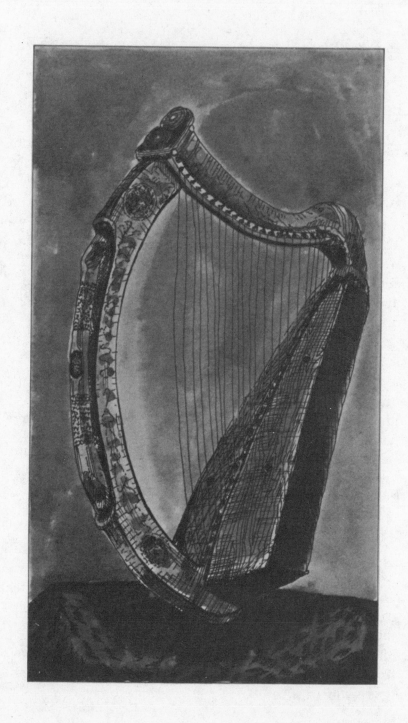

CHAPTER 3

SYMBOLS OF EIRE

LET SOMEONE so much as mention the Emerald Isle and there comes to mind words like shamrock and shillelagh, or perhaps to some, phrases like Penal Laws and coffin ships. Yet, a word that is truer to the heart of Ireland is Gaelic, the name of the language that has maintained Ireland's traditions from the time of the first settlers.

Because the Irish language between A.D. 1169 and 1919 had no State of its own, the nation's history has invariably been bandied about by historians who did not belong to the land or the land to them. As a result, many of us — even those who can trace their roots right back to the old sod — have never been aware that the traditions of the Irish people are the oldest of any race in Europe north and west of the Alps. Actually, it is only in recent years that scholars using the Gaelic language as a tool have been able to unearth the history of the Irish nation, rather than the history of a nation occupied by another country.

The Irish scholars and bards of old had the responsibility of preserving the records of Ireland's history along with many legendary and romantic tales. Records show that from the very earliest times the kings of Ireland made a point of maintaining a body of these learned men who were chosen for their excellent memories and their ability to recite numerous lines of verse and prose. They became the guardians of an oral literature which they in turn passed on to the scholars and bards of succeeding generations.

The coming of Christianity and the Latin alphabet brought about the beginnings of Irish literature as we know it today. However, it is thought that there was Irish literature for a thousand years or more before A.D. 600. Although much of Ireland's literary records were destroyed by the Viking and English invasions, some fragments of early Irish poetry have survived. Indeed, it is thought that the following lines taken from a poem written by a Milesian poet called Amergin, who lived hundreds of years before Christ, may represent some of the oldest surviving lines in any tongue except Greek:

> Who is it who throws light into the
> Meeting on the mountain?
> Who announces the ages of the moon (If not I)?
> Who teaches the place where couches the sun (If not I)?

In pre-Christian and early Christian periods the Ogham system of writing was employed. Ogham characters were slanted and perpendicular lines placed in relation to a horizontal line, usually scratched into stones, such as the Irish gallans or pillar-stones that commemorate the dead. *Gallan* may have come from the word *gol,* meaning "to cry or lament," and *lan,* "full," so that the whole word conveys sorrow or grief. Gallans are somewhat similar to the headstones used on graves today. In any case, it is apparent that Ogham was invented as a means of recording events long before the method of letters and alphabets was adopted.

Irish is, of course, a Celtic language. The Celtic languages were Gaulish, which died out at the beginning of the Christian era; Goidelic, from which descended Irish, Scottish Gaelic, and Manx; and Britannic, from which came Welsh, Cornish, and Breton.

One of the ancient titles given Ireland was Hibernia, a

term used by Caesar. Further proof of the nation's antiquity can be found in Plutarch's reference to the island as
Ogygia, meaning "the most ancient." In the sixth century
before Christ the poet Orpheus referred to it as Ierna, and
in Sanscrit writings Ireland is I Hirani, the "island of the
sun," that is, the island of sun-worshippers. Sun worship
was part of the Druidic religion practiced by ancient Celts.
Ireland has also been called Inisfail ("Isle of Destiny"), and
Scotia.

The last title, Scotia, has been the source of much con-
fusion. The fact is that the Scottish Gaels were originally
of Irish stock, and Scotland was known as Alba until
about ten centuries after the birth of Christ. The early
Irish Gaels who settled in "Alba" were known as Scots from
Scotia, and this name stayed with them, until finally Alba
became known as Scotland. The term Scotia is said to
have come from Scota, daughter of Pharaoh, one of the
ancestors of the Milesians, an ancient Gaelic race who
settled in Ireland.

Ancient manuscripts preserve a prayer that the Milesian
poet Amergin was supposed to have prayed for the safety
of the first voyage of Milesians going to Ireland. In the
poem he calls the island "the land of Eirinn." And the
people the Milesians found living on Eirinn were the
Tuatha De Danann, ruled at that time by their Queen Eire.

The Gaelic word *Eire* is thought to have been a name
given to the island by some of its earliest inhabitants, while
the English word *Erin* comes from the dative case, *Eirinn*.
Since the ancient form was *Eriu*, some have suggested that
the word possibly has a connection with the Aryans; others
connect it with an early Celtic race living on the island.

The name *Ireland* can be traced from Eber, or Heber, the
first Milesian king of the southern half of the island, and
Ir, whose family occupied the northeastern corner. However,

it was not until around the ninth century that the Scandi-
navian invaders, and later on the Saxons, began calling
the island Irland, Irlanda, or Ireland.

Over the centuries Ireland has been the scene of so
many bloody battles it is a miracle to think that even
twenty-six of its counties were able to survive as an independent nation. The struggle for independence was a long
and heartbreaking one, replete with tales of love affairs as
tragic as that of the Irish princess Isolde, whose story is
told in Wagner's famous opera. Toward the end of the
nineteenth century the Irish patriot, Charles Stewart Parnell,
a Protestant of the landlord class, came close to winning
Home Rule for Ireland, but ill health, along with his love
affair with Mrs. Kitty O'Shea, were instrumental in bringing
about the downfall of his brilliant career. On September
27, 1891, against the advice of his doctor, he delivered a
speech in County Galway and died a week later at the age
of forty-five.

The rise of the Separatist Party, *Sinn Fein* (pronounced
Shin Fayne, meaning "Ourselves Alone"), culminated in
the Easter Rising of 1916. Eamon de Valera, the only
major figure to survive the Rising, became the leader of
the movement and was elected President of the Provisional
Government of Ireland in 1917. There followed a guerrilla
war between the Irish and the British which eventually
ended in the Anglo-Irish Treaty of 1921. But it was not
until 1937 that the Bunreach na hEireann (Constitution of
Ireland) was enacted, changing the country's name from
Irish Free State to Eire. Subsequent developments led to
the Republic of Ireland Act in 1948.

A word about the government in the Republic of
Ireland: The Parliament (Oireachtas) consists of the
President of Ireland (An Uachtaran), House of Represen-
tatives (Dail Eireann), and the Senate (Seanad Eireann).

The two major political parties are the Fianna Fail (Soldiers of Destiny) and Fine Gael (United Ireland), the latter having formed a coalition pact with the Labor Party. The president is elected by direct vote of the people. The constitution which came into operation December 29, 1937, declared Ireland to be a sovereign, independent, democratic State and declares the national territory to be the whole of Ireland, its islands, and the territorial seas.

A brief explanation concerning the partition involves Lloyd George, Prime Minister of England as far back as 1919. Ignoring the fact that the Irish people had voted for an all Irish Republic in 1918, Lloyd George announced a bill a year later for a better government of Ireland without consulting any of the Irish representatives. In the end, Lloyd George was successful in pushing his bill through, and when the English Parliament passed the partition act, King George V made haste to Belfast to open the parliament of the newly partitioned six counties.

The story of Ireland's flag is an interesting one. During the 1916 Easter Rising, the Plough and the Stars was the flag of the Irish Citizen Army. This group, which originated during a labor dispute in Dublin in 1913, felt that their flag should contain symbols showing labor's near and higher ideals. The flag was a badge of courage to this group of men dedicated to the ideal that the ownership of Ireland, moral and material, was vested in the people of Ireland.

"Though I should mingle with the dust, or fall to ashes in flame," wrote Sean O'Casey in *Drums Under the Window,* the third volume of his autobiography, "the plough will always remain to furrow the earth, the stars will always be there to unveil the beauty of the night, and a newer people, living a newer life, will sing like the sons of the morning."

The present flag of the Republic of Ireland, standing for independence and opposition to British rule, comes in the

colors of green and white and orange. The green represents
old Ireland, the orange, new Ireland, and the white of
peace in the center of the flag, brotherhood and one nation.
The pledge of allegiance reads as follows:

> We are willing to fight for
>   the flag we love,
> Be the chances great or small.
> We are willing to die for the
>   flag above,
> Be the chances nothing at all.

Before the tricolor made its first appearance, the harp,
represented on Ireland's flag, had been the only cultural
emblem on a national flag in Europe. Originally, it was
shown in gold on a blue ground; later on, it was in gold
on a green ground. Ireland's official color was at one time
St. Patrick's blue, but by the nineteenth century green had
taken its place.

The harp in early times was referred to as a *cruit,* which
may have meant a lyre and not a harp. According to tradition, one of the early kings of Ireland who bore the name
of David took the harp of the Psalmist as his badge. The
harp, the oldest heraldic symbol of Ireland, is still used as
an official symbol, not only on the coinage and the Presidential flag, but on state seals and government mastheads.
There is an actual Irish harp, the Brian Boru Harp, dating
from the fifteenth century, which is preserved in Trinity
College.

The Irish people attach a special importance to their
national symbols, and the Gaelic language especially seems
to represent Irish traditions and national identity. Irish is
now taught in all the Irish schools. Street, road, and high-
way signs may be printed in English but they are also
shown in Gaelic. Many of the storefronts in towns and

villages sport Gaelic signs. An Irish American fortunate enough to be granted an interview with the President of Ireland is likely to be reminded of the fact that the country's leaders take great pride in their knowledge of the native language. Furthermore, it will be thoughtfully pointed out to him that it would be well to learn the traditional Gaelic greeting, *"Dia's Muire dhuit* — God and Mary be with you." The effort will be greatly appreciated by the president, who will respond with the words, *"Dia's Muire agus Padraig dhuit* — God and Mary and Patrick be with you."

If it is important to learn the Gaelic greeting, it is even more important to refer to the island by its proper title. There is a world of difference between the man who speaks of Eire and the man who speaks of Ireland. Eire is the country that men have gone out to fight and die for, a country whose people have a language of their own.

It is not surprising, then, that the national anthem is almost always sung in Gaelic. "A Soldier's Song," composed in 1907, with the music by Patrick Heaney, and the words by Peadar Kearney, an uncle of Brendan Behan, became the official national anthem by government decree in 1926, thereby supplanting the Fenian song, "God Save Ireland" and Thomas Davis' "A Nation Once Again." Like the tricolor, the popularity of "A Soldier's Song" dates from the 1916 Rising. Since it is more a march than an anthem, it is most effective when played by a military band.

Not so long ago, the ballad that told of the hanging of men and women for the "wearing o' the green" was considered the national anthem. But even though today's national anthem contains words like *tyrant* and *rifle's peal* and *cannon's roar,* it has a bold, rollicking ring about it that makes one feel the Irishman has come into his own at last and is trying to express the intensity of his joy as he sings in the Gaelic language, *Amran na bFiann.*

CHAPTER 4

ISLAND OF WOODS

IF WE WERE, by some strange means, allowed to visit
Eire between 10,000 B.C. and 9000 B.C., we would find a
country made up mostly of boggy grassland. As the climate
grew warmer bushes sprouted up, grassy tundra with
flowering plants such as the gentian carpeted the lowlands,
and herds of reindeer and Giant Irish Deer began to roam
the plains. Man appeared in Ireland as early as 6000 B.C.,
and perhaps before. That he existed at the same period as
the Giant Irish Deer cannot be doubted. The rib of one
such deer, presented to the Dublin Society over a hundred
years ago, shows evidence that one of its ribs had been
perforated with an arrow or sharp-pointed instrument.
Hunting this wild creature, whose antlers could measure
as much as sixteen feet in length, was likely a popular
sport for the early inhabitants of Ireland, and it is possible
the celebrated Irish wolf dog may have taken part in the
chase.

Around 6000 B.C. Ireland became separated from the
continent and formed a seabound country, an island of
woods. Although archaeologists again differ slightly in
their opinions, 6000 B.C. is generally given as the beginning
of the Stone Age in Ireland. Since Ireland's inland country
was heavily wooded at the time — it was said that the forest
was so dense a man could walk across the top of the trees
if he wished to get from one side of the island to the other

— Stone Age man was forced to cling to the edge of the island. He dined for the most part on shellfish, although he may have been able to kill a bird or snare a hare with his crude implements now and then. Many of these stone implements, such as the quern, a primitive mill used for grinding grain, and the spindle whorl, are preserved in the Cork Public Museum.

"This country of ours is no sand bank thrown up by some recent caprice of earth," said the respected nineteenth century patriot Thomas Davis. "It is an ancient land honoured in the archives of civilization." Indeed, the abundance of Celtic crosses and round towers scattered throughout the country provide a vivid history lesson for Irish schoolchildren, many of whom are familiar with the story associated with each and every landmark. Yet eight thousand years of history have left Ireland with much older memories than even those connected with Celtic crosses and round towers.

It is one of our ancestors' oldest characteristics, their remembrance of the dead, that has helped trace the sources of our early beginnings. Thousands of ancient stone burial places remain scattered throughout Ireland — dolmens, stone circles, huge burial mounds — that are called megalithic, that is, "built of great stones." Most of the megalithic remains date from the Neolithic or New Stone Age (since 3000 B.C.) and the Bronze Age (from around 1900 B.C.).

Some of the earliest monuments are located thirty miles north of Dublin on the banks of the Boyne River. In Newgrange, County Meath, excavations have revealed a large communal grave covering nearly an acre. Although extensive excavations have been undertaken in fairly recent times. the long and narrow passageways leading into what was no doubt a Druidic chamber were first explored in 1699, when a gentleman carrying away stones to repair a road

came upon a broad flat stone crudely carved and placed
edgewise at the bottom of a mound that rose to an elevation
of seventy feet.

Discoveries made at Newgrange continue to evoke questions. What is the meaning of the double and triple inter-
lacing spirals, or the zigzag carvings and geometric designs
that decorate the stones? What was the purpose of the huge
rock basins that appear in the tombs, or of the stone urns
found in the niches of the interior chambers that are some
twenty-two feet in diameter and are covered with "beehive"
domes? Initiating a series of excavations at Knowth in
July of 1967, Dr. George Eogan, archaeologist at Dublin's
University College, encountered for the first time an important burial passageway which seemed to have been
substantially untouched since it was originally sealed some
four thousand years ago. Knowth's passage graves give
investigators reason to hope they they will eventually un-
ravel some of the mystery surrounding the megalithic
remains.

Ireland's Bronze Age gives evidence of quite an advanced
culture with especially skilled craftsmen, judging by the
fine armor, weapons, and ornaments they left behind. About
fifty years ago an amber necklace belonging to the Bronze
Age was found buried under ten feet of bog in Skibbereen.
Another interesting find unearthed on the Hill of Tara in
Meath indicated a new type of burial. Here, in a tomb
covered with small stones and clay, were found various
food vessels and urns, giving evidence of cremation. In this
same tomb was the body of a youth whose neck was en-
circled with bronze and amber and faience, an artificial
stone of bright shimmering blue, a shade that found great
favor with the Irish long before green became the national
color.

Who were the earliest settlers of Ireland? Richard O'Connor writes, in *Portrait of a People*: "From the Fomorians who came to Ireland before the Deluge to the Milesians who came from Spain in the historical period the island was continuously inhabited." The Deluge referred to here is the biblical Flood, believed by some to have occurred as a result of the sinking of the great continent of Atlantis. O'Connor had a theory that the earliest Irish settlers were refugees from the doomed continent.

Ignatius Donnelly was an Irish American living in the latter part of the nineteenth century who also held that Ireland's settlers were part of the waves of population flowing from Atlantis. Donnelly managed to convince William Gladstone, then British Prime Minister, to help him raise money to outfit a ship and trace the outline of the sunken Atlantis in the Atlantic Ocean. Their fund-raising drive, however, was not successful and nothing came of the project.

Whatever actually happened in those dim days of prehistory, it is more generally agreed that the Irish race of today is descended from the Milesians (Gaels) who came to Ireland a thousand years before Christ. But when they arrived, according to legend, they did not find the island unoccupied.

One of the first colonies started in Ireland was made by settlers known as the Parthalonians, led by Parthalon, who are said to have left Greece for Ireland around 2500 B.C. Landing on the Dublin coast, Parthalon and his party were subsequently swept away by the plague and buried outside the city of Dublin in a place called Tallaghy, meaning "plague grave." They were followed by the Firbolgs, people of Gaelic stock who went to Ireland, also by way of Greece, perhaps a thousand years before the Milesians. The Firbolgs were later conquered by another people of Gaelic stock, the Tuatha De Danann ("People of the Goddess Dana").

The De Danann were a mystical people and more highly civilized than the Firbolg. It is said that when they landed in Ireland, they were guided in their choice of a settlement by an omen. Releasing a swarm of bees and observing where they landed, they erected their *baile,* or circular fort, there, giving the spot the name Cluan-mealla ("the plain of honey"), now in Tipperary. A castle was built on this very spot in later times and it was before this castle that Cromwell met his greatest defeat, losing about two thousand men. In West Cork, Cliodhana, a Tuatha De Danann fairy lady, is supposed to have drowned in Glanmore Bay, and at certain times one can hear her moaning over the lonesome sounds of the sea.

Under the leadership of Nuada Lamh Airgid ("Nuada of the Silver Hand"), the Tuatha De Danann defeated the Firbolg in the Battle of Moytura ("plain of towers"), commonly believed to be in present-day County Sligo. Tuatha De Danann kings ruled Ireland well; two of the most glorious live on in legend as Lugh and Dagda.

Soon after Dagda's reign the Milesians arrived. They, like the Firbolg, were dazzled by the culture and skills and magical powers of the Tuatha De Danann. Although the Milesians were superior warriors and eventually defeated the De Danann, they grew to honor them. In fact, the Milesians created a whole mythology around these wonderful people, and Tuatha De Danann heroes became the gods and goddesses of Milesian legends.

The Milesians were a Gaelic race who originated in Scythia, then a region of southwest Europe. According to tradition, a Scythian noble named Niall, who lived in the time of Moses, was banished from his country and went to dwell in Egypt. After the destruction of Pharaoh's hosts in the Red Sea, Niall was not wanted in Egypt, but because of this generosity towards Moses and the persecuted

Israelites, he was rewarded by the recovery of his son who lay at the point of death as the result of a snake bite. "One day," Moses told Niall, "you will live in a far-off western isle where no snake or reptile can live."

In the course of his wandering, Niall eventually reached Spain where he lived for many years, his tribe increasing. As time went on, Niall's descendants kept in mind the prophecy given their forefathers by Moses. Finally, under the leadership of Milesius, they had their opportunity when Milesius decided to send his uncle, Ith, with his son and 150 warriors, to Ireland. Unfortunately, the Tuatha De Danann became alarmed when the Milesians praised their land so highly, and attacked their ships, mortally wounding Ith. The Milesians retreated, and soon Milesius died, so it was left to his eight sons to avenge the slaying of Ith.

When the eight brothers and their band landed at the Slaney River in Wexford, they were again attacked by the De Danann and all the brothers perished except Eremon, Eber, and Amergin. Later on, however, the Milesians retaliated by defeating the Tuatha De Danann in the Battle of Taillte in County Meath. It is from the three surviving brothers that the Gaelic race in Ireland is said to derive. Thomas Moore, an Irish poet who lived in the early nineteenth century, described the first Milesian invasion in these words:

> They came from a land beyond the sea,
> And now o'er the western main,
> Set sail in their good ships, gallantly,
> From the sunny lands of Spain.

> Oh, where's the isle we've seen in dreams,
> Our destined home or grave?
> Thus sang they, as by the morning beams,
> They swept the Atlantic wave.

'Tis Inisfail — 'tis Inisfail!
Rings o'er the echoing sea;
While bending to heaven, the warriors hail
That home of the brave and free.

Then turned they unto the Eastern wave
Where now their Day-God's eye
A look of such sunny omen gave
As lighted up sea and sky.

No frown was seen through sky or sea,
Nor tear o'er leaf or sod,
When first on their Isle of Destiny
Our great forefathers trod.

The brothers divided Ireland between them, and from them dates a long succession of Milesian kings who ruled in Ireland. Thus began a long period of Celtic influence in Ireland, which was strengthened by further emigrations of Celts from continental Europe.

Celtic society was highly structured. The highest class, socially equal to kings, were the Druids, who were both priests and teachers — the keepers of all learning. They also acted as judges and were called upon to settle all disputes, so even kings could not act without the approval of their Druids.

Kings in Celtic Ireland ruled over a small petty kingdom called a *tuath*. They were, in turn, subject to over-kings. Many of the kings lived in *crannogs,* or lake dwellings, which were the forerunner of the moated castle. The crannog was a man-made island, constructed by forming a circular area with strong posts and filling up the enclosed space with earth and stones until the surface rose above the water level. A fortification was built around the area, and a house or houses erected to receive the lord and his

family, who were thus able to sleep peacefully without fear
of being attacked.

Noblemen during this era were primarily farmers. They
did not individually own land — the family unit was the
real owner — but they counted their personal wealth in
cattle. Under them were the commoners, who worked the
soil and grazed the cattle for their noble overlords. The
lowest class were the slaves, who had no rights.

The ancient Irish laws were called Brehon, and they
closely resembled ancient Hindu law. In Irish life the two
important institutions were the joint family and the petty
kingdom, or tuath. The family was a group which included
all relatives in the male line of descent for five generations.
Property was owned by the family, and the family was also
the unit that determined kingly succession. Under the
Brehon Law there was no death penalty, but a levying of
erics or fines, and the whole family of the accused individual
was held responsible for the payment of these fines.

At first glance this Irish system would appear to be a
fairly equitable one, the family group owning the land
collectively, and electing among themselves a ruler for the
tuath. However, the system was bound to have its defects.
For one thing, if a certain branch of a family had held the
kingship for four generations, they were not inclined to
relinquish their rights. Under these circumstances the other
branches, fearful of losing their royal status for all time,
were often tempted to slay their own kin. Also, since there
was no provision made for appointing a head of state after
the death of a king, there were times between two successive
reigns when the country had no sovereign. Both problems
contributed to the Irish people's inability to defend themselves in the invasions that would subsequently change the
course of Irish history.

There is an old saying that if you search back far enough

in a king's ancestry you will find a peasant and that if you search back far enough in a peasant's ancestry you will find a king. Considering the loosely styled form of government that existed in Ireland during the reign of Milesian kings, and the custom of joint rule which led to the establishment of numerous petty kingdoms, it is safe to say that this is particularly true in Ireland.

Who are those kings who now sleep in the royal cemetery of Brugh at Newgrange on the Boyne, or rest with Erin's warriors, saints, and scholars under the red earth of Clonmacnois?

The greatest of the early kings was Ollam Fodla ("Doctor of Wisdom"), the twenty-first Milesian king who reigned seven or eight centuries before the Christian era. Celebrated for his statesmanship, he established the Parliament of the Chiefs which assembled on Tara Hill every three years to settle the nation's affairs. Some three hundred years later, Ireland was ruled by a queen, Macha Mong Ruan ("The Red-Haired") whose father, Aod Ruad, was drowned at Assaroe Falls. The leading families of Ulster, Leinster, and Connacht trace their descent from Macha's foster son, King Ugani Mor ("The Great"); in fact, the name Leinster is said to have come from Ugani Mor's great-grandson, King Labraid Loingsech.

One of the greatest of the later rulers was Conor Mac-Nessa, King of Ulster. In his time, around the time of Christ, the warrior champions called the Red Branch Knights, led by Cuchullain, reached the height of their fame. In the second century A.D. lived Conn of the Hundred Battles. Conn divided Ireland with Mogha Nuadat, making a ridge of gravel running from Dublin to Galway the dividing line. Leth Cuinn was "Conn's Half" and Leth Mogha was "Mogha's Half." Cormac MacArt, Conn's grandson, rebuilt the palace of Tara and brought it to the

height of its splendor. During his reign this famous ruler
was assisted in war and peace by the Fian, or Fenians
("Companions of Finn MacCool"), whose motto was,
"Strength in our hands, truth on our lips, and cleanness in
our hearts." But Cormac, as we shall see, was not destined,
like his grandfather, to sleep in the royal burial ground at
Brugh.

From the reign of Cormac MacArt to the coming of St.
Patrick, Niall of the Nine Hostages, grandson of Muiredeach
Tireach, was Ireland's greatest king. Founder of the most
important and powerful Irish dynasty, Ui Neill, Niall reigned
from A.D. 379 to 404. His descendants ruled in Tara over
the five provinces of Ireland for almost six hundred years.
Then the high kingship was wrested from them by Brian
Boru of Munster, whose descendants gave way to O'Connor
of Connacht.

Kings of Munster in pre-Christian days were crowned on
the Rock of Cashel. The early Irish kings had a huge
palace on Cashel's impressive rock, which rises out of the
Tipperary plains to a breathtaking height of three hundred
feet. One of the square towers, built in the year 1108 and
ranking among the oldest constructions of the kind in Ireland, still exists. Within its walls the kings of Munster were
born and reared. The Irish historian Geoffrey Keating,
himself a native of Tipperary, indicates in his famous work,
The General History of Ireland, that Cashel was first
founded in the reign of Corc, king of Munster.

The name of the place which is now called the Rock
of Cashel was Sheedrum. . . . About that time there
came two swineherds to feed their pigs in the woods
about this hill, . . . and when they had continued on
the hill about a quarter of a year, there appeared to
them a figure as brilliant as the sun, whose voice was
more melodious than any music they had ever heard,

and it was consecrating the hill, and prophesying the coming of St. Patrick. The swineherds having returned to their homes, related what they had seen to their masters; and the story soon reached Corc, who repaired without delay to Sheedrum, and built a palace there which is called Lis-na-Lachree, or the fort of the heroes; and being King of Munster, his royal tribute was received on this rock, now called Carrick-Patrick; wherefore the rock was named Cashel — i.e. Cios ail — or the rock of tribute.

Irish kings had an abundance of fine gold ornaments. They dressed in clothes of woven wool, flax, and leather. For the most part they were wise and just rulers, but rank depended on wealth as well as birth, and since they lived in prosperous times, families were often set to warring against each other for power. Possession of the title of King of Tara was the cause of a great many disputes, not only between Leinster and Meath, but between the Ui Neill kings of Meath and Connacht and the kings of Leinster.

Tribal warfare went on until at last the Irish, perhaps bored with the incessant struggle for power and looking for new fields to conquer, began raiding Roman Britain. These Irish raiders were referred to by the Romans as Scotti, while the Britains called them Gwhddl. By a twist of fate, these overseas raids were to introduce a new element into the homeland, an element that was destined to change Ireland.

Cormac MacArt, grandson of Conn of the Hundred Battles, was one of the first to recognize the new element, Christianity. Cormac was given an early vision of the coming of Christianity, and he made the following plea to his people before his death: "Do not bury me in the pagan cemetery of Brugh, but rather bury me on the south bank of the Boyne at Rosnaree facing the east!"

CHAPTER 5

FROM KINGS TO CABBAGES

ALTHOUGH THE PROPHECY that had made such a profound impression on Corc, the king of Munster, was eventually fulfilled, St. Patrick first came to Ireland not as a saint, but as a slave. A group of Irish raiders, on one of their numerous forays into Romanized Britain, captured Patrick, brought him back to Ireland, and set him to herding sheep on the Slemish Mountain in the province of Ulster. It was there in that lonely mountain place that the love of God was kindled in St. Patrick's heart. After spending some seven years in captivity he managed to escape in a ship carrying wolfhounds to France. In the years that followed he studied under the tutelage of many teachers, including possibly St. Germain of Auxerre.

Here are the words of St. Patrick himself, telling of the voice of the Irish calling him to come back to them:

And there I saw in the night
the vision of a man whose name was Victoricus
coming as if it were from Ireland, with countless letters.
And he gave me one of them and I read
the opening words of the letter which were
the voice of the Irish.
And as I read the beginning of the letter,
I thought at the same moment I heard their voice —
They were those beside the Wood of Focult

which is near the Western Sea.
And thus did they cry out with one mouth,
We ask thee, boy, come and walk among us once more!

Patrick first came to Ireland in the year 389 during the reign of Niall. Then with the benediction of Pope Celestine I, he came back to Ireland in the Year of Our Lord 432.

Although St. Patrick was not the first Christian missionary to come to Ireland — St. Declan of Ardmore and others had been there before him — he was the most influential. Landing at Colp at the mouth of the Boyne on Easter Eve, on a night when it was the law that all fires should be put out, he and his followers kindled a fire on the Hill of Slane. When the High King commanded the lawbreakers to be brought before him, St. Patrick advanced to Tara, the seat of High Kings, chanting the twentieth psalm, "Some put their trust in hosts . . . ."

The flame that had been kindled on the Hill of Slane was to spread its light not only over all of Ireland but over other countries as well. The kings of Connacht and the kings of Munster became Christians, and in a comparatively short time, Christianity had spread throughout the Emerald Isle. St. Patrick's disciples and successors founded monastaries and built churches. Colmcille, or St. Columba, was one of the greatest missionary abbots, whose foundation of Iona became a famous center of learning. St. Columbanus founded monastaries at Luxeuil in Burgundy and Bobbio in Northern Italy. Irish monks helped evangelize tribes in Germany, Franconia, and Lithuania. At all these monasteries, including St. Gall, founded by a disciple of St. Columbanus, the monks built up important libraries and wrote scholarly works.

In the beginning, many of the monks went out in search of solitude, but inevitably they ended up preaching the gospel and setting up religious communities. One of the most famous is at Peronne in northeastern Gaul where St. Fursey is buried. So loved was this scholastic settlement by the Irishmen that it became known as Perona Scottorum, "Peronne of the Irish." It was the Irishman's love of learning fostered by centuries of tradition, combined with the art of writing, that diverted him from invading Britain as a raider to invading all western Europe as a missionary. Monasteries and schools were set up in England and English students came to Ireland for further education where the Irish welcomed them and provided them with books and teachers, often without asking payment.

This period, during the seventh and eighth centuries, was called Ireland's Golden Age, for it was an era when the fusion of Irish and Latin cultures manifested itself in intellectual accomplishments, exquisite gleaming altar vessels, and tombs richly decorated with gold and silver and precious stones. Toward the end of the Golden Age, Ireland was a land which had not been invaded since prehistoric times and which had been Christian for more than three centuries, a land described in these lines from a Latin verse written by Donatus of Fiesole, an Irish bishop living in Italy in the ninth century:

The noblest share of earth is the far western world
Whose name is written Scottia in the ancient books:
Rich in goods, in silver, jewels, cloth and gold,
Benign to the body in air and mellow soil.

With honey and with milk flow Ireland's lovely plains,
With silk and arms, abundant fruit, with art and men.
Worthy are the Irish to dwell in this their land,
A race of men renowned in war, in peace, in faith.

But though the Irish were not to be allowed to dwell in peace, or continue to be rich in silver, jewels, and gold,

they were held together during the disasters that were to
come by the most precious jewel of all, the gift of faith
bestowed on them by St. Patrick.

The first of these disasters came to Ireland in the shape
of a ship that was both fearful and beautiful. In A.D. 795
the Vikings arrived on Ireland's shores. In long low ships
with patterned sails, golden beak and gilded shields gleaming, they came gliding across the Irish Sea, a flotilla of
slender, shiny black swans. It was the monks who feared
them most, for in the past these helmeted Norse warriors
had often ransacked and burned monasteries, carrying off
jeweled shrines and other altar ornaments.

In fact, the prayer of one ninth century French monk
was, "From the fury of the Northmen, Lord deliver us."
The Viking raiders carried off countless relics, many of
which may now be found in the museums of Oslo, Bergen,
Stavanger, and Trondheim. Fortunately the Book of Kells,
that magnificent masterpiece that marked the culmination
of early Irish art, was not destroyed, although the Norse
invasions are thought to be responsible for its unfinished
state.

After numerous invasions and raids the Vikings built
the first fortified settlements, one on the Louth coast, the
other at the ford of the River Liffey. The Irish called these
defended bases *longphorts,* which suggests that the Norsemen began them with the building of a stockade around
their ships. The longphort on the Liffey was actually the
foundation of the city of Dublin.

One wonders why the Irish took so long to rout these
invaders, and the answer can only be found in the fact
that there was no single ruler in ninth century Ireland
who was responsible for the defense of the island as a whole.
There were a great number of small kingdoms, and the
island was divided into two halves: Leth Cuinn, dominated

by the Ui Neill king of Tara, and Leth Mogha, ruled by Egonachta of Cashel. Also, constant quarreling was going on between the kings themselves.

Yet, surprisingly enough, during these politically troubled times progress was being made in other areas. There were new developments in art and scholarship. Stone churches built with mortar were beginning to replace the wooden buildings; elegant bell-houses modeled on those found in Italy were becoming a feature of the Irish landscape. Beautiful works of sculpture were being created, among them the crosses of Patrick and Columba at Kells. In the meantime, the power of the kings of Tara had been strengthening, and Brian Boru became High King after the kings made an effort to patch up their difficulties. Under Brian Boru's leadership the Vikings were defeated at the Battle of Clontarf in 1014. But before the battle was over Brian Boru lay dead.

The Irish and the Vikings learned much from each other. The Irish learned of the Vikings' skillful ways with ships and horses, and had by now adopted their superior weapons. As for the Norsemen, those who stayed on were now largely Christians and took on Irish ways. The Irish language acquired Nordic words that were related to ships and trade. Even some of the place-names, while Irish in vocabulary and form, refer to the presence of Viking colonies. Baldoyle, for example, in County Dublin, means "country of the dark foreigners." Probably the most significant effect the Vikings had on Irish life was that the country's political and social center shifted from the midlands to the east coast, facing the Irish Sea.

The Irish Sea was quite capable of luring yet another invader to Irish shores, this time the Normans. One cannot help wondering if Ireland might not have risen to great glory in the centuries that were to come if it had not been for the Norman invasion. The historian, Goddard Orpen, in his book *Ireland under the Normans,* gives the following opinion:

Had Ireland been allowed to go her way unheeded by Europe, she might in time, and after much suffering, have evolved a better ordered system with some hope of progress in it, and the world might have been a Celtic civilization where Celtic imagination and Celtic genius, free and unfettered, would assuredly have contributed something towards the solution of human problems, which as it is, mankind has missed forever.

Unfortunately, the effect of the Norse invaders on Irish history was a lasting one, and with Brian Boru's death there was little hope of a unified Celtic nation. Besides, only 150 years elapsed between the Battle of Clontarf and the Norman invasion, so Ireland had little time in which to evolve a "better ordered system." This may have been impossible in any case, considering the lust for power that was embodied in the person of Dermot MacMurrough.

It all began with the struggle for supremacy between Murtough of Alech, the most powerful king in Ireland, and Rory O'Connor, king of Connacht. In this struggle, Dermot supported Murtough while Tiernan O'Rourke was on the side of O'Connor. During the struggle between the two factions, O'Connor defeated MacMurrough and reduced his power to a small kingdom centering around Ferns in Wexford. But Tiernan O'Rourke was not content with the mere defeat of his enemy. He was bent on destroying Mac-Murrough altogether, and with good reason. Back in 1152, MacMurrough had abducted O'Rourke's beautiful wife, Dervorgilla, and carried her away to his palace in Ferns. Some say that Dermot was Dervorgilla's first love and that it was not an abduction. At any rate, even though Dermot sent her home a year later, the memory of the dark deed remained to torture O'Rourke. In 1166, with the help of the north Leinster tribes, he attacked MacMurrough and captured Ferns.

After his defeat, Dermot fled to France to seek the aid of the king of England, Henry II. Henry did not offer direct help just then, but he did give Dermot a letter that invited all of Henry's subjects to rally to Dermot's assistance. The letter helped Dermot persuade the Welsh Earl of Pembroke, known as Strongbow, to assist him. Strongbow agreed after exacting a promise from Dermot that he would give him the hand of his daughter, Aoife, and the succession to his kingdom of Leinster. In 1169 Dermot led a small group of Normans, Flemings, and Welsh in the first Norman invasion of Ireland.

The Norman invasion marked the beginning of the end of Rory O'Connor, the last of the High Kings, who was to die in 1198 as a pilgrim in Cong. But although Strongbow finally managed to achieve supremacy over the Norse and Gaelic Irish, his position was to be threatened by still another opponent, his own royal master. Henry II had been closely following the progress of Strongbow's men as they risked their lives and fortunes to accomplish a conquest of Ireland. Now that they had succeeded, he was fearful that a rival Norman dynasty might be set up in Ireland.

Henry sailed for Ireland in October of 1171. Arriving in Waterford he made his way up through the country with his retinue. The Irish, except for the princes of north-westerly parts of the country, paid him homage. Possibly because Pope Adrian IV, a friend of Henry's and the only Englishman ever to sit on the papal throne, had approved Henry's expedition, Irish bishops, including the Archbishop of Dublin, also submitted. It was a bloodless conquest for Henry. Taking up residence in a palace just outside Dublin,

Henry received and entertained the Irish kings who came
to pay homage to him, overwhelming them with his generous gifts.

In 1172 Henry returned to England. No sooner had he
gone than the barons to whom he had granted land renewed
their offensive against the Irish. This offensive led to the
eventual adoption of the Treaty of Windsor. In the treaty,
signed by Henry in October, 1175, Rory O'Connor pledged
himself to recognize Henry as overlord and Henry accepted
Rory as High King of the unconquered areas. But instead
of pointing toward a peaceful solution, the treaty only
paved the way to bloodier battles. Obviously, since Rory
was king in name only, it was impossible for him to enforce
authority even within his own territory in Connacht, and
for all of the O'Connor's continued evidence of loyalty,
his lands were besieged and conquered by the Anglo-
Norman army. Furthermore, despite the treaty he had
signed, Henry began to give away lands that belonged to
the ancient Irish, while his barons kept on seizing more
land.

Now there began a systematic purging of Irish kings and
chieftains, the Anglo-Normans going so far as to plunder
church property, such as the ecclesiastical center at Lis-
more. But in spite of all this destruction, the Normans
were also responsible for bringing in new religious orders
to Ireland, including the Dominicans, Franciscans, Augus-
tians, and Carmelites. In the end, many of the Norman
nobles, weary of battle and anxious to prepare themselves
for the inevitable, founded abbeys where they retired to
spend their last days in prayer.

Some historians suggest that the Normans brought a measure of peace to the country. If so, it was an uneasy peace,
and the price exacted too high, for it was about this time
that the Irish common people became vassals, and the

descendants of dispossessed kings and chiefs began to melt into the peasantry. One cannot but think it a pity that the Normans and the Irish, who shared a common religion, could not have merged to form a unified nation that would be strong enough to prevail against any enemy. In the beginning, this seemed a likely possibility. There was much intermingling and even intermarriage between the two factions, and eventually new generations of Normans began to adopt the Irish language, names, and customs. But in retrospect, the dominant result of the Norman invasion was that it began England's involvement in Irish affairs.

During the reign of Edward II (1307-27), the subjection of the Irish Church to England by virtue of Pope Adrian's Bull, *Laudabiliter,* along with the failure of the English Crown to impose any semblance of peace, caused the chiefs of Ulster to enlist the aid of Edward Bruce, brother of the king of Scotland, Robert Bruce. Landing in Antrim in 1315 with six thousand Scots, he joined the O'Neills. The two combined forces marched south, defeating the English Viceroy de Burgo and destroying all traces of English rule in the south of Ireland. Having scored a series of impressive victories, Bruce was crowned King of Ireland. Although his army was later crushed by Sir John Bermingham at Limerick and he himself slain at Dundalk in 1318, the Crown's position in Ireland had become considerably weakened, and the English were forced to occupy a much more limited area of the country.

Then in the winter of 1348, the Black Death, a plague which had destroyed more than one-third of the population in Europe, descended upon Ireland. When the plague struck Dublin and Drogheda it almost completely depopulated both cities within a few weeks. The Black Death caused panic among the English settlers and many of them fled back to England. Manors were deserted, fields left untilled. Eventually, the plague burnt itself out and the land which had been cleared by the English settlers became a wooded area again.

Meanwhile, both before and after the plague, a Gaelic revival was taking root throughout Ireland, and the government in Dublin was becoming disturbed. An attempt had been made to revive the old high kingship, and although the attempt was not particularly successful, the Irish did exhibit a distinct military advantage. By now they had their own new-styled armies and weapons. They also had the help of the Gallowglasses, a group of mercenary soldiers brought over from Scotland. The Irish had still another advantage. At this point, the financial resources of the English colony, reduced by the loss of territory to Gaelic Ireland and by the migration of settlers, were not adequate to maintain an army that would be successful against the Gaelic chieftains.

It seemed as if Ireland, known to the Europeans in the past as a land of saints and scholars, had a good chance of reclaiming her own at last. During this Gaelic revival many of the greatest books were written in Irish. It was a time when the poets and scholars had as their patrons some of the Gaelic noble families. Even the Anglo-Irish nobility were sponsoring Gaelic men of letters. But alas, by 1366 the government in Dublin was so alarmed at the degree of assimilation that had already taken place that it passed the famous piece of legislation called the Statutes of Kilkenny. This law prohibited the families of Anglo-Norman settlers in Ireland from adopting Irish surnames, language, dress, manners, or customs.

By the time Richard II came to the throne in 1377 the English had suffered such a loss of power in Ireland that MacMurrough Kavanagh, King of Leinster, had become virtually king of Dublin and was receiving from that city an annual tribute. England, although engaged in a war with Scotland and involved in a long-term struggle with France, nevertheless sent Richard II on an expedition to Ireland. With the largest army ever seen in Ireland backing him — thirty thousand in all — he was still unable to put down the Irish, and the ensuing contests caused a French chronicler to say, "The Irish cannot be conquered while the leaves are on the trees." While fighting the Irish in Leinster bad news from England forced Richard to sail home, where he found he had been deprived of his throne and kingdom by the Duke of Lancaster. Richard II was the last English king to come to Ireland during the Middle Ages.

Although Ireland was left alone for a time during the fifteenth century, this was no longer true after Henry VIII came to the English throne. In his efforts to gain control of Ireland, he was responsible for some of the most significant and deplorable changes ever made there. Under his pressure, many of the Irish lords swore allegiance to Henry and gave up their lands to the Crown, receiving them back as feudal grants. Some of the lords went so far as to agree "to learn English, to cease wearing distinctively Irish garments, and to establish uniformity of language and dress through the dominion."

Henry's policy of granting English titles to the great lords created further rebellion. Under Henry's rule, the old Brehon Law disappeared, to be replaced by English law. Such a radical change was bound to lead to tribal difficulties but, as Henry knew full well, the best means of destroying a nation was to divide it against itself.

It must have been painful for the Gaelic people to see their fellow Irishmen being seduced by all the pageantry and pomp of Henry's court. Yet they were to witness an

even more painful scene. Henry became aware of the great
wealth of the monasteries and, during the period between
1536 and 1539, ordered them destroyed and confiscated.
Having enriched himself and his English friends, he began
giving some of the confiscated monasteries to his new
loyal earls. But even though Henry introduced the Reformation to Ireland, and had an act of Parliament passed to
make him Supreme Head on Earth of the Church in Ireland, he never attempted to destroy the Catholic religion.

This, however, was not true of his daughter Elizabeth.
"Divide and conquer!" said Henry. "Suppress and starve,"
replied Elizabeth. Elizabeth had more than a passing degree
of interest in Ireland, for her mother, Ann Boleyn, had
been reared in Ireland by her cousins, the Butlers. Elizabeth,
a staunch Protestant, was a proud and aggressive woman
who had every intention of seeing to it that the whole of
Ireland became Protestant. To accomplish this, she set up
a plantation system. Within a short period of time Elizabeth had arranged to have foreigners brought in to replace
the dispossessed Irishmen. These people preferred to be
called settlers, but were in fact, land-grabbers, for they
were allowed to occupy homes already built on land
already developed.

While Queen Elizabeth's tactics were leading to an idea-
logical struggle, the struggle of Catholic against Protestant,
rebellions were taking place all over Ireland, particularly
in Connacht and Munster. Eventually, the Spaniards and
the Italians came to assist the Irish rebels, making England
all the more determined to crush Ireland. In 1600 Lord
Deputy Mountjoy came over to put down the rebellion in
Ulster.

It has been said that Mountjoy made a black desert of
Ulster. He destroyed cornfields and burned houses. His
successful ventures came to a climax in 1601 at the Battle

of Kinsale where he finally defeated the Irish. The victory
at Kinsale was a decisive one for the English. But for the
Irish it was to mean, with the overthrow of O'Neill and
O'Donnell, the downfall of the last of the Gaelic lordships
and the end of the Irish world.

Following the Battle of Kinsale, O'Neill and O'Donnell,
earls of Tyrone and Tyrconnell, had been allowed to return
to their own lands and live among their own people. However, after several years they could no longer abide living
under the subjection of the English Crown, so in 1607,
they, along with ninety other leading men of Ulster, went
into exile on the continent. Soon after the flight of the
earls, the government began setting up plantations on a
larger scale than ever before. The land in Armagh, Cavan,
Donegal, Derry, Fermanagh, and Tyrone was confiscated
and parceled out in lots of from one to two thousand acres,
at easy rents, but only on the condition that those who
received the grant had to bring in Protestant tenants to
cultivate the soil. Taking the land from the Catholic
Irish and handing it over to the Protestant immigrants was
a familiar policy, and one well calculated to weaken resistance to English rule.

King James, son of Mary, Queen of Scots, raised hopes
in Irish hearts, but alas, he could not manage the pressures
brought to bear on him by the powerful anti-Catholic forces.
Things began to look brighter when Charles I, at war with
Spain, and having financial difficulties, promised to grant
the "Old English" in Ireland certain concessions in return
for a sizable loan of money. The "Old English" were an
influential group of people who, though English by descent,
were Catholic in religion. The fact that the government
considered all Catholics to be disloyal had been creating a
serious problem for these people. Naturally, they were
willing to loan the money to Charles.

As it turned out, Charles reneged on his promises and the "Old English," distrustful of the English Parliament, formed an alliance with the Catholic Irish. Calling themselves the Confederate Catholics, they adopted a motto, "Ireland united for God and king and country." For several years these Confederate Catholics engaged in rebellions, until England, bringing her own civil war to an end with the execution of Charles I, turned her attention to the Emerald Isle once more.

In 1649 Oliver Cromwell, current symbol of English power, landed in Dublin with his Puritan army. It has often been said that there is nothing in the annals of history to surpass the brutality of Cromwell's army in Ireland. He began by marching on Drogheda where he massacred the garrison and butchered the townspeople. The thousands of men, women, and children who survived were sent as slaves to labor in the Barbados. As a result of Cromwell's successful sieges, Ireland inevitably fell into England's hands again. Now there was created not just a Protestant community, but a Protestant upper class, by transferring the sources of wealth and power from Catholics to Protestants. By May 1, 1654, those under sentence of confiscation were forced to leave their homes and transplant themselves west of the Shannon — "to hell or Connacht."

James II came to the throne in 1685, reviving the hopes of the Irish once more, but he was a king with "one shoe English and one shoe Irish." His actions were primarily motivated by a desire to regain his throne; thus he was committed to keeping Ireland under the subordination of the English Crown. Several notable members of the English Parliament asked William of Orange, husband of James II's Protestant daughter, to invade England and help them get rid of his Catholic father-in-law. Aware that his cause was collapsing, James fled to France, and in March of 1689 he landed at Kinsale with French money and arms to embark on what was to be described as a war between two kings.

William himself, coming over to Ireland with about thirty-six thousand troops, defeated James in a battle that took place about three miles above Drogheda. Fighting continued until in 1691 the Dutch general, Ginkel, crossed the Shannon at Athlone and scored an impressive victory. Limerick, which had managed to hold out until then under the gallant leadership of Patrick Sarsfield, finally attempted negotiations. In October, the Treaty of Limerick was signed by Sarsfield. But although the terms of the treaty clearly stated that Catholics were to enjoy religious liberty, the English Parliament engaged in further land confiscations and continued to discriminate against Catholics.

It was at this time that the Penal Laws were passed, laws that resulted in almost one hundred years of persecution of Christians by Christians. The following are some examples of laws passed to penalize Catholics:

Catholic schoolmasters were forbidden to teach or send their children to any foreign country to be educated.

All orders of priests, Jesuits, and the like, were to leave the country before May 1, 1698. (Subsequently, many bishops and hundreds of the regular clergy left the country and were forbidden to return under penalty of death.)

No Catholic church should have a steeple or bell.

If a Catholic had a horse worth above five pounds, any Protestant might get possession of it by offering five pounds.

If a wife of a Catholic became a Protestant, she could claim separate support and one-third of his property.

No Catholic could buy land or take a lease for longer than thirty-one years.

Eventually, the public offering of the mass was forbidden, and priests had to retreat to isolated valleys or some lonely hill, where sentries kept watch for the possible arrival of the law. Sad to say, there were those who made a living by being priest-hunters, and sometimes the English soldiers, coming upon a mass gathering, slaughtered the people who were unable to escape and tortured the priests. It was during this period when Catholics were not allowed to build churches, that the custom began of referring to the place of worship as a chapel.

Without dwelling on the indignities our ancestors had to endure in those dark days, it is nevertheless necessary to know that such things happened if we are to understand the desperate measures taken by the Whiteboys and the Raparrees and the famous Fenians who were to come upon the scene later. We cannot but have a tremendous amount of admiration for those persecuted people. Threatened from every direction, they never once lost their faith, or that indomitable spirit that is so much a part of every Irishman.

By the end of the eighteenth century the English found themselves in a somewhat dispirited state, the old Empire having at last fallen to defeat in America. The Irish had naturally felt sympathy for the American revolutionaries; in fact, many of the Irish who had gone to America helped fight the war against England. With England's defeat, Irish optimism again prevailed and rebellion became the order of the day. But for all of the courageous efforts of the French officer, Wolfe Tone, and the work of the patriot, Robert Emmet, the rebellion of '98 was not only unsuccessful, but was to lead to the Act of Union.

Under the Act of Union, passed January 1, 1801, Ireland and England became one. The Irish Parliament of

Dublin was no more and the English Parliament was now legislating for both England and Ireland. The terms of this act, which has often been described as a brutal rape rather than a union, were opposed vigorously, but with no success. The Act of Union became law.

The effects were disastrous. Because of the free trade existing between the two countries, England was now able to use Ireland as a market for surplus goods. As a result, Irish industry collapsed and unemployment became widespread. Worse than that, Catholic emancipation, which the people had been led to believe would follow, did not come to pass. The very day he received the news that the Act of Union had been put into effect, Daniel O'Connell, then twenty-five, wrote in his journal, "I was travelling through the mountains from Killarney to Kenmare. My heart was heavy, and the day was wild and gloomy. The deserted district was congenial to solemnity and sadness. . . . My soul felt dreary at the loss Ireland had sustained . . . ."

Addressing a meeting of Protestants in 1809, this struggling lawyer advised the group that the union had cost Ireland ninety million dollars of revenue at this point and that absentee landlords were spending more than two million pounds outside the country each year, money which had been wrung from the peasants. In his speech, he warned these men that the situation could only end in bankruptcy and famine. "Union," O'Connell cried in despair, "is a crime to begin with and must continue to be, unless crime, like wine, improves with old age."

Giving up his law practice, O'Connell devoted his efforts toward repeal of the Act of Union, and toward Catholic emancipation, which was finally achieved in 1829. To accomplish repeal was somewhat more difficult, especially when Sir Robert Peel became Prime Minister, for Sir Robert, dubbed "Orange Peel," was opposed to both repeal and Catholic emancipation. The situation came to a climax with the mass meeting held by O'Connell at Tara, the ancient seat of Irish kings in Meath.

Unfortunately, O'Connell's attempt to bring about reform by peaceable means alarmed the English goverment, which would have been much less apprehensive if the people had resorted to violence. Consequently, when O'Connell announced an even larger meeting to be held in Clontarf, the government set their plans in motion. The day before the meeting was to be held, warships entered Dublin Bay and troops were stationed at all approaches to the meeting place. O'Connell, remembering the hangings and torturings and floggings that followed in the wake of the rebellion of '98, held to his creed: "Human blood is no cement for the temple of liberty." Yet, in spite of the fact that he ordered his followers to return to their homes, he was arrested a week later, convicted by a packed jury, and sent to prison.

By this time the Irish people, facing the loss of another leader, had been under the domination of the English for nearly seven hundred years. At least three times the native aristocracy had been conquered and dispossessed, and although many fled to France or Spain, many remained to be forced down by poverty to the economic level of peasantry. Under these circumstances, it was not surprising to find that until the famine it was quite common for peasants in mud cabins to make wills bequeathing their estates, estates that had long ago been confiscated from their forefathers.

During the pre-famine years, Ireland was already suffering from unemployment and a shortage of farm land. To make matters worse, by 1841 Ireland had a population of over eight million, one of the most densely populated countries in Europe. The Irish peasant, who for centuries had been deprived of any sort of livelihood but that of working the land, was now allowed to do so only in order to make revenue for the landowners. Yet, the holdings at this time were so small — in Connacht, 64 percent of the holdings consisted of five acres or less — that a man considered it a miracle if he managed enough revenue to pay his rent. In most cases, the butter paid the rent, a strip of linen and the wool of three sheep were usually sufficient to clothe his family, while potatoes and milk maintained the diet of the household.

But in spite of the fact that this simple diet produced rosy-cheeked children with strong teeth, the Irish in general had a poor opinion of the potato. Sometimes they expressed their feelings in song:

> *Pratai ar maidin, pratai um noin,*
> *'s da n-eireochainn i*
> *Meadhon oidhche,*
> *Pratai a gheobhainn!*

> Potatoes at morning,
> Potatoes at noon,
> And if I were to rise at midnight,
> Potatoes I'd get.

In the days before the famine, although the people of Ireland were forced to work very hard just to stay alive, early marriages were the custom. Girls often were married at sixteen and boys at seventeen. For one thing, neither men nor women achieved full status in the community until they were married. The couple, guided and advised by their parents both before and after marriage, invariably ended up with a large family. This fact helps explain the density of Ireland's population in the pre-famine years.

But no matter how persistently one searches the records, it is impossible to find any sort of logical explanation for the famine itself, the aftermath of which can only be described as a tragedy of errors. Although the famine years cover a period from 1845 to 1849, there had been a series of potato crop failures beginning as early as 1770, and by 1839 crop failure was again universal throughout Ireland.

At the height of the famine it seemed to be the fashion for British officials to issue statements indicating that reports concerning the alleged failure of the potato crop were highly exaggerated. Indeed, when one of the British officials finally wrote to Sir Robert Peel to advise him that the reports had not been exaggerated, but actually may have been understated, Peel reminded the official of the Irishman's eternal tendency to exaggerate Irish news.

What is most ironic is the fact that the hundreds of people who were dying in ditches by the roadside were starving to death in a land of plenty. In the second year of the famine, Ireland was producing sufficient food, wool, and flax to feed and clothe eight million people. And in the summer of that same year, ship after ship sailed down the Shannon carrying wheat, oats, cattle, pigs, eggs, and butter. But as one Irish farmer in Cork explained, "A man would have to be desperate to resort to eating up his rent." This seemed to be the attitude of most of the people, for they had a horror of eviction, the aftermath of which they described as "death by slow torture."

During the course of the famine, evictions took place all over Ireland. In March 1846, in one mass eviction in the village of Ballinglass, County Galway, seventy-six families, numbering three hundred people in all, were forced to sleep in "scalps," holes dug in the earth and roofed over with sticks and pieces of turf. It was later discovered that these evicted people were actually not in arrears, but in fact had their rent money ready.

In that same year when autumn was at hand, hordes of starving people who had been relying on nettles and cabbage leaves crowded the barren fields, their fingers combing through dead stalks for anything that might remain. As time went on, the roads became thronged with people who were fleeing from a land they never would have thought it possible for them to leave. Taking with them a few salted herring, or some treasured momento — often so humble an object as a piece of whitewashed plaster broken from the outside wall of a cabin — they joined the procession that would lead them to Waterford, or Killala in County Mayo, or Cobh, or Dublin, ports where they might board one of those antiquated and overcrowded vessels that were given the name "coffin ships." A barque of this type called the *Elizabeth and Sara* sailed out of Killala with two hundred seventy-six passengers, although it was capable of carrying no more than half that number. The *Elizabeth and Sara* took eight weeks to reach Quebec. During the course of the journey, passengers starved, the water supply became depleted, and forty-two persons died.

On May 30, 1847, Mr. Robert Whyte embarked in Dublin on a brig carrying Irish emigrants, among them a party of tenants from County Meath who had been evicted by their landlord. Whyte traveled as a cabin passenger and kept a diary of the voyage, which he entitled *The Ocean Plague.* The diary revealed the carelessness of the doctors who conducted medical examinations of the passengers prior to embarkation and allowed many ill people to board, including one man dying of consumption. Other notes indicated shortage of food, and food not properly cooked, which caused many stomach ailments. On June 15 fever broke out. One hundred and ten passengers were shut up in the hold without doctor, medicine, or water. When the men came up on deck to demand food for their ill wives and children, a mate fired his blunderbuss and forced the men back into the hold.

The diary mentions that although the ship arrived in Quebec in July, the sick were not taken off until August 1, by which time many had died. The sick and dead were transported from the ship to Grosse Isle, where there was no pier of any kind. "Hundreds were flung on the beach, left amid the mud and stones to crawl on dry land as they could," wrote Whyte.

In one of the last passages of his diary, Mr. Whyte tells how he had gone to the funeral of the wife of one of the Meath emigrants. "After the grave was filled up, the husband placed two shovels in the form of a cross and said, 'By the cross, Mary, I swear to avenge your death. As soon as I earn the price of my passage home, I'll go back and shoot the man that murdered you — and that's the landlord.'"

Unfortunately, the conduct of government officials, particularly during the latter part of the famine (1847-1849) only served to contribute to the sufferings of the people. Lord John Russell and his advisers, for example, forced famine-stricken applicants for relief to give up their every possession, thus creating additional armies of paupers. As a result, Irish people suffered a complete loss of confidence in the English goverment. Because Ireland thereafter became the guilty conscience of the ruling class, there was more reason than ever for the English to suppress knowledge of Irish history.

Out of the estimated two and a half million who met their death from starvation during the "Great Hunger," at least a million were Irish-speaking. With the continuing emigration of millions of others, those left behind knew not only the loneliness of losing close kin and neighbors, but another loneliness, that of losing touch with the Irish language, the main link with their ancient history and culture. During the post-famine years when, as John

Mitchel, founder of the newspaper the *United Irishmen,* so aptly put it, "A calm still horror was all over the land," the Irish were often referred to as the "Silent People." Indeed, toward the end of the nineteenth century the Irish language was close to extinction in many parts of Ireland.

Yet all the while, at a time when Ireland's soul was said to be sleeping, there were men seeking out hidden treasures, poring over unsifted manuscripts, making every effort to kindle sparks in peasant souls. The Society for the Preservation of the Irish Language was formed in 1876. Then in 1893 Douglas Hyde and Eoin MacNeill, attempting to revive the Irish language, return to the native culture, and de-Anglicize the country, founded the Gaelic League. By the early part of the twentieth century, English-speaking people in Dublin from all walks of life were learning to speak and read and write in Gaelic.

During this period of their country's awakening, young men and women took to spending their holidays in Irish-speaking districts so that they might practice speaking Irish with those who had somehow still managed to cling to the ancestral language. Often, too, they went to summer school to learn the native dances and to learn the words and tunes of folk songs that had been sung by their ancestors. Some of them went so far as to wear traditional Irish costumes fashioned of blue-green, Irish-manufactured material, and embroidered with designs out of the Book of Kells. It mattered little to them that a few of the more unimaginative might see fit to deride them with remarks such as, "Will you look at those Irishers trying to look like stained glass windows!" They were too busy becoming involved in their new quest for freedom, and discovering in the process what it was to be of Irish descent.

CHAPTER 6

WHAT IS AN IRISHMAN?

LONG AGO at a time when Cormac MacArt found it necessary to resign as High King of Ireland, he took it upon himself to instruct his son Cairbre, so that he would be able to
faithfully perform his duties as High King. In his reply to
Cairbre, who had asked him what he did when he was a
young man, he stressed certain qualities that are characteristic of the Irish race. "I was fierce in the battlefield,"
said Cormac. "I was gentle in friendship."

That the Irish were fierce in battle cannot be denied.
Various military leaders, including George Washington,
have not hesitated to say that some of their best soldiers
and officers were Irish. However, the old saw that "the
Irish are never at peace but when they're fighting" has a
meaning that goes beyond purely military exploits. On the
eve of America's Civil War, for example, Colonel Michael
Corcoran of the famous Fighting 69th peacetime militia
company created quite a tempest when he refused to parade
his men in honor of the visiting Prince of Wales. Some
fifty years later, the Irish-dominated Central Labor Union
came near to dynamiting the Brooklyn Bridge when its
opening was inadvertently scheduled on the birthday of
the "famine queen," Victoria.

Obviously, the sensitivities behind these actions can
best be understood by those who are familiar with Ireland's
long history of oppression. The Irish are of an excitable

and impulsive nature. Perhaps it is the latter quality that makes it possible for them to be gentle in friendship, and so generous in sharing whatever they might have with others.

In the olden days, anyone who had partaken of food in an Irishman's home was considered to be secure against harm or hurt from any member of the family, and no one was ever turned away. Since with the coming of Christianity the Irish considered Christ to be in the person of every guest, to close the door against anyone was to run the risk of having Christ close the door against them. Later on, and even during the famine years, the Irish continued the practice of opening their door to the wandering traveler. Indeed, one of the old Irish songs contains the lines, "We've an extra potato right hot on the fire, for one who may be passing through wet bog and mire." Hospitality, the pride of the ancient Irish, still exists in Ireland today. Whether the wayfarer be friend or stranger, he can be sure of receiving a hail of *Cead mile failte* — A hundred thousand welcomes!" should he approach the door of a country cottage, and it is not often he will be able to leave without having partaken of both food and drink.

The Irish are a naturally democratic people, and there is a distinct lack of affectation among them. Those who have acquired a considerable amount of formal education do not show off their learning, but rather tend to gracefully conceal it. Other traditional attributes associated with the Irish include courtesy, a high sense of honor, and ease of manner. Irish children are taught at a very early age to be truthful, courteous, and respectful — in other words, trained to show consideration for others. Such virtues, like chickens that come home to roost, often bring rewards to the parents who instilled them.

"If you are kind to your parents," Irish children are told, "you will have a long life." And hadn't Cormac, grandson of Conn of the Hundred Battles, given his own son similar advice back in the third century when he said, "Do not deride the old, though you are young."

In Ireland it is rare to find an aging parent being cast aside by his offspring. Even if it required a miracle to provide food for an extra mouth, the Irish son or daughter would sooner starve than shift the obligation elsewhere. "It's easy to halve the potato where there's love," says the old Irish proverb.

Back in 1830 there was one Irish daughter-in-law who was not willing to go along with the old proverb, for she bitterly resented the presence of her husband's father in the home. Torn by anxiety over her increasing brood of children, she indulged in constant tantrums until to her intense relief the father-in-law, wishing his son to have peace in his family life, decided to leave the house.

On the morning the old man was to take to the road the son begged him to stay. Attempting to soothe him, the old man said, "God will give me enough while I live, for He that feeds the sparrows will put it into the hearts of good Christians to give me that little."

The daughter-in-law began fixing a bag of food for him to take with him, glancing nervously now and then at her seven-year-old son who was sitting in a corner of the kitchen sewing his bib into a bag.

"What are you doing?" the father asked the boy.

"Making a bag for you to go beg — when you're as old as Granddad," he replied.

At that the daughter-in-law burst into tears and asked forgiveness of them all. Thus the old man was saved by the remark of a sensitive and compassionate child.

That the Irish are a compassionate people is shown in their treatment of the mentally ill. Mr. and Mrs. S. C. Hall, an English couple who wrote a series of books on Ireland in 1842, made a strange but interesting observation regarding the attitude of the natives toward these unfortunate people. "One might imagine that the Irish, like the Turks, believe insanity to be an inspiration, judging from the tenderness and care they evince towards the poor wandering idiots, who rarely provoke a harsh or an unkind expression from the peasantry." ·

Cheerfully fed and sheltered by the country people, these mentally ill were referred to by the Irish as "innocents" or "naturals." Often too they had special names for them, such as Reddy the Rhymer, or in the case of a woman who wandered alone along the seashore, a poetic Irish name which meant "the storm bird." Whenever a farmer or fisherman caught a glimpse of this woman's red cloak fluttering in the breeze they would know a tempest was at hand, for her visits always took place at twilight just before the onset of a storm. It was said she never spoke a single word until the sun went down and even then she kept repeating one phrase over and over, "Beauty fades, death comes — beauty fades, death comes."

The evening chanting of this particular "innocent" may have been an expression of her desire to come to terms with the inevitability of the day's ending, and the ending of life itself. The Irish people in general have a philosophical outlook which enables them to face the tragedies of life with a reasonable degree of grace. Between the 1880s and the rising of 1916 when the Irish rebellion was taking the form of a land war, families were evicted from their homes, and the remains of many burnt houses with roofless walls loomed up, blackened and broken, to desecrate the landscape. Yet in spite of the fact that they were surrounded by memories of famines and frustrated insurrections, the Irish people, secure in their belief that the difficulties of this world would be compensated for in the next, still managed to retain their natural tendency toward happiness.

The Irish are a witty and charming people, with a talent for indulging in the sort of dialogue that would be quite at home on the stage of a theater. Without a doubt, they have a unique way of putting words together. But conversation is more than a mere interchange of words. It is a game of wits Irishmen play. So subtle is the manner in which the game is played that the Irishman who has been away from his native land for too long a spell may find he needs to sharpen his own wits if he wishes to play the game with any degree of success.

Not long ago a priest who had been in America and Japan went back to Eire for a visit. On his first day in the country he wandered about letting his camera capture the half-remembered scenes of his childhood. Pausing to rest he stood alone on a bridge surveying the distant mountains. Finally, he decided to hike up the mountainside to take additional pictures. But no sooner had he reached the desired spot than he realized he had left his light meter on the bridge and had to go back.

With relief he found the meter had not disappeared. but this time he wasn't alone on the bridge — an elderly man was standing nearby. Attempting to begin a conversation, the priest remarked how lucky it was that the light meter was still in the place where he had left it.

"Tis many a man it would suit," said the old man dryly.

After making further futile stabs at conversation, the priest asked the man if he knew any spots in the neighborhood where he might be able to shoot some scenic pictures.

The old man hesitated for a moment, his eyes seeming to take in the sweep of green fields, the distant lavender hills, and the runaway brook rustling with water lilies. Then he said with a sigh, "Sure it would be hard to know what's in another man's mind."

It is apparent that the Irishman, for all the joy he takes in trading words, simply refuses to do so on a superficial level. He is blessed with an extraordinary degree of perception, and will be able to tell in an instant if you are talking off the top of your head.

Because they have this talent for self-expression, the Irish may show impatience with those who do not share the gift. Although the virtue of patience was high on the list of Cormac's code of ethics, it must be said that it is not a trait possessed by all Irishmen, who have often been heard to exclaim, "I could crawl the wall when I hear that man murdering the language."

"If you be too talkative, you will not be heeded," said Cormac to Cairbre. And since the Irishman is inclined to be gregarious, he may often be accused, and rightly so, of not knowing when to stop talking. He has also been accused of not knowing when to stop drinking. What about the Irishman's drinking habits? In truth, he is not the most skillful drinker in the world. The trouble is, he is intoxicated before he so much as takes a drink! Combine his explosive nature with the imbibed spirits and there is bound to be produced an effect that is all out of proportion to the amount of consumed liquor.

The Irish in America were often stereotyped as heavy drinkers. The fact is, many of them belonged to the Temperance Society and never touched a drop of liquor. On the other hand, those who did indulge preferred to do their drinking in public so that they might enjoy social intercourse with others. As a result the Irishman's drinking was more conspicuous than members of other ethnic groups who preferred to drink their beer or wine in the privacy of their homes. Be that as it may, it must be admitted that the Irish had no trouble whatsoever finding an excuse for drinking. Some of them drank heavily to forget the disappointments of their lives. Others drank for the glory of life, for the glory of God, or to oil the machinery of their minds so that their thoughts might flow freely.

In fact, the Irish were the first to be skilled in the art of distillation. In the early days, the fiery liquid was called *uiscebeatha,* which was the local translation for "water of life," *aqua vitae* in Latin. Distilled on a broad scale by monks, surgeons, or "barbours," whiskey was in the beginning primarily used for medicinal purposes. It was not until the sixteenth century that domestic distillation became common. During the seventeenth century Richard Stanhurst was singing the praises of whiskey with these words: "It scowereth all scurf; it sloweth age; it cutteth flegme; it pounceth the stone; it expelleth gavel; it keepeth the head from whirling, the mouth from maffling, the stomach from wambling, the heart from swelling, the belly from wirtching, the guttes from rumbling . . . it is a sovereign liquor."

With such a good advertising campaign, whiskey, if risky, was bound to be popular. And even though reports of Irish drinking may be somewhat exaggerated, it is still no doubt a popular pastime in Ireland. "Taking the country as a whole," writes Anthony Butler in *The Book of Blarney,* "there is about one public house or saloon for every sixty drinkers." But for all of that, it is apparent to anyone familiar with the country that the Irishman seeks out these "spas" for purposes that go beyond the need for quenching his thirst. Many an old man in an Irish townland, seeking to escape the solitude that was once prized so highly by the great Cormac MacArt, uses the pub as an antidote for daytime loneliness. And in an Irish pub in the evening one may hear discussions on theology, literature — over half of the population is writing — or you might pick up interesting scraps of conversation that end like this: "Oh, *m'anam le Dhia* — My soul to God! What excuse can a man give for returning home at such an hour. At three o'clock of a mornin' would freeze the words in your throat!"

The Irishman may love his home, but it would appear, at least in some cases, that he spends a great deal of time away from it. Not just because of his affinity for the pub, but because he is more at home in the company of men than in the company of women. Let a nice day present itself and himself won't hesitate an instant before deciding to get in a few hours of fishing. The gate latch may need fixing; the fence may be sagging. But as far as the Irishman is concerned, the fence will be there long after he is gone, but he can be sure this day, so uniquely decorated with sky, sun, and sea suds, will never pass his way again.

Which brings us to another characteristic of the Irish — their disregard for material possessions. Somehow, the Irish people never seem to concern themselves with the acquisition of material things. Few possessions have been passed from one generation to another. Even if a family did possess a few valuable pieces of furniture they found it quite painless to part with them. During the latter part of the nineteenth century — and even later — it was not uncommon to find a family selling a set of eighteenth century chairs so that their son might avail himself of a college education. The Irish have inherited a fairly good self-concept, a pride of race, a long memory of historical and legendary events — and these are a more important legacy than material goods.

Here we are forced to deal with an aggravating aspect of the Irish nature. Let someone ask him what he would choose to be if he could not be Irish and he will immediately reply, "Dead!" The truth is, the Irish are so proud to be Irish they are inclined to irritate their fellowmen with their incessant boasting. Forgive the Irishman if he boasts of a name like O'Hara or O'Gara, or holds you captive for hours while he informs you of the brilliance of his son the politician, or the accomplishments of his daughter the nun. If he is capable of being loyal to his family, he is also capable of being loyal to his country.

One of the most predominant Irish traits is the quality of faithfulness. There are, in fact, fewer divorces in Ireland than in most, if not all, other countries. There are those who will be quick to say that many couples stay together because of their religious beliefs. While this is true to some extent, it is not the complete answer, for there has always been a deep attachment in Irish marriages. Time was when a second marriage was considered an insult to the dead spouse, and if in spite of this prevailing attitude a man did remarry, his neighbors felt compelled to apologize for him.

If the quality of faithfulness was sometimes carried to extremes, so too was the quality of family loyalty. Many a young woman marrying a son of the old sod has tried in vain to cut through the barrier that separated her from her Irish spouse's flesh and blood family. As far as being clannish is concerned, the Irish come second to none. An Irishman who emigrated at an early age would, for understandable reasons, usually settle in an area where other relatives had settled before him. Since he had to work doubly hard to give an account of himself in a strange new land where there abounded plenty of preconceived notions about the Irishman's character, or lack of it, he was forced to depend on his own people, not only for the pleasures of socializing, but also to support some degree of emotional security.

The almost claustrophobic closeness of the family unit, along with the interdependence of related families, eventually caused the Irish to be accused of having an inflated opinion of themselves. Fortunately, such clannish tendencies are fairly rare these days. In most families a prospective daughter-in-law is given a warm welcome. Especially if she is lucky enough to have a name like O'Meara or O'Farrell.

One hears a great deal about the luck of the Irish. Lucky they may be, but a closer observation leads one to believe pluck would be a more appropriate word. Contrary to certain prevalent opinions, an Irishman can be a hard-working individual when the necessity presents itself. Most of us have heard about the number of Boston Irishmen who became self-made millionaires. But few people know of the contributions made by Irishmen who settled in the little towns and villages throughout America. The records are there for us all to see if we care to take the trouble to look them up. They reveal the history of many a man who started out with a small parcel of land and ended up with a farm for each of his sons, having furthermore managed to secure a proper education for each member of his family. That these Irishmen left a mark on the community is indicated by the numerous obituary notices in small-town papers which include lines such as these:

The church was filled with a great throng of people who came from near and far to pay a last tribute to the memory of a respected citizen, a good neighbor, a faithful friend.

No lines of praise remain to honor the "Black Don-nellys." The interesting, if somewhat gory, true story of Canada's most barbaric Irish feud began back in Tipper-ary when young Jim Donnelly's father received a letter from a friend telling him of the golden opportunities that awaited him in the New World. Although the elder Don-nelly never did get to Canada, the dream of doing so had been firmly planted in his son's mind. Along about the summer of 1842, with little thought of what fate had in

store for him, Jim and some of his pals went to Clonmel
to attend the fair. Fun and frolic were to be found there,
along with generous helping of poteen, and in no time at
all there developed a faction fight. Jim was giving a pretty
good account of himself when one of the fighters tore
the shillelagh from his hand. The next minute a girl named
Johannah Foley was jabbing him in the ribs and thoughtfully supplying him with another weapon.

It wasn't long before he and Johannah were married,
and for the next three years Johannah worked right alongside her man in the fields. She also gave birth to two sons,
tended the household chores, and even found time to take
part in a shillelagh fight now and then. But all the while
she kept putting aside a regular amount of money which
one day would add up to enough to take them all to the
New World. Came a night in the winter of 1845 when the
snow was coming down in such a way as to suggest to
Johannah that "the auld woman was plucking her geese,"
and off the family went to sail for London, Ontario.

No matter how successful they might be in the years
to come, both Jim and Johannah would have undoubtedly
agreed — had they been given the chance — that none of
it was worth the travail it brought them. In Biddulph
Township, near the village of Lucan, Jim got off to a
bad start by settling on privately owned land. With the
indomitable Johannah beside him, and himself acting in
a manner that set the natives to saying, "When that
Donnelly glares at you, you seem to hear the sound of
shovels digging your grave," it took a mighty brave man
to take issue with Jim's error in judgment. By the time
the stormy couple had birthed and raised four more sons
and a daughter, they were known as the terror of the
township. Then in the early morning hours of February
4, 1880, the Donnellys — at least those who were in the

house at the time — were brutally murdered by a mob
of revengeful men who had never been able to accept
them as friends or neighbors.

Needless to say, the Donnellys were no more typical of
the race than was the stage Irishman of long ago. But they
did exhibit — at least Johannah did — certain traits
peculiar to the Irish. For one thing, Johannah possessed
the gift of humor. There was, for example, the time her
son Willy carried a note home from his teacher complaining that Willy brought an unpleasant odor to school
with him. Did Johannah rush out to the drugstore to seek
out products that might make her Willy more acceptable?
Of course she didn't. She merely sat down and calmly
composed a note of her own.

"Teach Willy!" she admonished his teacher. "Don't
smell him. Willy's no rose!"

It was Johannah's cleverness that saved her husband's
life when he was under threat of being hanged for killing
another man in a quarrel. At her bidding Jim hid out in
the woods, Johannah herself agreeing to take over the
farm chores until things cooled down. Each night at the
stroke of twelve she put a candle in the window to let
him know it was safe to come home for a good hot meal
and extra provisions. On nights when the constable and
his deputies paid unexpected calls, she somehow managed
to light three candles as a prearranged warning signal
without arousing the suspicions of the law. During one
of those nocturnal visits she even succeeded in getting
the constable to place the three lighted candles in the
window.

Johannah was an intensely loyal woman. There was
nothing she would not do for her family. She had a lot
of common sense, too. Once her middle son went off on
an adventuring tour. Coming home months later he

plopped himself down in a chair by the fireside with this statement: "Mom, I've come home to die."

"You're a liar," said Johannah. "You came home to eat." And no sooner had she put things in their proper perspective than she went to fix him a decent meal.

If Johannah lacked some of the gentler traits, we must remember she was born and raised in the Galtee Mountains during an era when toughness was a necessary ingredient. Schooling was not easy to come by in those days, especially in such isolated areas as the Galtees. In that lonely mountain place where Jim and Johannah grew up, it is more than likely that neither of them had ever heard of an Irish king named Cormac MacArt. Deprived of any sort of education in their own land, and deprived of even one offer of friendship in the New World that had once held such promise, it is possible that Johannah Foley and Jim Donnelly were forced to draw their philosophy of life from the old Irish proverb which claims, "Better the fighting than the loneliness."

CHAPTER 7

UNDER THE HEDGEROW

FEW IRISH AMERICANS are aware of the difficulties our ancestors encountered in their quest for knowledge. Since education was at a particularly low level in the early part of the nineteenth century, it is fortunate that our great-grandparents had such a great reverence for learning. In truth, there were periods in Irish history when they had to somehow manage to educate themselves, and often at the risk of their lives.

In 1831, the British government established the National Schools. Although the new system of education marked the beginning of free primary education at public expense, the schools were referred to by the Irish as "Foreign Schools." As a passage from the ballad "Galway Bay" puts it, "The stranger came and tried to teach us their ways. They scorned us for being what we are."

The trouble was, the English were trying to teach the Irish their ways in a language the Irish did not understand. And even after the Irish child managed to gain some knowledge of the English language, he discovered that there was nothing "national" about a system of education where the following verse was hung in every school:

I thank the goodness and the grace
That on my birth have smiled,
And made me in these Christian days
A happy English child.

One can imagine the wrath of an Irish parent whose child came home from school innocently mouthing the words of this rhyme. It was natural that these schools would be successful in accomplishing at least one of their objectives, that is, to play a major role in the decline of the Irish language.

Just how prevalent was the use of the Irish language before the British government established the National Schools?

Back in 1799, almost everyone in Ireland spoke Irish. By 1825, although only about 500 thousand people used Irish exclusively, at least another million used it among themselves but had sufficient knowledge of English to enable them to carry out certain commercial transactions.

No one had foreseen, however, that knowledge of the English language placed an effective weapon in the minds of a people who would at last be able to communicate their wrongs to the world. It was a weapon that would not only be instrumental in bringing about a sense of national unity, but would also allow for the spreading of the tremendous flow of literature that was to come out of Ireland, some of which would be conceived during the flowering of the Hedge Schools.

Before getting to the Hedge Schools, it might be well to review briefly the history of education in Ireland. During the Middle Ages it was the monasteries that dispensed learning. By 1310 Irish students were entering the monasteries in such great numbers that a Parliament at Kilkenny passed a law forbidding religious orders within the Pale to accept anyone who was not English. In 1321 they added a supplementary measure which decreed that no monastery should refuse an Englishman. Finally, in 1380 a law was initiated which forbade monasteries to receive any Irishmen. Then came the Reformation, and after Henry VIII was declared Supreme Head of the Church in Ireland, the monasteries themselves were suppressed, monks expelled, and century-old buildings confiscated and destroyed.

After Cromwell subdued Ireland, the Cromwellians were upset about the "Popish School Masters" who were teaching Irish youth, "trayning them up in Supersticion, Idolatry, and the Evill Customs of the Nacion." Off went the schoolmasters to slavery in the Barbados. With the Penal Laws there were even harsher restrictions placed on education, and for nearly a hundred years after, Catholic schools and schoolmasters were outlawed. Rewards were offered to informers, and anyone over the age of sixteen could be brought to court and examined under oath concerning suspected Catholic schools. Even heavier penalties were inflicted on those who sent their sons abroad to school. In time it was only the clerical students who were able to reach Irish colleges in Paris, Salamanca, Rome, and other centers of learning. These clerical students, often forced to make the journey in smugglers' boats, were quite ready to risk their lives in order to be educated for the priesthood.

Where, one might well ask, did these men get their preliminary education? Some of them may have been educated at the Bardic Schools. Or they may have belonged to a family who still retained, somehow or other, the services of the bard. The Bardic Schools represented a highly developed system of education, providing the nearest approach to a university education. The medium of instruction was, of course, the native tongue, and Irish language, literature, and history were studied. Brehon Law was also a part of the curriculum.

An interested description is given of a Bardic School in the preface to the Clanrickarde Memoirs, published in London in 1722. Clanrickarde was primarily a school of poetry, open only to students who were descendants of poets and were of some distinction in their clans.

The school was situated in a quiet spot away from families and friends of the students so that their studies would suffer no interruption. The school building was a simple construction with no windows, and furnished with a table, couch and chair for each student, who had a cubicle of his own. On the evening of the first day, the students were given a subject on which to write a poem; then they withdrew to their cubicles to compose their poems in complete darkness. There they remained till next evening when candles were brought and they wrote down their compositions. They were given to their professors in the assembly hall and examined by them. On Saturdays and the eves of Feasts, the students were entertained by the gentlemen and rich farmers of the neighborhood. The school was open from Michaelmas to the 25th March, when the students returned to their homes, each one carrying with him an important document, namely, an Attestation of his Behavior and Capacity, from the chief Professor, to those that had sent him.

Over the centuries the Bardic Schools produced a long succession of poets, historians, and brehons, or judges. These schools grew out of the druidic tradition, and the coming of Christianity had very little effect on them, although they naturally no longer trained Druids. Furthermore, despite the fact that the wars of Henry VIII and Elizabeth fairly well depleted the fortunes of the Irish chiefs and Anglo-Norman lords who had been patrons of the Bardic Schools, they still managed to survive for a time. The poet Edmund Spenser in the late sixteenth century was aware of them. Banished to Ireland after writing a witty ditty about one of Queen Elizabeth's suitors, Spenser not only completed *The Faerie Queene,* but still found time to express his disapproval of the bards. One can scarcely blame him. The bards were in a position to arouse the resentment of those who had been dispossessed of the lands now occupied by the poet.

It is generally believed that Bardic Schools lasted well into the seventeenth century, after which they became known as "Courts of Poetry." Although these courts were little more than gatherings at which poetry was discussed and recited, they served to preserve some of the tradition of the Bardic Schools and at the same time helped keep alive the craft of versifying. That the Bardic Schools may not have been as exclusive as has often been thought is evidenced in the writings of a distinguished London doctor who spent several years in Ireland prior to 1767. Having attended many "Courts of Poetry" sessions, he had this to say of them:

In Ireland they have bards to this day, among the inland inhabitants; and even among the poorest of the people: — and it is a very common practice among them when they return from the toil of the day, to sit down, with their people around them, in bad weather in their houses, and without doors in fair, repeating the histories of ancient heroes and their transactions, in a style that, for its beauty, and fine sentiments has often struck me with amazement.

The Hedge Schools did not actually come into being as a result of the decline of the Bardic Schools. It was the suppression of any ordinary sort of education, first under the Cromwellian regime, then under the Penal Laws introduced in the reign of William III, that was responsible for the origin of the Hedge Schools. Although they have nothing in common with the Bardic Schools in either content or method of instruction, they furnished students with a more than adequate education. Existing as early as

the seventeenth century, they were not referred to as Hedge
Schools until possibly the early part of the eighteenth
century, when the law forced them to go underground. At
this time any householder caught harboring a schoolmaster
was dealt with harshly; consequently, classes often had to
be held out-of-doors. Hazardous this may have been, but
as a manner of gaining knowledge it had many advantages.

Classes were held in an isolated spot on the sunny side
of a hedge which served to screen participants from the
glance of anyone who happened to be passing by. Here
the schoolmaster, seated on a large stone, sowed seeds of
knowledge to his pupils who were stretched out in various
comfortable shapes on the green grass of Erin, their voices
rising and falling to mingle with the incessant hum of bees
or the far-off call of a lark. And always, a sentinel must
keep watch for the suspicious-looking stranger who might
be inclined to report their unlawful activities.

During periods when laws against education were relaxed,
school could be held in a byre (barn), or a small low
hut. In certain areas, a sod house was scooped out of the
banks on the roadside. On cold winter days a fire, kept
alive by the donations of two sods of turf per day by each
student, was built in the center of the sod school. Smoke
made its way through a hole in the roof, a custom that
caused the natives to comment, "You can't cross a ditch
or you'll fall down a chimney." Around the fire children
gathered, sitting on a circle of stones which surrounded it.

While the schoolmaster would allow no excuse for neglect
of study, discipline was not unduly severe. William Carleton,
the early nineteenth century novelist, loved the bustle and
busy hum of what was apparently a fairly progressive
school. Carleton felt that a child was capable of more
intense study and abstraction in the din of a schoolroom
than in partial silence. On his first day in Hedge School,

at the age of six, he learned the whole alphabet and a few simple spellings. Because his criticisms of the National Schools emphasize many important aspects of education that we are only now beginning to understand, it might be worthwhile to include a few of the observations he recorded in his *Traits and Stories.*

"There is something cheering and cheerful in the noise of friendly voices around us. A boy should work with others. Do not send him in quest of knowledge alone, but let him have cheerful companionship along the way."

Defending the schoolboy's tendency to joke, his occasional outbursts of merriment, or even a little horseplay, Carleton writes, "It is an exercise to the mind and he will return to his business with greater vigour and effect."

Inevitably, Hedge Schools came in for a great deal of criticism too, the attacks coming primarily from writers with pronounced anti-Irish views. "Too much rehearsing," said one Commissioner of the Board of Education in 1825.

What the commissioner failed to understand was that this particular method of teaching stemmed from a shortage of books. A schoolmaster kept all the up-to-date information he needed in manuscript form. Since a shilling often represented three days' wages for an Irish farm laborer in those days, books were rarely bought. However, when printers were finally able to produce books that could be sold cheaply, the Commissioners began to question the ability of the schoolmaster, and denounced the type of books found in the Hedge Schools as capable of breeding revolutionary tendencies.

A list of what was generally known as the "cottage classics" leads us to believe the books did indeed make strange bedfellows:

Montelion, Knight of the Oracle, Parisimum and Parisemes, Irish Rogues and Rapparees, Ovid's Art of

*Love, Moll Flanders, The History of Witches and Ap-
paritions, Alibaba, The Devil and Doctor Faustus,
Jack the Bachelor* (a noted smuggler), *Freney* (a
notorious robber), *Seven Sleepers, Fair Rosamund and
Jane Shore* (two prostitutes), *Don Quixote, The Vicar
of Wakefield, Travels to the North Sea, Life of Buona-
parte.*

While many of these books were unsuitable, none of the
critics saw fit to point out that some schoolmasters were
classical scholars and poets as well. A great number of
these men were descendants of the poets and scholars who
were scattered among the common people when the clan
system on which Irish culture was based broke down in the
seventeenth century. In many cases, Protestant parents were
so impressed by the wit and knowledge of the schoolmaster
that they preferred to send their own children to him rather
than to schools run by teachers of their own denomination.
Oliver Goldsmith, writing *The Village Schoolmaster,* ended
his poem with these lines:

> And still they gazed, and still the wonder grew,
> That one small head could carry all he knew.

The father of the well-known author, Maria Edgeworth,
had this to say about the teaching ability of the Hedge
Schools: "I am certain it will be found that not only the
common, but the higher parts of Arithmetic, are better
understood and more expertly practiced by boys without
shoes and stockings than by any gentlemen riding home
on horseback or in coaches, to enjoy their Christmas
idleness."

The curriculum of these crudely built schools included,
along with the three Rs, not only such subjects as history,
geography, bookkeeping, surveying, and mathematics, but
Greek and Latin as well. Students learned to spell and

write before they were introduced to the subject of reading. Mathematics as taught in these schools was of a practical nature and enabled many of the students to eventually assist surveyors in computing laborers' wages.

The popularity of the Hedge Schools was due to the willingness of an already impoverished people to make sacrifices so that their children could secure an education. In 1824 there were 7,600 independent schools under lay Catholic teachers in Ireland, most of which were of the Hedge variety. There were numerous endowed schools too, mainly Protestant, such as those of the Erasmus Smith Foundation and the schools of the Kildare Place Society, all receiving Parliamentary grants. The Presentation Sisters, Sisters of Mercy, Sisters of Charity, and other religious orders also contributed to the furtherance of education at this time. In fact, the latter foundations, along with the Christian Brothers, have made significant contributions all over the world, and particularly in America.

The School of Christian Brothers made it possible for Catholic boys to obtain an education at a time when education was almost beyond the reach of any Roman Catholic. The principal support of the school was derived from subscriptions collected annually in the city and vicinity of Waterford.

But if our great-grandfathers suffered hardships in their effort to receive an education, what of the teachers who taught them? The life of the schoolmaster was, in fact, more a bed of thorns than roses. The schoolmaster with the smallest classes and poorest clients was lucky if he made forty pounds a year. To make matters worse, the tuition was not always paid with money, but with sods of turf, a kish of praties, a dozen eggs, fowl, bacon, or milk, or at Christmas and Easter, a roll of fresh butter. Actually, there were times when a parent was too poor to pay anything, and occasions when some simply refused to pay at all. Using the weapons of satire to discomfit the defaulter, one unhappy schoolmaster composed this lament: "Miserable is my business and most poor my lot. But I promise to them, to each rustic boor in the land, that long will it be until my like comes among them again."

The poor man not only had to put up with the problems of unpaid tuition; he was the victim of some mud-slinging, too. Here are a few of the barbs flung out at him:

He is the center of the mystery of rustic antiquity, the cheap attorney of the neighborhood, and, furnished with his little book of precedents, the fabricator of false leases and surreptitious deeds and conveyances.

He is frequently the promoter of insurrectional tumults; he plans the nocturnal operations of the disaffected; writes their threatening proclamations studiously misspelled and pompously signed: Captain Moonlight, Lieutenant Firebrand, Major Hasher, Colonel Dreadnought, Night Errant, Grant Commander of the Order of the Shamrock Election.

According to P. J. Dowling in his book, *The Hedge Schools of Ireland,* there is no evidence to substantiate the charges of insurrectional intentions. On the other hand, the schoolmaster, with his knowledge and gift for imagery, was often called upon to speak on behalf of a candidate seeking public office, a practice which would hardly have added to his popularity in certain quarters. On one occasion the hedge schoolmaster, James Nash, making a political speech, may have both impressed and confounded even his most sympathetic listeners when, defying the enemy of the land, he cried out, "Let them come on! Let them draw the sword! And then woe to the conquered! — every potato field shall be a Marathon, and every boreen a Thermopylae!"

Yet no matter how he might have been viewed by those

who feared the power of the teacher as much as they feared the power of the poet, the schoolmaster had a high social standing in the community. More than that, he was regarded as a friend. In times of stress or difficulties, it was the schoolmaster the Irish people sought for counsel, and like the parish priest, he was always included in important family festivities. And since he was such a prominent figure at every christening, wedding, wake, and funeral, it is not too farfetched to suggest it was his very attendance at these functions that brought about the accusations of inebriation.

We do, however, find a mass of evidence supporting the belief that he did not confine his talents to the schoolroom. Here are a few examples of moonlighting activities taken from the diary of John Fitzgerald, a Cork city schoolmaster:

7 Jan. — Constant smart rain the whole day and most part of the night. Drew marriage articles between Thom. Wood and Bridget Murphy and got 8s. 2½d. for my trouble. . . . Crouch gave me two pots of porter at my fireside. I wrote a letter for him to J. D. Maindue, M.D. Esq., Bloomsbury Square, London.

18 April — A cold, dry windy day. Ed Parks was appointed City Goaler in the place of Thom. Sharpe . . . . Wrote a petition for the journeyman horseshoers to raise their wages, and got 2s. 1½d. for my trouble.

29 June — Cloudy, cool weather. Captain Brick sent for me to go to Evergreen, I suppose to draw his will, but when I went to his house he adjourned the business till tomorrow morning. After I came home Miss Wrixton sent me a posey and some salad. Write a petition for Barth Mahony, and got 2s. 8½d. for my trouble.

29 August — A fine pleasant day; very heavy rain most part of the evening. Began to teach Whetman's son and Parker Dunscombe at Mr. Hinck's school, and

is to give me a guinea a quarter in the future, but I
don't know how it will be with regard to the quarter
now going on. Sam Hobbs forced me against my will
to drink a tumbler of red wine in his house. I taught
Henry Fortescue at Mr. Maguire's house this day, and
I drew three presentments for John Raymond, but he
gave me no money for them. I drew a fourth present-
ment for Cornelius Sweeney on the new account, which
remains yet unpaid.

Another diary kept by Humphrey O'Sullivan is considered to be an important document, as it contains many
interesting observations on weather, Irish botany, orni-
thology, fairs, markets, and the author's comments on politics, history, war, and peace. In his efforts to find a remedy
for the potato blight, Martin O'Sullivan, a poet-schoolmaster, achieved world fame. Convinced that the blight came
from atmospheric electricity, he tried suspending a network
of fine copper wire over certain potato beds. So successful
were his experiments and his book *Electro-Culture of
Potatoes* that he was soon engaged in lengthy correspond-
ence with scholars in several seats of learning from Chicago
to St. Petersburg.

So beautiful were the songs and poems written by the
eighteenth century Kerry poet-schoolmaster, Owen Roe
O'Sullivan, that he was known to his contemporaries as
Eoghan an Bheil Bhinn, meaning "Owen of the Sweet
Mouth." Owen often engaged himself in the task of writing
love letters for village swains. Sometimes he even went so
far as to write his classroom instructions, or his announcements advising the villagers he was coming to teach in a
certain area, in rhyming verse.

But for all of the schoolmaster's tendency to be a "jack-
of-all-trades," he derived more prestige than pay from his
extra duties. It was fortunate he was content, for the most

part, if his income was sufficient to provide him with a
shirt, a small coat and breeches, pen, book, and candle.
The writer and historian Seumas MacManus, himself a
teacher of a mountain school in Donegal during the latter
part of the nineteenth century, composed a poem in memory of these hedge schoolmasters which ends with these
lines:

> The grass waves green above them; soft sleep is theirs
>   for aye;
> The hunt is over, and the cold; the hunger passed away.
> O hold them high and holy! and their memory
>   proudly pledge,
> Who gathered their ragged classes behind a friendly
>   hedge.

As for the poor scholar who left his native place and
wandered about the country to seek more advanced schooling, he was often deprived of even the basic needs. It was
a difficult life at best for these young men who were
usually either preparing themselves for the priesthood or
for the teaching field. How well these verses from Padraic
Colum's poem, *A Poor Scholar,* convey the feelings of
those wandering young scholars:

> My eyelids red and heavy are,
> With bending o'er the smould'ring peat.
> I know the Aeneid now by heart,
> My Virgil read in cold and heat,
> In loneliness and hunger smart.
> And I know Homer, too, I ween,
> As Munster poets know Ossian.
>
> And I must walk this road that winds
> 'Twixt bog and bog, while east there lies
> A city with its men and books,

With treasures open to the wise,
Heart-words from equals, comrade-looks;
Down there they have but tale and song
They talk Repeal the whole night long.

You teach Greek verbs and Latin nouns,
The dreamer of young Ireland said.
You do not hear the muffled call,
The sword being forged, the far-off tread,
Of hosts to meet as Gael and Gall —
What good to us, your wisdom store,
Your Latin verse, your Grecian Lore?

And what to me is Gael or Gall?
Less than the Latin or the Greek.
I teach these by the dim rush-light,
In smoky cabins night and week.
But what avail my teaching slight?
Years hence, in rustic speech a phrase
As in wild earth a Grecian vase!

Dressed in scant clothing, the poor scholar carried a
satchel of grey linen made in the manner of a soldier's
knapsack. The satchel was, of course, filled with books.
His inkhorn was suspended from his buttonhole, and two
or three ill-cut pens were stuck in a twist of twine encircling
his neck. Devoid of worldly goods, the scholar was completely dependent on the generosity of strangers. Because
of the Irishman's veneration for the scholar, he had no need
to worry where his next meal was coming from, though it
was the Irish country people who extended the warmest
welcome to these knights of the road. As one contemporary
put it, "Blessed with a potato to eat and a potato to share
with a stranger, a poor Hibernian is happy."

A lad who embarked on such a journey was usually one

who had excelled in the Hedge School, then stayed on for a longer period of study. When he completed the prescribed courses, he was given a letter of recommendation called "A Pass" which listed in detail the physical and mental attributes of the bearer. Starting in the village of his birth, he traveled throughout Ireland, visiting each village, spending time in every school, and making it a point to examine historical points of interest. Often, a scholar would in time return to become a schoolmaster of his own village. Others, who were preparing themselves for the priesthood, had to gain the knowledge necessary to qualify for entrance to a seminary, either in Ireland, or abroad where they received their education gratis.

Poor scholars continued their wanderings in search of knowledge long after the introduction of the National Schools, as is evidenced by the writings of an English-woman, Lady Chatterton. Observing some of these scholars when visiting Ireland in 1838, she described them rather unkindly as "that interesting race who feed their minds with crumbs of learning that fall from Hedge Schools, and their bodies with the stray potatoes they pick up in the farm-house."

It was inevitable that the era of wandering scholars had to end, for it was difficult to maintain the Hedge Schools after the National Board of Education was established in 1832. Since the fees in the National Schools were lower than in the Hedge Schools, parents were inclined to send their children there, while teachers in both town and country schools, lured by a regularity of salary unknown to them in the past, eventually went to teach in the National system.

In the beginning, however, the Irish child not only had to struggle to decipher the words of the verse that hung on the walls of his schoolroom, but was forced to change his customary matinal greeting from *"Dia Dhuit — God be* with you," to the more conventional, English "Good morning." But the teachers in the National Schools, unable as they were to speak even one word of Gaelic, must have had their unhappy moments too. Trying their best to teach their pupils some sort of acceptable English, they were at the mercy of an inspector who often visited the schoolroom, ridiculing them if their pupils gave less than perfect answers. As time went on, knowledge was given and knowledge absorbed, which is a credit to the teacher as well as the pupil.

Today's happy Irish child is in many cases bilingual as soon as he escapes the cradle. Recently, the first all-Irish kindergarten was instituted in Bray, just outside of Dublin. Organized by *an Condradh,* under the direction of Padraig O'Fearail, *cathaoirleach,* the school has already enrolled a large number of children from three to five years old, who are taught games, rhymes, and dialogue in Irish.

Actually, it was not until 1910 that Gaelic was reintroduced into the curriculum. The curriculum of primary education in the National Schools, which are at present under the direct supervision of the Catholic and Protestant clergy, is similar to that of other European countries, differing mainly in its concern for two languages. The history, music, and traditions of Ireland also play an important role in the life of the Irish schools. Under the School Attendance Act of 1926, every child between the ages of six and fourteen is required to attend a National School or other suitable school.

In Ireland it has always been extremely important that the male offspring receive as much education as the law, or the financial situation in the family, allowed. But up until the latter part of the nineteenth century this was not necessarily true as far as the female children were concerned. In many cases, after receiving a certain amount of education, she was expected to occupy herself with piano-playing and embroidering. She also had to practice hemstitching and crocheting. With the arrival of the twentieth century, however, parents began to realize that a university degree could represent security for their daughters as well as for their sons. Those daughters whose parents could afford the cost of boarding school, or who were fortunate enough to earn a scholarship, were quick to take advantage of the changing attitudes. The young woman who, for one reason or another, was forced to continue dealing with the practical aspects of life — such as learning to stuff cushions with seagull feathers — might console herself with the knowledge that it was a type of training well calculated to prepare her for what many Irishwomen dream of — a long and happy marriage.

Chapter 8

LOVE AND MARRIAGE

IN THOSE PRE-FAMINE days when a man had to work from darkness to darkness to make even a modest living for his family, the incidence of early marriages was extremely high in Ireland. After all, who could resist the proposal of a young swain who possessed that secret weapon of the Irish known as blarney. With no education beyond what he received from the National School, one such rustic romantic had little difficulty when it came to the language of love, as he proved in this letter written to the light of his life: "Far away from where I am now there is a little gap in the hills," he wrote, "and beyond it, the sea; and 'tis there I do be looking the whole day long, for it's the nearest thing to yourself I can see."

The English were inclined to disapprove of these early marriages, and considered the Irish totally lacking in responsibility and indifferent to consequences. Perhaps it does seem that the young lovers gave no thought to the future. But in a nation where, by 1820, one-fourth of the rural population depended on such a precarious means for a living as the conacre system, to await a time of security could only mean to wait forever. The conacre or rood-land system consisted of renting a piece of land from a farmer, sometimes as small as a quarter of an acre, and giving a part of the crop to the farmer in payment of rent.

So if the early marriages were unwise, they did seem to

fulfill a natural desire on the part of the young people to achieve a degree of independence. Neither men nor women achieved full status in the community until they married. But more than that, marriage represented, and perhaps a bit unrealistically, the promise of some measure of beauty and order in their lives, a condition as necessary to the Irishman as the very air he breathes. Then, too, the marriages were usually sanctioned by the parents whose own frail hopes were invested in their grandchildren.

Anyone who has ever observed the Irish at close range knows that one of their most outstanding characteristics is their love of children. The sensitive writer Walter Macken knew full well that the population explosion among the Irish came about from something more than religious concepts. Writing of that period when people were forced to live on a few roods of potatoes and few days of work a year, he made this observation in his novel, *The Silent People*: "When they could create nothing else, to create a child of their own was as precious as finding a jewel in a turnip field."

The fact that the Irish value their children as a vain woman values her jewels may explain the reason why they tended to cling to certain old superstitions. For example, it was thought that the fairies often exchanged their own offspring for the offspring of a mortal woman. Back in the early part of the nineteenth century when superstitious practices were quite common in Ireland, a young woman about to become a mother would consult the pishogue. A pishogue was the wise woman of the village, a purveyor of charms, old saws, and other rural incantations. For a fee she would give the young woman something to keep the good people out of her home for the first nine days.

Actually, the poor expectant mother must have kept busy all day long, that is if she expected to do the host of things required of her to avoid having a fairy changeling end up in her crib. Woe to her if she forgot to put a horseshoe on the doorpost, cross a plate of salt, put a prayerbook under her pillow, peel the seven roods of hazel in her first pain, cut a notch in a black cat's tail, pour a cup of sweet milk out of the first pail when milking. or break a new potato on the hearthstone.

But even after the child's birth, the mother was faced with other stringent requirements if she expected to preserve the infant from evil influences. Upon first opening its eyes, the child must gaze upon a blaze of candlelight to make certain it would prefer deeds of light to deeds of darkness. And foolish was the mother who cut her baby's nails instead of biting them. For who would want a thief in the family? Foolish, too, was the mother who neglected to toss the first lock of hay at haymaking time. And if she should by chance see the print of fairy feet on sea sand, she would be considered careless indeed if she kicked the marks away. After all, wasn't it just as easy to sing "Wave, wave, wash out"?

We can imagine the anxiety of the young woman who, upon first holding her child in her arms, was expected to look for telltale signs. A mole above the mouth was a good omen, since it gave promise that the child would have a soft tongue and winning ways. But some marks were thought to be "Devil's Crosses," while a baby born with a tooth would be a bitter bite. And pity the mother who found a mole under her baby's left ear, a certain sign its owner was slated for hanging. Nine hairs plucked from the tail of a wild colt and bound around an infant's ankle nine days after birth would make him swift and sure of foot. Needless to say, the mother herself needed to be fleet as a deer to accomplish this feat.

Wise old pishogues were sometimes called upon by men,

often just before a young man got married. Living in
Kildare during the early part of the nineteenth century was
a wise woman called Poll the Pishogue, who was supposed
to have great powers of divination. On one occasion a
young man consulted her to find out what sort of woman
was destined to share his life.

"Go home and wait till May eve," droned Poll the
Pishogue. Then she proceeded to furnish him with further
detailed instructions.

Home went the young man to await May eve. That night
he put his right garter round his left knee, his left round
his right, and tied his thumbs in a cross with a sliver of
bark peeled from a rowan tree. Then it was off to the
churchyard, where he picked up the third snail he met
under an ivy leaf. Taking it home, he put it between two
plates, leaving the twist of rowan tree on the top plate.
Now he could hardly wait to see what was written on the
plate, for Poll had assured him it would contain the initials
of his wife's name. But alas, on May morning when he
rose before sunrise and lifted off the top plate, he was
unable to make out the letters, for he could not read.

In haste he went back to old Poll, who told him to take
the plate to the schoolmaster, who made out the letters GV
on the plate. As it turned out the young man married
Grace Vourney, herself the third daughter of the schoolmaster who had helped the young man read the initials on
the plate.

It must be said that all the above superstitions were not
prevalent in all of Ireland, certain ones being peculiar to
an area. For the most part the old attitudes did not survive
the crisis of the famine. There would have been little
chance of their surviving in any case, because of the vigilance of the now well-organized priesthood. There is one,
though, that seems to have survived unto this day: One

still looks with wonder on the seventh son of a seventh son, for his mind is said to contain great knowledge.

Another practice that persisted in Ireland was abduction. The practice seems to have lasted for a longer period of time in Ireland than in England, in spite of the fact that in 1707 forcible abduction was declared a capital offense, for which the penalty was hanging. However, some cases referred to as abductions were not actually abductions at all. Sometimes a girl whose parents were opposed to her choice of husband arranged to have her lover break into her home and carry her off. In such a case what could the parents do but accept the returning couple, now married, with open arms.

Unfortunately, there was little romance involved in many of the abductions. In those days it was not always a woman's face that was her fortune. To be an heiress was often to be in danger. Fear of hanging did not deter the adventurous, for was poverty not worse than death? Such, at least, were the sentiments of the Earl of Chesterfield, once Viceroy of Ireland, whose solemn adjuration was, "Be more afraid of poverty than of the Pope." Besides, there was something daring, even admirable, about an abduction, and the abductor was often envied rather than despised. Ballads were written about them, and more often than not the guilty got off scot-free.

There were times when an adventurous young man succeeded in getting a young woman's fortune, and her love too. Not so with Garret Byrne and James Strange, who abducted the Kennedy girls in the eighteenth century. Here was a case that began with love and ended with two young men, whose greatest crime had been idleness, being hanged in Kilkenny on December 2, 1780. On their last night in Newgate Prison, Garret, James, and Patrick, the brother of James and an accessory to the crime, contemplated their past lives, while outside the prison walls the bellman asked the Lord above to have mercy on their souls. On that last night Garret Byrne, who had actually loved the girl he had abducted, addressed his Katherine — whose main fault was that of allowing herself to be influenced by her mother and her shrewish sister — in a long, sad poem from which this verse is taken:

> Ungrateful Katherine! source of my undoing.
> Could naught content thee, but my very ruin?
> Say! Did I ever seem to love you less,
> Or show propensity for fickleness?
> Ah, Katherine, no: that crime I charge to thee.
> From which proceeds my present misery.

Affairs of young love, even those that did not seem to have the slightest chance of lasting more than a month or two, did not always end so tragically. Long ago in Ireland an heir of the princely Desmonds of Kerry was caught in a storm while hunting, and sought shelter in the house of a poor man who lived on his property and had the name of MacCormac. He fell in love with MacCormac's daughter and subsequently took her in marriage. Although he was ostracized by his people for marrying beneath his station, an Irish poet came to his rescue, composing a song that has him addressing his family in these lines:

> You who call it dishonour
> To bow to this flame,
> If you've eyes look but on her,
> And blush while you blame.
> Hath the pearl less whiteness
> Because of its birth?
> Has the violet less brightness
> For growing near earth?

It is apparent that marriage was the wished-for destiny of many of the young people, and that it mattered not whether they were rich or poor. During the period when all the laborer had to do to make provisions for marriage was to rent a quarter of an acre from a farmer, it was inevitable that there should be many early marriages. But the famine, hard enough on farmers, almost completely eliminated the laborer. In fact, statistics show that even though the number of farmhouses increased slightly in the famine decade, more than 300 thousand one-room cabins were swept from the land. Since that time the landless laborer has remained a small minority of Ireland's rural population.

Thus, as the nineteenth century progressed, the men of Ireland tended to marry at a much later age and sometimes not at all. But for all of that, the old custom of matchmaking was still very much a part of the scene. Matchmaking varied from place to place. While there are some instances where a recognized matchmaker acted as a go-between, most marriages were arranged by the parents. Meeting at the fair or in the house of the intended groom, the parents would discuss the pros and cons of the proposed alliance, the father of the young man wanting to be sure the girl's dowry would be sufficient to match the young man's holdings, and vice versa.

There were times when these first overtures were made by friends of the young man, who would visit the girl's house for the "drawing down" of the match with her parents. But no matter who was responsible for getting the young people together, the favorite time for the visits was between Christmas and Epiphany (January 6), this with a view to having the wedding take place the following Shrovetide, the three days just before the opening of Lent. After the preliminaries were observed, a sort of inspection tour was undertaken, a custom called "walking the land." This accomplished, the visiting party would then partake of the hospitality of the house in order to make certain there were no miserly tendencies in the young man's family.

There are those who will tell you the marriages were arranged without the couple's knowledge. The truth is, in most cases the young people had already been carrying on a courtship at parties, fairs, and surprisingly enough, sometimes even at wakes. However, where land and livestock were involved, there may have been a tendency to ignore romantic considerations, and in certain areas it was not uncommon for relatives to marry, a necessary condition if families were to keep the land or enlarge the patrimony. A common saying was, "A blanket is better off being doubled." This attitude turned out to be a blessing for the girl not endowed with beauty. A dowry of cows or its equivalent in cash or "dry-money" was quite capable of turning a plain girl into a mighty attractive one.

After the formalities of the matchmaking were accomplished, there was nearly as much excitement at the home of the young man as that of the bride. While she was being fitted for a wedding dress, he would be eagerly awaiting the arrival of the tailor. The tailor, inordinately proud of his craft, boasted that it was the oldest craft in the world, for hadn't the first tailor sewed clothes of fig leaves for Adam and Eve? The smith, however, confounded the braggart by asking him who it was that made the needle that sewed the clothes. At any rate, while the "nanty-maker" was fashioning gown and cloak for the bride-to-be, her intended husband was working himself into a nervous breakdown wondering if the tailor had met with some delay.

A dilatory man was the tailor. Traveling from house to house, and often an expert storyteller, he stoked the furnace of his imagination with coals of gossip that fell around him as he sat stitching and snipping at the kitchen table. The trouble was, he had a way of promising a suit for a certain day, then invariably the day showed up with nary a sign of suit or tailor. His independent airs stemmed from the fact that he was indeed indispensable; his pride in himself was fortified by the memory of an old Brehon Law which pointed up the value of the tailor's needle by the awarding of a heifer in compensation for a lost needle. Nevertheless, the young man hadn't the slightest reason to worry. There were two occasions when the tailor made a point of having the new suit ready on time, being willing to stay up all night if necessary in order to accomplish the task. One was the wedding, the other a funeral.

Came the day of the wedding and the young man would once more be anxious. If the sun saw fit to shine on the bride it was a lucky omen, but a rainy day foretold hardship. And who would be so foolish as to marry on a Saturday, an unlucky day no matter how you looked at it. Those who married in the harvest, the wise old owls predicted, would spend all their lives gathering. But to hear a cuckoo on the wedding morning, or see three magpies, brought a promise of all the luck one could handle.

The bridegroom's party, consisting of the fiddlers who had slept at his house the night before, and some ten to twenty of the groom's relations, would mount their horses and make their way to the bride's home. The women were carried on pillions behind the men. Single men rode ahead of the others and were met by other single horsemen belonging to the bride's party, after which they all raced furiously toward the bride's residence, each hoping to win the coveted bottle of liquor.

It may come as a surprise to some to find that in former days the marriage ceremony was not always performed at the church but at the house of the bride. Of course, there were occasions when the celebration itself would be held in the place in which the young couple would live, or in the groom's house, the latter being customary when the young couple planned to live in *his* parent's house. If it happened that the young man was marrying into the house of the bride, a custom called *cliann isteaen,* the wedding would then naturally be held at the home of his bride. In such cases, the man would be expected to bring a suitable amount of money into the union.

At the bride's house, both bride and bridegroom were presented with a plate of oatmeal and salt. Each took three mouthfuls as a protection against the power of the evil eye. This customary ritual was, for the most part, merely an indication that the festivities were about to begin.

Irish weddings were a time of much merrymaking. There was always plenty to drink, but any actual sign of drunkenness was regarded as an insult to the people of the house as well as to the young couple. As a matter of fact, a friend of the family was always at hand, whose responsibility it was to see that everyone had something to drink and to curtail the drinking of anyone who showed signs of overindulgence. Whiskey, milk, wine, and tea were available, and in later years, porter. And since a wedding was considered an occasion of joy, there was no sense of shock on hearing an old woman or an old man say, "Ah, sure I have the pledge. I'll have a half of wine!"

A typical wedding ceremony of long ago might be that of the joining of Nora and Patrick. The wedding guests are gathered around the table which extends the full length of the barn. The priest is in his place of honor at the head of the table next to the bride and groom. Plaintive tunes are being played by the musicians. Friends of Nora's mother, who have helped serve the ham, fowl, bacon, and other delicacies, bustle about in their white aprons. For now the meal is over and it is time for the table to be cleared. As soon as the cloth is removed, the priest rises to begin the marriage ceremony.

Suddenly, Nora's mind is wild with anxieties. Well, all is well, isn't it, she asks herself. We did not meet a funeral on the road. And the sun is shining as bright as a lamp in the house of the gentry. But what if a woman is the first one to wish her joy. A man should always be the first one to do that. She searches the barn and her mind for an enemy. Spiteful women have been known to jump up and kiss the bride, thereby bringing a hail of bad luck down on her head. But oh — the priest is getting on with the ceremony, and everyone is crowding around the table so they may have the honor of having their names recorded as witnesses.

The ceremony goes on in the age-old language of the church, and the priest finally ends it by commanding the husband to "Give your wife the kiss of peace."

Everyone begins crowding around the table, struggling to get the first kiss. But here's Patrick now, offering a mere whisper of a kiss, for they've brought in the bride's cake and the priest is blessing it. The cake is served. In return for a slice of cake, each guest places a donation for the priest on the table in front of him. Wine and punch is passed around, and amidst cries of "Slainte," a toast is proposed for the bride and groom:

Health and long life to you,
Land without rent to you,
A child every year to you,
And death in old Ireland.

The fiddlers now change to dance tunes instead of the plaintive national airs. Music swirls around the barn, dust rises in the air as wedding guests merrily tick off the steps of the reel, stirring up scents of hay with their dancing.

"Look, Patrick," cries Nora. "Father Conroy is dancing the jig." Breathless, not from dancing but from worrying that Patrick will forget and burst into song, she gives him a sidelong glance. For everyone has stopped dancing now to begin the singing. But of course, Patrick knows it's unlucky for a man to sing at his own wedding.

As a matter of fact, Patrick is looking over her shoulder. "The strawboys have arrived," he tells Nora, bending down to give her a tight squeeze.

And sure enough the strawboys are coming in the barn door. The strawboys always came to weddings, though usually not until later in the evening. Disguised in old clothes, their faces blackened with burnt cork, they were sons of neighboring farmers. And now here is their leader heading straight for Nora to wish her joy and ask her to dance while his companions searched for other partners. The dance finished, the strawboys avail themselves of the host's hospitality and go on their way. At the same time the priest regretfully bids his adieus and goes off to perform still another wedding ceremony.

Nora and Patrick's wedding was of the sort that could be managed by a small farmer of the early nineteenth century. But take the case of our rustic swain who penned the romantic letter to his love. A laborer living in a one-room cabin, his marriage feast might consist of nothing more than a dish of potatoes and a jug of sweet milk, unless he had kind and generous neighbors.

As for Nora and Patrick, they could look forward to having some time alone together, since the bride was not to have any contact with her mother for a number of days. But on the Sunday following the wedding, called Bride's Sunday, friends who had been invited to the wedding accompanied the newly married couple to chapel. The young couple were further honored by being invited to the bridesmaid's house for tea and dinner.

On the first May-day after the wedding, the young men and women of the parish would go to the woods and cut down the tallest tree they could find. Garnishing the tree with ribbons and placing a large ball decorated with colored paper and gilt in its center, they carried it to the bride's house. They set it up before the door and proceeded to dance around it. This enchanting custom, an offshoot of druidism, is now unfortunately no longer observed in Ireland.

After the May-day ceremony, Nora would probably set her mind to dreaming of the child they might have, and if she still carried the superstitions of her ancestors she would take special care with Patrick's jacket, because wearing this jacket during childbirth was thought to allow the husband to share some of the pain.

Pain would be known to the two of them from the very beginning of their lives together. There would be the pain of parting, for Patrick, after planting his small garden of potatoes and oats, would have to go about the countryside looking for work to sustain them during the summer months. Nora would tend the crops while he was away. In her spare time she would continue to knit, and embroider bed covers, which she would sell to futher supplement their income.

In Ireland long ago, this was the way of life for young couples, whose greatest wealth was music, beauty, and love. They were the sort of people that caused Walter Macken's Dualta in *The Silent People* to say, "Visiting you is like a cloverfield in summer."

CHAPTER 9

TEA AND TURF FIRE

ALTHOUGH THE PEOPLE of Ireland were often thought of
as being poor, their lives, as Old Font, a character in Bryan
MacMahon's novel *Children of the Rainbow* put it, "were
thronged with the small beauties." It is no wonder, then,
that a man returning from his labors in other men's fields
was so anxious to get back to his own home and sit by his
own fireside. Indeed, if our ancestors could but return to
earth to furnish us with further facts concerning the old
Irish ways, one of the first things they would be likely to
tell us is that "Home is where the Hearth is."

No matter how small a house might be, there was always
room to sit around the hearth, for the fireside was not only
the center of domestic activities but also the center of social
activities. It is here the family gathered in the evening, and
here where, in the cheerful glow of turf fire, they listened
to the tune of a fiddler and the voice of a ballad singer
raised in song, or where a child, sitting still as a stone, listened to his grandfather tell stories of long ago. Here too,
the wandering *bacach,* or beggarman, warmed himself while
he munched on Irish soda bread and made it clear that he
would not be averse to spending the night on the bench by
the hearth.

That the hearth was the focal point of the house is
evidenced by the fact that the position of all other rooms
was described in relationship to the wall behind the fire-

place, which usually separated the kitchen from the main bedroom. A woman who happened to be in the main bedroom was "above in the room," and conversely, if she chanced to be in the room at the other end of the kitchen, she would be "below in the room."

The custom of locating the hearth at the exact center of the house is very old. A twelfth century artist who drew the interior of the great banquet hall at Tara shows a line of hearths running right down the middle of the floor. Picturing the nobles and their ladies gathered around the fire to gossip and inhale the delicious smells coming from the cooking pots, we are reminded of the Japanese style of preparing the meal at the table in front of the guests. Proof that nobles and ladies assembled around the fire to indulge in cocktail gossip is found in a passage from an ancient Irish law that says one cannot claim damages when scalded by the soup if the cook has made certain to shout, "Look out! Here goes the fork into the cauldron!"

In the more humble dwellings of later times, the seats flanking the fireplace were given to honored guests. On nights when there were no guests, it was the man of the house and the woman of the house who occupied these special hearth seats. There they could be close to the little openings in the wall that held the man's pipe and the wife's knitting. In some cases, the woman of the house, known as the *bean-a-tighe,* may have tucked her snuffbox in with her knitting, and it is possible the grandmother may have had a pipe stashed away somewhere, too. Even in the days of our own great-grandmothers, there were a few hardy souls who considered a few puffs on a pipe to be as natural as knitting.

Of course, all hearths are not the same, but vary in different locales. The extremely large ones of Munster and south Leinster, for example, have two chairs on either side of the fire. In Connacht and west Munster the seats are of stone, while in Cork and County Kerry we find a large wooden seat resembling a cobbler's bench. But no matter what the arrangement, there is always room to sit around the fire in the room that usually served as a combination kitchen and living room.

A charming custom long associated with the Irish people is the practice of gathering around the fireplace to say the evening rosary. The bean-a-tighe had the honor of leading the family rosary. She also composed the after-prayers that were designed, for the most part, to effect the release of souls from purgatory. But on the nights when the bacach chose to make his visits, he had no more qualms about taking over the bean-a-tighe's place in leading the rosary than he had in taking over her bench by the hearth. Not only that, but when it came to composing the after-prayers, he often became so enamored with his improvisations that he kept the family captive for a half hour or more while he knelt at the hearth praying for the sailors and soldiers, the boys and girls in America, and of course for the poor and homeless.

While the hearth is a symbol of Irish hospitality toward strangers, the turf fire itself has still another meaning, that of family continuity. When the fire went out, it was thought that the soul went out of the people of the house. Although keeping a turf fire burning day and night meant a lot of extra work for the man of the house, the women and children of the family were more than willing to go to the bog and help with the turf-cutting. Actually, the bog was not as cheerless a place as might be imagined, especially if the harvesting of the turf took place in May when the tiny white flowers called *cean-a-bhans* were dancing over the marshy brown earth. To make the task all the more pleasant, neighbors often joined together in a gathering called a *mihul* and made a picnic of the occasion. During the course of the day's work a contest would suddenly spring up to determine who was the strongest and swiftest turf-cutter in the townland.

Each bog bank had to be stripped or cleaned for the cutting. A bog that had been cut away to a great extent resembled a huge chocolate layer cake. Each and every sod of turf was molded into irregular brick-like shapes and then carried to high clear ground to be dried by sun and wind. Many a day it took in the bog to harvest a year's supply of turf, but somehow the people managed to take joy in their work. There are men still living in Ireland who remember those days when the bog was alive with music and laughter and the sound of friendly voices hailing a newly proclaimed turf-cutting champion.

Another feature of the old-style Irish farmhouse, and indeed, another symbol of Irish hospitality, was the half-door. It was a godsend for the housewife, who could watch the pot boiling as she held forth on subjects ranging from the fall of Rome to the falling of a new bride's cake. The season of the half-door spawned many a poet and philosopher, for the view from its swinging top was well calculated to stir the imagination of a child.

Devised originally as a way of admitting light and keeping out animals, the door became a magic vantage point where one might receive the blessings of a priest, and where sun and stars traced patterns on the kitchen floor. Shreds of gossip were tossed in and out of the kitchen along with the blessings. "Failt romhat! Durid suas chun na tine!" was the greeting usually extended the visitor. In turn, the visitor would say, "God bless this house," or if there were a child in sight, "God bless this child," though a birthday or special saint's day might call for an entirely different sort of greeting.

Naturally, a child garnered his earliest memories from the scenes enacted above the half-door, and from others that took place in the vicinity of the hearth. Most of the memories were pleasant ones, but he would not be likely to forget the night before he was to begin his first day at school. No amount of gazing into the constant fire would be enough to quell his anxiety that night. And when at last he went off to his bed in the loft, he would pray the winds would come to tear off the roof and blow it away, and himself with it, so that he might be spared making the morrow's journey into the unknown.

The following morning he might very well experience an unexpected lifting of his spirits, for as he carried the creel of turf to his mother, the fire would be roaring and blazing. There was fresh milk and oatmeal stirabout, or porridge, laid out for him too, and as always, the pot of tea was warming itself on the hearth. Furthermore, on that auspicious morning his mother surprised him by serving him a cup of hot tea with buttered farls, or sections, of hard bread. By lunchtime he would have a new worry — would his lunch packet contain a chunk of the hated india-bread, or would he instead have oaten bread? Oaten bread was respectable enough, particularly when it was made with ground almonds and raisins and honey, but india-bread, eaten only in poorer times, was a symbol of poverty. In fact, india-bread was associated with the famine days. To bring it to school was to run the risk of being "codded" unmercifully. However, the despised india-bread had one redeeming feature. It was useful for pelting the codders on the way home from school.

Obviously, the boy whose lunch consisted of only a few chunks of india-bread could get pretty hungry on his way home from school. But there were any number of the Irish country people who might be having tea at that time of the day. And he might just happen to stop at a neighbor's house at the exact moment she was taking a loaf of Boxty bread out of the pot oven. Boxty is a kind of potato bread. Before it is baked it is always marked with a cross so that it can be divided into sections, or farls. Known as "Dippity" when served with milk and salt, Boxty is traditionally eaten in Ireland on All Hallow's Eve, or the Eve of All Saint's Day. So too is colcannon, a mixture of mashed potatoes and cabbage, which is served with melted butter. A boy growing up on the simple but tasty foods of the Irish country people could not but answer "yes" to this old Irish verse:

> Did ye ever ate colcannon that's
>   made from thickened cream,
> With greens and scallions blended
>   like a picture in your dream?
> Did ye ever take potato-cake or
>   boxty to the school,
> Tucked underneath your oxter
>   with your book and slate and rule?

If the tailor happened to be staying at his family's house, however, a boy would hardly be inclined to stop and take tea with a neighbor on his way home from school. Whenever the tailor stopped at the house you could be sure there would be at least a hundred thousand welcomes tossed out over the half-door, what with the neighbors coming to call, and sometimes getting fitted for a suit. On those rare occasions a boy could be certain there would be many nightly gatherings around the fireside.

But whether or not there was a guest in the house, the meals were always served in an interesting manner. In many houses, particularly in the north and west, food was served out of a basket, or kish. The basket, steaming on top of a three-legged pot of water, kept the potatoes from cooling off. At mealtime the family sat on low stools around this basket, sharing the steaming warmth exhaled by the three-legged pot. The potatoes were always cooked in their jackets; consequently, they had to be peeled, either with the fingers or with a knife. They were then dipped into a bowl of hot salted milk and eaten.

In an Irish home, tea was served at just about any time of day. What was called High Tea might include a variety of breads, meats, and even a hot dish, along with some sort of Irish cheese cake, made with either sweet curds or cottage cheese. Oddly enough, tea did not come into general use until a few hundred years ago, when Britain won the battle with France for mastery over India. As a result of this victory, a market had to found for the great tea production of India and China. Consequently, every effort was made to get people to drink tea instead of coffee. At the time, coffee cost one and tenpence a pound in Ireland, while tea was twelve shillings a pound. A century later coffee was still the same price but tea was down to three shillings a pound.

"The newest of food and the oldest of drink," says the old Irish proverb. Indeed, our ancestors were never inclined to favor preserved food. Potatoes and oatmeal were the staple food in an Irish household, and milk and honey the twin compliments to any Irish meal.

Soda bread, made with flour, buttermilk, soda, and salt, and traditionally cooked in an oven with glowing turf sods on top to give all-around heat, was a specialty of the Irish housewife. Another dish frequently served was blood pudding, sometimes called drisheen. It was made with sheep's blood combined with milk, chopped mutton suet, bread crumbs, and seasoning, and then steamed before eating. Drisheen was, no doubt, a substitute for meat. During the periods when he was not so much as allowed to snare a hare, and when the farm animals helped pay the rent, the Irishman probably knew instinctively that he needed to supplement his diet. In the famine days he also ate nettles, chopping them and suffocating them with porridge.

But even though nettles and other wild growths were boiled and eaten during the famine days, they were ordinarily used as a flavoring referred to as "kitchen." Onions, leeks, and garlic were also enjoyed, as were watercress, sorrel, dulse, a seaweed used in soup, and sloke, or sea-spinach. The only other vegetables besides potatoes that proved popular were cabbage and carrots. Fortunately, there was an abundance of wild fruits, such as raspberries, strawberries, crabapples, and whortleberries. And always there was plenty of shellfish, including cockles, mussels, and periwinkles, the tiny saltwater snails that were boiled in seawater and then dug out of their shells and dipped in finely ground oatmeal before they were eaten.

Irish children learned early in life that they must contribute in some manner if there was to be enough food in the house to sustain the family during the winter months. But whether they fished, or searched for snails, or went off to the hills to gather wild whortleberries, they always made a game of it. A boy, of course, had to help with the farm chores. If there were no girls in the family, he might also be asked to help out with the butter-making.

Butter played an important role in the Irish household economy. Every farmhouse had its churn, and in most areas it was a matter of housewifely pride to keep the churn immaculately clean at all times. In the process of helping with the butter-making, a boy could very well be introduced to some of the old Irish superstitions concerning this milk product.

Lumps of butter were sometimes thrown into the lake

or springs through which cattle were driven. This was done to ward off evil and thereby induce an abundant flow of milk. Milk was often thought to have been stolen by fairies, or the butter bewitched by them. Often a live cinder was put into the churn to guard the butter from its enemies. No person was to take live fire out of the house while the churning was in progress. If he did try rekindling his pipe at the hearth, he was forced to take a hand at the churning before leaving, thus ensuring that the butter and churn were preserved from all harm.

As time went on, a boy learned a lot more about life than its superstitions. The boy who went so reluctantly to school that first day would be more likely than not to discover — and especially if he was the oldest or only son in his family — that his mother had an occupation in mind for him that required more than a minimal degree of education. Most everyone knows of the Irish mother's desire to have her first son become a priest. But not everyone knows that the desire did not always stem purely from religious reasons. During many periods of Irish history, becoming a priest was the only way a lad could be assured of getting a fairly decent education.

Such a lofty ambition required dedication, and a boy had to spend a great deal of time studying in a chair pulled up to the kitchen table. The table, used primarily as a working area, and sometimes for playing cards, was usually placed against the wall, and with good reason. To shake hands across the table was considered unlucky, and with the table arranged in such a manner, it was nigh to impossible to do any handshaking over it.

The kitchen was a comfortable and cheerful room in which to study one's lessons. The glow of the turf fire seemed to soften the surroundings, giving it an overall pastel effect, like a watercolor drawing. Light from a paraffin wall lamp blossomed on the copper pans hanging on the hearth, shed itself on the fire irons, pot-lifters, and trivets, and brought into sharper focus the huge crane that was used to swing the pot away from the fire.

There was a picture of the Holy Family on the wall. In the picture, the Mother wore a blue dress and red mantle, and like the Irish children themselves, St. Joseph, Mary, and the child Jesus had bare feet. One of the oldest and most interesting pieces of furniture in the kitchen, dating from the Middle Ages, was the dresser. On its shelves were the gleaming blue willow pattern dishes, scrubbed wooden piggins, and lustre jugs, bowls, and teacups that had been in the family for decades. In one corner of the room was the flour bin, with one compartment for flour and the other for "yella meal," or corn meal, and the beetle that was used for pounding potatoes and for washing clothes in the stream. There was also a large chest that held oatmeal which children used to stamp down with their bare feet to squeeze the air out and thus prevent it from turning musty.

While he was studying his lessons at the table in the kitchen, the boy would probably be occasionally distracted by the low-voiced tones of his father and mother. They would likely be speaking in Gaelic, which they often did when they didn't know he was listening. As he grew older he would learn that they had been punished for speaking the Irish language when they were children. And he would begin to wonder, and wondering he would become anxious to learn something more about the history of his country. During those nightly gatherings around the hearth, he would listen more carefully to the conversation that went on among the older people. If it was necessary for him to journey to the hiring fair, he might get a job in a place where he would learn something about the Irish who lived in another part of the island.

As time went on, he would begin to take a closer look at the world around him, noticing things that had escaped him in the past. He would notice the special shapes and colors of the landscape, see history in cromlechs and Celtic crosses and in the heathery hills where he had once picked whortleberries, and where the ruins of old houses that had been deserted after the famine still remained. Now when he looked at the fuchsia-laden hedges by the roadside he knew why the Irish called the fallen flowers "Tears of God."

He would observe the farmhouses more closely, noticing their similarities — they were built in a long rectangular shape, stemming from the superstition that "A house to be lucky must not be more than one room wide" — and their differences — some roofs had sloping sides and were thatched with beautiful golden oat straw, while others were low and rounded at the top and were thatched with wheat or flax straw. He loved the way the lime-washed walls of the houses changed color in the changing light. But his new reflective mood would not prevent him from continuing to participate in the activities that were constantly taking place around him. He could still take joy in the mihul, and in the roof-thatching gatherings that took place when a man in need of a new roof called all the neighbors together for a day of work that ended in a night of singing and dancing.

Whether he garnered his knowledge at the fair, the turf-cutting or roof-thatching gatherings, or from the activities that went on around his own fireside, there was something he would carry with him for the rest of his life, and that was the memory of neighborly love. Nor would he ever forget the words of the Irish blessing that was given at the end of each and every one of those neighborly gatherings: "That the roll call this day twelvemonths may find us all present and none absent."

CHAPTER 10

COME TO THE FAIR

FOR CENTURIES, cattle-raising has played a significant role in the survival of the Irish race. In the early days, the people grew crops with which to feed the animals, and in summer drove the beasts to where the grain was growing, reserving some of the grain for winter needs. During the summer months they camped in *buaile* or booleys, and for the rest of the year preferred to live in rural or family groups. Due to this semi-nomadic way of life, there were no large towns or cities in Ireland until the ninth century, so it is not surprising that the Irish often gathered together for fairs — not just to arrange cattle deals and settle disputes, but to engage in social activities.

The custom of assembling for fairs goes back a long way. According to ancient records, fairs took place as much as fifteen hundred years ago. Fairs held at places like Tara, Taillte, and Uisneach were originally political councils, where kings and nobles met to discuss national affairs. Forty-seven kings and their nobles showed up at one such an assemblage in Carman, County Wexford, bringing with them their followers and retainers as well as a number of commoners. Tents were pitched for the occasion, sod and wattle huts were speedily put together, while a few hardy souls slept in the open air. And as usual, the warriors slept under the shelter of their chariots.

Though councils were indeed conducted at these early

gatherings, fairs served many other purposes as well. They
were markets where one could buy or sell wares; they were
the occasion for endless races, sports, and athletic contests;
and they were an opportunity to hear the bards and poets
recite Ireland's history and the deeds of past great warriors
and heroes. The yearly fair at Taillte was especially important for its athletic contests, which were called Ireland's
Olympic Games. They traditionally took place during the
first week of August.

One of the most colorful contests held during the Olympic Games was the ancient game of hurling. This unique
and exciting sport was played as much as three thousand
years ago. Later on, it was Cuchullain's performance on
the hurling field that won him the attention of King Conor's
court. A dangerous sport, one that has often been referred
to as a form of anarchic hockey, it is said to be the fastest
ball game in the world. To play it, a man needs to possess
extraordinary athletic abilities: he has to have a quick eye,
a ready hand, a strong arm, and be an excellent runner and
wrestler as well. In its expressiveness, vigor, and intensity,
the game is especially suited to the Irish character. In
ancient times as now (to this very day this national sport
continues to maintain its amateur status) hurling was
played purely for the love of the game, and to express pride
in the homeland.

Gaelic football, though not as old a sport as hurling, is
said to be the origin of rugby football in England, and of
the version played in America. The Gaelic form of football,
however, differs from others; for example, players are permitted to catch the ball and box it with the hands as well
as kick it. President de Valera, himself once a participant in
the game, remarked that it, too, was a game well suited to
the Irish temperament, particularly because of the "hard
cut and thrust of attack and counterattack and the sheer

pleasure of getting to grips with your opponent." Other sports in the olden days included horse racing, road bowling, rounders, from which baseball evolved, and coursing, that is, hunting with the hounds. Carvings found on ancient pillars remain to illustrate the love the ancient Irish had for hunting. A carving on a pillar in Clonmacnois, for example, shows a trapped stag.

There is also much to be learned from the carvings found on ancient churches and crosses. These carvings, along with the old illuminated manuscripts, reveal much about our ancestors' manner of dress, even as far back as a thousand years. Before the coming of the Normans, the type of dress for professional men and men of wealth consisted of two main garments. The first was a long tunic with sleeves that reached halfway down the shin. The second garment, a long sleeveless cloak fitted to the shoulders, was worn over the tunic. The cloak reached to the knee and was sometimes fastened with a large brooch or pin.

Farmers, soldiers, and hunters wore a pair of tightly fitting trousers and a short jacket. Some trousers were similar to a football player's shorts. Other were fastened below the knees, like knee-breeches. Others reached the ankle and had a strap under the instep.

By Queen Elizabeth's time, Irishmen had taken to wearing elaborately pleated shirts tucked into tightly fitting belted trousers. The shirt, though of a shade called saffron, was actually a beautiful daffodil yellow. The sunny color came from the flower of the autumn crocus especially grown for dyemaking.

The most splendid of all garments was a man's cloak. Of rich woolen material dyed a bright color, the cloak often had a fringe around its edge or a ripple of fur around the neck. So popular were Irish cloaks that in 1504 over two thousand of them were exported to Bristol. Even

Spenser spoke of the convenience of the cloak, although
in a somewhat high-handed manner: "It is a fit house for
an outlaw, and an apt cloak for a thief. When it raineth,
it is his pent-house, when it bloweth, it is his tent, when it
freezeth, it is his tabernacle."

Cloaks were popular with women,too. Indeed, the cloak
continued to be the Irishwoman's characteristic garment all
through the nineteenth century. Large enough to envelop
the whole person, the Irish cloak falls in graceful folds, its
hood serving as a protection for wind and rain. Pictures
of our great-grandparents often show the grandmother
wearing such a cloak with its hood thrown back to reveal
the white frilled bonnet, a symbol of her married status.
Although many cloaks were lined with contrasting jewel-
toned shades of satin, those still worn in certain parts of
Ireland are apt to be made up of the more somber colors.

In the past, however, women of Ireland were very much
inclined to favor the brighter colors. Ankle-length dresses,
fashioned of wool — or silk for very special occasions —
came in sparkling jelly bean shades of blue, red, green,
black, and yellow. Gowns of the very earliest times were
often of white linen with beautifully embroidered decora-
tions of gold. Sandals, dyed and decorated, were worn too,
though the Irish, it must be confessed, were much inclined
toward barefootedness, more out of a desire for comfort
than from economic reasons.

The woman of the house, if she happened to be super-
vising her husband's preparations for a trip to the fair,
would be sure to see that his shirt front and cuffs were
stiffly starched and white as snow. By the early part of the
nineteenth century, the men of Ireland were showing a great
attachment to the tailcoat. The tails of this coat were so
long that a man often found it necessary, when walking, to
throw them over his left arm. This, then, might very well

be what he would wear when traveling to the fair some hundred and fifty years ago when our ancestors were still paying strict heed to the old Irish proverb, "Even if you have only an old puck goat, be in the middle of the fair with him!"

The road to the fair was often beset by dangers. Fenced in by ancient taboos and customs, an Irishman was obliged to take part in many rituals before he so much as took leave of the house. Even at the risk of having his white shirt front become limp as boiled lettuce, he was sprinkled with holy water while speaking the words of the folk prayer, *An Mhairbhne Phadraic*: "In the name of the victorious Father and of the Son who suffered pain, may Mary and her Son be with me on my journey."

No sooner was he on his way than he had to watch for other portentous signs. If he met a funeral he took three steps backwards with it. Catching a glimpse of a red-haired woman, he would do well to give up the trip entirely, and if he happened to forget something, no good could come of his going back to the house for it. To forget would have been easy, since he had to remember to take with him salt, a fire-ember, soot, or a sprig of hazel, any one of which was capable of protecting him from evil spirits. On the brighter side, if he chanced to find a white button on the road or meet a weasel, he could expect to encounter good luck along the way.

Driving or walking along the road, he would inevitably come upon a cairn, a small heap of stones marking the place where someone had died. Pausing to throw one more small stone on the cairn, he would again take time to pray. "I throw this stone from my hand to the heap for good luck. May God bless the souls of my father and mother, and especially the soul of the person who died here."

A woman had to watch her step on the way to the fair,

too. If pregnant, she was not likely to stop in a graveyard, for if she turned her ankle on a grave her child would be born with a *cam reilge,* or clubfoot. Pregnant or not, she had to quell any high-spirited urge to whistle, since a whistling woman and a crowing hen were certain to bring bad luck to the listeners. In truth, the latter belief caused many a hen to be left at the crossroads.

Numerous were the superstitions concerning crossroads. They were not only burying places for unbaptized children and animals, but a place where it was said people sometimes went to give themselves up to the devil. As it was often customary to hold dances at crossroads, it may be the clergy brought the devil onto the scene, perhaps to discourage what they considered to be a sinful form of entertainment.

In the olden days, Irish country people computed the length of the journey by the number of rosaries recited as they made their way to the fair. On the road, the traveler would likely see cartloads of turf being taken to the fair to be sold. Often they were decorated with a bush or holly branch for good luck. Gay red ribbons were tied onto the horses' tails, not only for the purpose of luring Lady Luck, but also to stress the festive nature of the occasion.

The horse, as many know, is the national animal of Ireland. If anyone could be said to be crazy over horses, it would be the Irish, for the love of this animal has been a part of their tradition for a very long time. Men and women alike share in this love of horses. In fact, there are those who think something is radically wrong with a woman who dislikes horses.

Irish horses, like Irish soldiers, took part in battles from Flanders to the Crimea. Napoleon's famous white horse Marengo was bred in County Wexford. A horse, the Irishman will tell you, is a lucky animal. The horse, at least in Ireland, also has the ability to see ghosts. Try as you will you can never get him to trot across a spot where an evil deed has been committed, though it is sometimes helpful to lay down a rug, or cover the spot with a layer of grass or straw. Another interesting aspect of Irish horse lore concerns the belief that horses had human speech before the Flood. There are many who even believe the animals can understand human speech.

To this day there are people in Ireland who have the gift known as *cogar i gcluais an chapaill,* that is, the ability to gentle the fiercest of wild horses. No one knows exactly how it is accomplished, for it is always done in secret, but some say it is done by breathing into the horse's nostrils. Others tell us the gentling is accomplished by whispering certain words into the animal's ears. According to a Kerry-man, who professes to know the secret of how to get along with this beloved national animal, "You should always talk to a horse the same as if he was a Christian."

On the way to fair a hundred years or more ago, the horse would likely be pulling a two-wheeled jaunting cart, or perhaps the famous "low-backed car." However, since the Irish people never thought anything of walking fifteen or twenty miles, it was not uncommon to find many travelers making their way to the fair on foot.

The fair itself not only afforded people an opportunity to gossip with friends, but was a wonderful place to shop. Shops were stocked with laces, gloves, and other trinkets. In every *booreen,* lanes that were out of the way of traffic, were rows of canvas-covered stalls. White sheets were spread out over counters containing apples, gooseberries, plums, seagrass, meat pie, oysters, and boiled periwinkles. There were tents where one could pause for a cup of tea, and wicker baskets filled to the brim with orange-colored cockles.

Many of the big fairs had swing boats, merry-go-rounds, and maggies — wooden effigies that could be shot at for three shots a penny and five for tuppence. One of the most popular gatherings was the Harvest Fair. Boys and girls came to this autumn fair from villages miles away. Summer's work was done; everyone was in a festive mood. At the Harvest Fair, the black arts man gathered crowds of people around his tent to show them his magic tricks, while in other hideaways, fortune-tellers filled young minds with dreams.

While younger men were playing games of chance or looking over the current crop of pretty colleens, older men were talking quietly among themselves. Some of them were joking in an effort to hide their anxiety. Would the buyer give them a fair price for their cattle? When attempts were made to strike a bargain, the conversation was laced with remarks made by a third party, called a tangler or blocker, who had a reputation for being a crooked dealer. To complete a transaction, the buyer would spit on the palm of his hand and slap the seller's hand. Then the money was paid and the cow marked with the buyer's mark. Sometimes the seller asked for a good luck penny which was also spat upon by the buyer before he gave it to the previous owner of the cow. After the business formalities had been observed, the men would be ready to listen to the pipers and flute players and fiddlers who might eventually lure them into the dancing tents.

There was hardly a man at the fair who did not carry a blackthorn stick. The blackthorn stick was designed primarily as a walking stick, but it was also used in the faction fights that took place at Irish fairs long ago. As any man would explain if you asked, "A man without a blackthorn stick is a man without an expedient." A good many Irishmen spent hours practicing with these sticks so that if they did become involved in a fight they would be capable of dealing with the opponent. Sometimes a young man about to leave for the fair would be startled to have his father suddenly knock the stick out of his hand with a quick jab of his own stick. "This will teach you to mind yourself," the father would then say mildly. "You must learn to hold the stick properly so that the stranger you might meet at the fair won't be after taking you by surprise."

Faction fighting, once considered a form of sport similar to fencing, is no longer a part of the Irish scene. Furthermore, festivals and sporting events have all but taken the place of the great fairs of long ago. Greyhound racing, horse racing, and numerous horse shows, including the Connemara Pony Show held in July, are all popular. The Irish Sweeps Derby is held in County Kildare, the Fairyhouse Races at Fairyhouse, County Meath, and the Sweeps Hurdle at Leopartstown, just outside Dublin. Each year the All-Ireland Hurling Finals are played at Croke Park, Dublin, attracting as many as ten thousand spectators. The All-Ireland Football Finals are also played in Croke Park. Galway holds its yearly West of Ireland Speed Boat Championships, and the West of Ireland Amateur Open Golf Championships are held in County Sligo.

There is one fair held yearly in County Kerry, however, that still manages to recreate the carnival memories of the old-time celebrations. The Puck Fair begins on the tenth of August, which is, appropriately enough, called Gathering Day. On the evening of this day, the people meet at the bridge to form a procession. From there they proceed to the square carrying a billy goat in a cage mounted on a lorry, or truck. The billy goat, decorated with brightly colored ribbons, is chained by its horns to a high platform, and there, surrounded by a generous supply of cabbages, he presides over the fair. There are those who see Puck as a symbol of fertility and good luck. But the popular explanation tells us that the Puck Fair commemorates an occasion when the noise of goats warned the Irish of advancing English forces. At any rate, Puck's reign is short, for on the evening of August 12, Scattering Day, he is lifted off his cabbage throne.

Ballinasloe in County Galway is well-known for its great horse, cattle, and sheep fairs. Most famous is its October Fair, which begins on the first Tuesday of October and lasts through the four following days. Irishwomen who might happen to be attending the October Fair would likely be wearing suits or coats made out of homespun material, such as is found in Galway, Mayo, Donegal, or the Aran Islands.

Indeed, a distinctive garment worn by the men, women, and children in any part of Ireland is the Aran sweater, first made some five hundred years ago. The island people needed something to keep them warm and dry, so the fishermen took time off from weaving their nets and turned their skills to knitting these waterproof sweaters. They are made from *bainin,* the unscoured, unbleached wool taken from the small shabby native sheep. The wool is oiled, combed, and spun, and then knitted with goose quills. Religious symbols and folk motifs are woven into the sweaters. Actually, there was a time when each family created its own particular pattern. Since the bodies of lost fishermen might be in the water for a week before being recovered by their families, the characteristic pattern was of great help in identifying the bodies.

In many small villages of Ireland, there still remain vestiges of the street sale where a collection of old clothing, pots and pans, farm tools, and other items of a practical nature are laid out on tables. These days, however, most of the fairs are conducted for the purpose of marketing cattle. And although the great fairs of long ago were, for the most part, more celebrative than those of today, there was a certain type of fair that held not a single note of joy — the hiring fair.

A hiring fair was usually held on the twelfth of May. On this day, boys and girls stood in the market square while the prosperous farmers and their wives looked them over. The boy who wished to be hired for the summer months would wait anxiously, and then breathe a sigh of relief when the hiring man finally said, "He is wee, but his neck is good. Bought and sold for three pounds!"

A boy introduced to his first hiring fair would find himself growing up in a hurry. But he may also have experienced a sudden sense of maturity while attending the Harvest Fair. For as the Fian, or Fenians, were recruited at the great fairs of old, so too were young men recruited at fairs in later days. There in the gloomy secrecy of some byre, a young man often knelt to take his first oath of love and loyalty to his own Dark Rosaleen — another of the names used to symbolize Ireland. It is not surprising, then, that when the fair was over the young man's mind might stray from thoughts of the lovely colleen he had dallied with a while back, and turn instead to more serious matters.

Even today, the Irish boy who for one reason or another has taken on the responsibilities of the family farm is sometimes plagued with somber thoughts. Indeed, many a young man, coming home from the cattle fair at the end of a long day, might very well be pondering on these lines taken from Padraic Colum's poem, *The Drover*:

> O farmer, strong farmer,
> You can spend at the fair,
> But your face you must turn
> To your crops and your care.

CHAPTER 11

FEAST DAYS AND FESTIVALS

THERE IS AN OLD Irish saying, *Na dein nos agus na bris nos.*
It means, "Neither make nor break a custom." One Irish
custom that is not likely to be broken is the practice of
observing feast days and festivals. Certainly, the female
patron saint of Ireland will continue to be honored as long
as there is an Irishman left to speak her name. In rural
Ireland, St. Bridget's Day was traditionally the first day of
spring and of the new year. St. Bridget's Feast falls on February 1, at the start of the agricultural season, a day that
was originally an important pre-Christian festival. It is
appropriate that the saint's day should fall on February 1,
the day when the people began the tilling of the fields,
because Bridget herself had a great love for the land, and
took part in tending the crops and caring for the cattle.

A great many old customs and beliefs are associated
with St. Bridget's Feast. In the olden days, people would
perform no work on that day that involved turning or
twisting. There would be no spinning, for example, or
digging, or ploughing, or, in fact, any form of work that
required the use of a wheel. To invoke a plentiful supply
of fish for the rest of the year, shellfish was brought into
the houses and put in the four corners of the floor. In
some areas of Ireland, young boys went from door to door
carrying a churndash and asked for gifts in the name of
St. Bridget.

On the evening of the saint's day, the oldest daughter of the family brings a bundle of rushes to the door. Playing the role of the saint, she calls out, "Go upon your knees, do reverence, and let Bridget enter." Immediately, those who are inside the house answer, "Greeting, greeting to the Noble Lady!" The girl then brings in the rushes and distributes them among the family. Everyone, down to the smallest child, fashions a cross from the rushes. The crosses are sprinkled with holy water and hung in various rooms in the house, and also in the byre. That night, a cloth known as a *brat Bhride,* or Bridget's cloak, is left outside. This cloak is said to acquire healing powers as it lies out on the steps during the night. There is also a custom of throwing a sheaf of oats against the doorstep "to drive away hunger" and to guarantee that the family will have sufficient food to carry them through the year.

In many parts of Ireland it is the youngest child who is allowed to play the leading role in the ceremonial rituals that are observed on Christmas Eve. It is the custom of the Irish to set a tall candle in the window of their homes so as to light the path for the Holy Family. Usually, it is the youngest Mary in the house who is given the honor of lighting this candle. On the night of the Savior's birth, the littlest Mary stands at the hearth holding a sliver of bog-pine. At the exact moment the Angelus bell rings, she takes a light from the fire and carries the flame to the candle. If there is no Mary in the house, the honor of lighting the candle is still given to the youngest child, who, as the Irish point out, will live the longest and send the custom furthest.

The long litany of Ireland's saints includes St. Stephen, whose feast is celebrated on December 26. In some parts of Ireland, the custom of abstaining from meat on St. Stephen's Day is still observed to honor this saint, who is supposed to have saved the people from the plague. On St. Stephen's

Day it is customary for the young men of the parish to go
from door to door carrying a holly bush on which is placed
a dead wren, or a representation of one. The young men
sing a song that begins:

> The wren, the wren, the king of all birds
> St. Stephen's Day was caught in the furze;
> Although he is little, his family is great,
> So rise up, landlady, and give us a treat;
> Bottles of whiskey and bottles of beer,
> And I wish you all a happy New Year.

Another interesting custom in the old country is associated with the twelve days of Christmas ending on January
6, the day known as Small Christmas, or Nollaig na mBan
("Women's Christmas"). Christmas holly is taken down
and burned on Nollaig na mBan. Then twelve candles are
lighted in every home in honor of the twelve apostles. Time
was when it was thought that the first candle to go out
signified that the person who had lighted it would be the
first one in the family to die. The eve of this feast, Oiche
na dTri Rithe, the Night of the Three Kings, corresponded
with the wedding feast of Cana. The Irish saying was:

> On the night of the Three Kings
> Water becomes wine,
> Clusters of rushes become silk,
> And the sand becomes gold.

This enchanting belief, when passed on to descendants
of Irish immigrants in America, seems to have suffered
in the transfer. In America, it was on New Year's Eve that
the Irish American child often tried in vain to keep awake
so that he might participate in the miracle of the wine. If
he happened to be familiar with the Irish superstition
regarding the New Year, he would look with favor on any

dark-haired person who visited the home that day — that
is, if the visitor was led outside and asked to come back in
again. In the old days, no Irishman would risk losing his
luck by giving money or milk away on New Year's Day.
Neither would he allow the ashes or floor sweepings to be
put out. And of course, no one would think of digging a
grave or burying the dead, for it was feared that this might
set the pattern for the coming year.

Many were the taboos associated with Good Friday. No
nail was to be driven on this day, and no wood burned.
The sun on Good Friday was said to grow darker after
noontide. No one was allowed to drink milk on that day —
this was probably a form of fasting — and any cakes that
were baked had the sign of the cross of them. Yet, it was
considered lucky to plant seed potatoes. Women and girls
took their hair down and allowed it to hang loose.

On Easter Sunday holy water was sprinkled on the fields.
Surprisingly enough, the people made a practice of drinking
the holy water. If the festival of the Virgin Mary (March
25) chanced to coincide with Easter Sunday, it was considered a bad omen. Although St. Bridget has always been
known in Ireland as "Mary of the Gael," the Mother of the
Savior is also venerated by the Irish. Back in 1879 the
Catholic Church of Knock in County Mayo was the scene
of a series of apparitions. In the wake of the apparitions,
a number of miraculous cures took place in the village. To
this day, there are pilgrimages to Knock every Sunday of
the summer season. The Virgin Mary is also honored in an
August festival, and as always, many patterns and local
festivals take place on her feast days.

Obviously, the Irish have great respect and reverence
for their saints' days. This is particularly true in the case
of Ireland's beloved patron saint. *Ni dire bradan fearna i
lar na caise ne le Padraig i Lar an Earriagh* is an old Irish

saying that leads one to believe St. Patrick's feast day was associated with hope, and with its offspring, joy: "As the sturgeon or salmon swims exactly in midstream, so does St. Patrick's Day fall exactly in midspring."

Just how was St. Patrick's Day celebrated in the old days? First of all, it was the custom to sow the grain as near to his feast day as possible. The older men celebrated the feast by gathering together in the public house to drink *pota Phadraic,* or St. Patrick's pot. St. Patrick, by the way, did not disapprove of drinking, though any evidence of excess was likely to arouse his ire. Indeed, he had a brewer in his own household. So, too, did St. Bridget, who was often praised for the quality of her brewed ale.

On St. Patrick's Day, at least in former times, the father of the house took a charred stick and marked the arm of each member of the family with a cross. As he made the mark he said, "In the name of the Father and of the Son and of the Holy Ghost." Crosses were also made out of colored ribbon and worn on the breast. As any Irishman knows, the shamrock is supposed to have been used by St. Patrick as a means of explaining the Trinity, but the custom of wearing the shamrock may be fairly recent.

St. Patrick's staff, however, is more appropriately associated with the saint. According to tradition, St. Patrick acquired his famous pastoral staff while on a journey from Germanus to Rome. In the midst of his travels, he stopped at a house on an island in the Tyrrhenian Sea. In this house lived a young married couple who, astonishingly enough, had children and grandchildren who were old and decrepit. The couple had been married at the time of Jesus, and He had visited their home. After partaking of their hospitality, Jesus blessed them, saying they would remain new and young until the Judgment Day. On departing He left His staff, with instructions that it be given to

St. Patrick when he too passed that way. So it was that at the age of sixty, St. Patrick received the Staff of Jesus, and with it, an injunction from a young, old man to "Go and preach in the land of the Gael."

St. Patrick's famous pastoral staff remains preserved to this day, as does the story of a time when he used it somewhat improperly. The story begins at Royal Cashel where he was about to baptize King Aongus. As was customary, Patrick thrust his staff into the earth — or so he thought. When the ceremony was over, he discovered that he had thrust the sharp iron point of his staff right through the king's foot. "Why did you not tell me this?" he cried in anguish to Aongus, and the king answered, "Because I thought it was a part of the ceremony."

St. Patrick, in his Confessions, tells of the difficulties he encountered in his missionary work. A man of only moderate learning, he felt humble upon finding himself among so many learned men in Ireland. In the beginning, the four bishops, Ailbe, Declan, Ciaran, and Ibar, were not the least bit inclined to accept St. Patrick as their patron. Despite the fact that the saint had spent his seven years of slavery learning the Irish language and nurturing his Irish spirituality, these bishops considered him a foreigner. It was not until Declan was admonished by an angel that he finally came to do the will of St. Patrick.

During those years of missionary work, St. Patrick performed many miracles. As an old Limerick man remarked over a hundred years ago, "Every miracle he performed had the humanities in it." However, in the story of Beamon's Candle, we find him in a situation where he is compelled to cast out, rather than create, light. In those days there was a woman called the witch of Beamon who lived in a cabin on Carrigogunel, the "Rock of the Candle." The witch of Beamon was the only dweller on this rock, which overlooked Limerick city. While she lived, and even after, a candle flung its light around the adjacent countryside. Whoever chanced to look at the candle between sunset and sunrise became a corpse by morning.

The light of the candle was greatly feared by the people, and to such an extent that they were afraid to open their doors to travelers. St. Patrick came to their rescue, and in the instant that he extinguished the light, the witch of Beamon gave such a great cry it shook the branches of trees and cause the waters of the Shannon to erupt in a niagara of weeping. When St. Patrick then took possession of Carrigogunel and made a monastery of it, the people beseeched him to change its name because of its ominous connotations. "No," said St. Patrick. "Let it be called the Rock of the Candle while Ireland is green."

Also associated with Ireland's patron saint is the famous St. Patrick's Purgatory, a Christian shrine situated on an island in Lough Derg, a lake stretching out among the mountains of Donegal. During the Middle Ages, pilgrims who had committed terrible crimes came to this shrine to do penance. Many came merely to pray. To this day, tens of thousands of people from all walks of life come to the island between June and mid-August to make a three-day retreat. Legend has it that Christ Himself revealed the island to St. Patrick. It is said that Christ told St. Patrick that whoever would spend a night and day on this island would witness both the torments of hell and the joys of heaven. It has also been claimed that Dante's *Divine Comedy* was inspired by this island.

Possibly it is because of Lough Derg that the legend of the snakes came about. After St. Patrick had banished all the snakes except one, he managed to entice the last offender into a box with an offer of wine. Chiding the saint for his lack of fair play, the snake pleaded to be released. "I promise to let you out on the morrow," said St. Patrick, and with that he threw the box into Lough Derg. Ever since then, it is said that children often hear the voice of the snake rising out above the waves of the mountain lake. "Is this day the morrow . . . is this day the morrow?"

St. Patrick himself may have had nothing to do with the origin of the snake symbol, but he did influence the type of Catholicism that is practiced in Ireland today. Irish Catholicism from its very beginning was quite different than the Catholicism of other countries. Indeed, one of the most distinguishing features of the Celtic mythology is that its dogmas are cheerful, its view of the spiritual world devoid of Gothic gloom. This caused a great deal of conflict between Rome and Ireland. Even as far back as the tenth century, there was an awareness of this conflict, as was expressed in the following poem translated from the Irish by Frank O'Connor:

> To go to Rome —
> Is little profit, endless pain,
> The Master that you seek in Rome,
> You find at home, or seek in vain.

Father Peter O'Leary (1850-1920) has given us a first-hand account of Ireland's unique approach to religion in his autobiography, *My Story*. Of this great Land League and Gaelic League priest, who was a native of Cork, his contemporaries said, "He was a little God to us all." Fearless and courageous, as were many of the priests in those days, he was one of the first to make an effort to restore the Irish language by teaching it to the young. This saintly and humane man couldn't be described better than in the lines of the following verse, which indicates the type of man Irish people consider to be a good priest:

I'd like a priest, fine, cheerful, merry,
Full of faith and charity, good natured,
Who'd be kind to the poor and gentle with his flock,
But I'd not like a boor in the fair livery of
   The Only-Son.

The story of Father O'Leary casts doubt on the opinions of those who suggest there is an austere tradition in Irish Catholicism. As for those who go so far as to trace the tradition of austerity back to St. Patrick, they seem to have lost the argument altogether. It is highly unlikely that a man who included in his poem of blessings the words "Blessings of happiness be upon you all" would be at home in such an atmosphere.

St. Patrick's Day in Ireland is observed in a somewhat different manner than it is in other countries. In Ireland, St. Patrick's Day is a holy day. The churches are jammed, and all over the land there can be heard the joyous sounds of Irish voices singing "Hail Glorious St. Patrick," a simply magnificent hymn which contains these lines:

All praise to St. Patrick
Who brought to our mountains
The gift of God's faith,
The sweet light of his love!

Commemorative parades are also held in Ireland to honor the feast of St. Patrick. The tradition of holding parades in his honor may very well have originated with Irish Americans in America. Here is a description of an early St. Patrick's Day celebration in a midwestern American city:

The first St. Patrick's Day celebration of which there is any record was that of 1853 when upwards of 300 men joined in a procession wearing green scarfs over their right shoulders and sprigs of shamrocks in their hats. The parade formed at the church after Mass and marched through the streets to the stirring notes of fife and drum.

According to old newspaper accounts, the Irish Catholic Temperance Society was well represented in those early St. Patrick's parades. As time went on, it would appear that members of the Temperance Societies were not as much in evidence. Nowadays, it is heartening, even touching, to see members of other ethnic groups walking side by side with their Irish friends, exhibiting a remarkable spirit of brotherhood. It is also interesting to note that in recent times St. Patrick's Day parades have become more of a family affair, with families marching together and holding a banner on which is written the name of the clan and the name of the clan's county. Even small children take part in the processions in order to show their regard for the land of their ancestors.

Children still take part in processions in Ireland, too, especially on December 28, the Feast of the Holy Innocents, or Children's Day. Also called Cross Day, it was once a day when the Irish would never think of getting married, or digging a grave. The people of Ireland may have abandoned many of these old folks beliefs, but the country is to this day often referred to as the "Showcase of Catholicism."

Speaking of the spirit of Christmas, and the tendency of other countries to indulge in the crude commercialism of this great Christian feast, an Irish priest recently remarked, "Christmas is still Christ-Mass in Ireland, its sacred character the dominant note of the holy time." And who can fail to take joy in the natural beauty of these lines taken from a poem in which the Irish poet, Patrick Kavanagh, recaptures a Christmas scene from his childhood:

Outside the cow-house my mother
Made the music of milking,
The light of her stable-lamp was a star
And the frost of Bethlehem made it twinkle.

My father played the melodeon,
My mother milked the cows,
And I had a prayer like a white rose pinned
On the Virgin Mary's blouse.

In many respects, Ireland is a country where religion is as it should be — simple. Traditional customs associated with the Mass have become a way of life. Approaching the church on Sunday, or any other holy day, the Irish say, "Hail to thee, O church of God, in which lives my Savior, Jesus Christ. May Mary and the twelve apostles pray for me today." When departing the prayer is, "Farewell, O Mary, and farewell, O Christ! May Ye preserve my soul until I come again." Commemorating a time when public celebration of the Mass was prohibited, the people in certain parts of Ireland still cling to the old custom of having Mass said in the house. The visit from the priest, called the Station, is held at a different house in the village or townland each year.

The stations of the cross were — and still are — a vital part of the Irish religion. So, too, are the holy wells. Everywhere in Ireland there are holy wells and it is not uncommon to see people praying near them, creating, as they pray, little piles of stones that will be counted on the last day. Stones of atonement! A well of rosaries! A hail of Aves and Paters falling down and around the soft air. Surely there are times when Ireland would still seem to be an island of saints.

So numerous were the saints who lived and prayed in Ireland that it would be impossible to list them all here.

Some of them were scholarly saints, whose minds became almost inaccessible towers of learning. But they fulfilled a need all the same. So, too, did St. Patrick, who was able to reach the less educated people and spread his message of love in such a way that he is honored by both Catholics and Protestants.

Most of the Protestants in the Republic belong to the Church of Ireland, which is a member of the Anglican. Communion and has its administrative center in Dublin. Once the official church, but disestablished in 1870, it has no legal ties with the Church of England. Other religious groups include the Presbyterians, Methodists, Unitarians, Quakers, and the Jewish community, which is concentrated in the cities of Dublin and Cork.

It is safe to say that certain feast days and festivals in Ireland have almost as much appeal for Protestants as for Catholics. This is particularly true of May Day, St. John's, and Michaelmas, which are all associated with a season. Beliefs associated with May Day originally stemmed from fear of blight and ban, in the days when people employed many charms to protect their butter, their animals, and their crops. Green branches and flowers were carried into the house and scattered around doors and windows on the Old May Day, May 12. Associated with this custom was an old Irish song which began, "We have brought the summer with us." The song is still popular in Ireland.

The Feast of St. John (June 24) may very well have its origin in the pre-Christian festival of midsummer. In ancient Ireland, the village inhabitants often gathered together and built a huge bonfire. Cattle were driven between two bonfires to protect them from disease. In later days, boys and girls gathered together on Midsummer Night and built a bonfire on the top of a hill. Around this fire they danced and sang. When the dancing was over, each boy and girl took up a burning brand and proceeded to make a charmed circle — around the crops, around the cattle, and even around the houses — with the sacred fire.

Michaelmas in September not only commemorates St. Michael the Archangel, but also marks the end of summer. A common saying used to be, "Summer is summer until Michaelmas." Galway has for centuries been associated with the feasts of Michaelmas, May Day, and Midsummer Eve. During the celebrations for May Day and Midsummer Eve, nobody was allowed to travel in a coach under the Spanish Arch unless they had been born in Galway. Anyone who had not been born in Galway had to get out of the coach and walk. As they walked under the arch they were to make a silent wish. This tradition is still observed in Galway. And on Midsummer Night, the young people still gather around a bonfire, usually built on the square just outside the Spanish Arch, and dance throughout the night.

Actually, there are so many feast days and festivals in Ireland it would almost seem there is one for every day of the year. There is a film festival in Cork, an Opera Festival in Wexford, an Amateur Drama Festival in Athlone. The International Festival of Light Opera in Waterford is the only annual international competitive festival of its kind; it attracts competing companies from England and Wales as well as from Ireland. For the gourmet, Bundoran in County Donegal offers the May Lobster Festival, while in September Galway offers their prized sea delicacies at the Galway Oyster Festival.

People from all over Ireland, and even from Europe, attend the Galway Oyster Festival. Held on the coast of Galway Bay, the season's first shellfish is brought from the sea to the sound of fiddle music. The Queen of Connemara, who is chosen to preside over the day's activities, presents

the first oyster to the mayor. To further celebrate the
opening of the oyster season, banquets are held in the
evening.

The "Kingdom of Kerry" is famous for a festival that is
unique in Ireland — their annual beauty contest. And
where else would the Rose of Tralee be selected but in the
village of Tralee itself? Lasting for the better part of the
week in late summer, the festivities begin with the playing
of a harp by a woman who must belong to a Kerry family
in which harp-playing has been a traditional occupation
for generations. During the course of the week, a circus is
brought to town. There are horse races, too, and competition in singing, dancing, and storytelling. The beauty contest is worldwide, with girls coming from Ireland, Britain,
the United States, and even from such distant places as
Australia. But although the girl chosen to be the Rose of
Tralee must be lovely and fair, she must also be of Kerry
descent.

The fact that the ballad "The Rose of Tralee" is so well-
remembered has more to with a pair of star-crossed lovers
than with the Kerry beauty contest. It was William Pembroke Mulchinock who composed the ballad. Living just
outside the village of Tralee, William fell in love with a
girl who was a maid in one of the nearby houses. Since a
romance with an Irish servant girl could hardly be tolerated
by the Pembroke Mulchinocks, in no time at all William
was sent to join a regiment in India.

And so the young man soldiered, his thoughts remaining
on the girl he left behind. Three years passed before he
returned to Tralee. As he came into the village, he saw a
funeral procession passing down the street. It was the
funeral of the girl he loved, who had died, it was said,
of a broken heart. In the public park just outside Tralee
there is a memorial to these ill-fated lovers. On the marble

stone beneath a carved cross is this inscription: "To the memory of William Pembroke Mulchinock and the Rose of Tralee. She was lovely and fair as the rose of the summer."

CHAPTER 12

THE WAKE AND THE FUNERAL

THE IRISH, with their characteristically poetic nature, have a theory that after death the soul escapes from the body in the form of a white butterfly. And the memory of one who has died is often perpetuated with a verse or phrase that gives some indication of the sort of person he or she was when living on earth. Patrick Kavanagh is laid to rest in a typical Erin cemetery where wind ruffles the wild grass, and where, appropriately enough, butterflies streak the air like white lightning. On a simple stone cross above the poet's grave is carved his birthdate, October 21, 1904, his death date, November 30, 1967, and below it these words: "And pray for him who walked apart on the hills loving life's miracles."

But where do Irishmen go when they die?

Catholics in Ireland, for the most part, believe in the doctrine of Purgatory. Yet viewing the history of Ireland, the only country in western Europe where religious persecution was visited on a group who formed the majority of the population, it would appear that many of its people served their sentence of Purgatory while still on earth.

Oddly enough, there is no indigenous word in the Irish language to express hell, while heaven literally signifies "the isle of the noble." Certain gifted Irish individuals who have sought out the mystery of that final tomorrow are said to have seen this isle. Situated off the western coast of

Ireland, it is described as a region of perennial spring and endless pleasure. Phrases in the poems of Ossian describe heaven as a "grey stone rising amidst beauteous verdure," and presents us with a picture of "the warrior sleeping beneath the green sunny hill on the margin of a blue rolling lake, the warm beam of the sun above him."

Since the Irish accepted the doctrine of Purgatory, at least after the Christian era, one would hardly expect to find them acting in such a manner as to risk serving a sentence in that halfway house to heaven. But they did all the same. Indeed, the custom of laying curses on one's enemies was once prevalent in Ireland, despite the old Irish proverb that says, *"Fillean an feal ar an bhfeallaire —* Wait till you see now. Curses come home to roost."

Ordinarily, a curse laid by an innocent or genuinely wronged person brought no evil upon the one who uttered it. On the other hand, if the malediction was visited on an innocent victim, it often turned out to be a boomerang and further pointed up the truth of the admonition, "Let he who is without sin cast the first stone." At a place called Kilmoon, in the northern part of County Clare, it was said the stones could cause the mouth of the one who uttered the curse to become crooked. Even St. Patrick was known to have cursed the wretch who stole his goat to make a bodhran or drum, out of the skin. There are those who say the sound of that ghostly goatskin bodhran is still heard along the Boyne in the dark of night.

Although most people did not generally approve of the custom of laying curses, the way ancient Irish law operated offered the victim little chance for vindication. Thus, the injured party often felt he had to take the law in his own hands. In fact, the practice persisted in some areas of Ireland well into the nineteenth century.

Many a story has been told of the poor traveling widow

who sought sanctuary in an unused cabin on the property of a rich landlord. There, she and her infant were supplied with food brought by kindly neighbors. The landlord eventually heard of her presence, flung her from the land, and burned the little cabin. When the infant died of starvation, the mother brought a curse down on the landlord's head. It was so effective that for seven generations none of the landlord's male heirs were allowed to die in their beds, but met death by suicide, or in battle, or at sea, leaving seven widows with young children.

Sometimes a curse was contained in the funeral lament, as in the case of a widow whose two sons were executed for treason on the testimony of a perjured informer, a young man by the name of Hugh. In her combined keen and curse verse, the anguished woman described how the falsehoods of Hugh shook the court to its foundations, shook the earth and the skies, and caused a bolt to fall from heaven, blasting the bloom of the trees and stopping the song of the birds. Then she went on to say:

> Evil befall the grand jury, and the judge,
> Evil befall the twelve who tried you.

Another keener combined lamentation with curse to poetically describe the dead man, saying he was swift and sure of foot and could look the sun in the face like an eagle. "There have been full and plenty in his father's house," she sang, "and the traveler never left it empty, but the tyrants had taken all but his heart's blood, and that they took at last." Then, kneeling with her hands clasped together, she cursed the one who had aimed the fatal bullet.

Actually, the Irish were more inclined toward charms than curses, and even then they did not resort to that expedient until they had exhausted all other logical methods for curing an illness or overcoming some sort of difficulty.

Perhaps the most common charm was the one used to banish toothaches, because the only alternative was to allow the local blacksmith to painfully extract the tooth. The following verse, chanted three times and with the utmost concentration, is found in the Latin manuscripts of the Middle Ages:

> As Peter sat on a marble stone
> The Lord came to him all alone.
> "Oh Peter, Peter, why dost thou shake?"
> "Oh, Lord, it is my tooth doth ache."
> The Lord said, "Take this for My sake
> And never more your tooth will ache."

Many of the basic remedies for illness were astonishingly effective. One of these simple cures, once dismissed as quackery, was salicyl, a product of the bark of a type of willow, used as a remedy for rheumatism. Another drug used traditionally in Ireland to alleviate the symptoms of heart ailment was the extract of foxglove, digitalin. Perhaps the most interesting and ingenious medication was penicillin. Long before it was discovered by Sir Alexander Fleming, the Irish country people made a practice of keeping a loaf of white bread or a piece of bacon in a damp part of the house, and using the resultant growth of mold to heal sores or wounds.

Elements of magic and religion were sometimes combined with the cure, the rituals no doubt having the same sort of psychological effect that a trip to the doctor or a placebo might have in our own times. There was, for example, the practice of going around the midsummer bonfire twice, taking three meals of nettles in May, and of course, drinking blessed Easter water on Easter Sunday. Forge water was also a commonplace remedy, probably because of its iron content. Relics of the saints were often used and many ill people sought relief by lying in the supposed tomb or bed of a saint.

Those who were ill would not be inclined to favor the idea of showing any improvement on a Sunday, since this was regarded as an ill omen. Close observation had also led the Irish to realize that a patient was doubly ill at night. To visit an invalid when one was returning from a funeral was considered the height of folly. Nor was it wise to allow milk or fire to go out of the house while a person was ill, since the fire was symbolic of the life of the patient. And as this old proverb shows, the doctor was never called until the eleventh hour: *"Dearbhrathair don Bhas fios a chur ar an dochtuir* — Sending for the doctor is brother to death."

Two o'clock in the morning was considered a lonesome hour and many people died at that time. The Irish always said that souls left the bodies with the turning of the tide. Indeed, the Irish have made a point of preserving many elements of their original attitudes toward death. In early literature a female goddess named Morrigan was said to have haunted the battlefields. Later on, we find the *badhb,* or crow, symbolizing death. There is the story of the dying Cuchullain whose moment of death was heralded by a bird who perched on his shoulder. A statue depicting this incident still stands in the General Post Office in Dublin. In Ireland it is considered an omen of death if a bird perches on the windowsill of the sick room, while the Irish-American is inclined to think it a death omen if a bird gets into the house and is allowed to fly out again.

Other ominous signs include a dog howling outside at night, or a raven or crow seen flying over the house. But the most common omen was at one time the eerie wail of the Banshee. It was thought that most of the old Irish families had one of these spirits attending them. Appearing

as a beautiful woman gowned in white, this phantom of the
night is referred to in the lines of an ancient bard:

> The Banshee mournful wails
> In the midst of the silent, lonely night
> Plaintive she sings the song of death.

On occasion the Banshee was heard at noon, "when mid-
day is silent all around." Sometimes the voices of several
of these maidens of death were heard together, their melancholy voices mingling with wind song sounds, like "Aery
tongues, that syllable men's names, on sand, and shore, and
desert wilderness."

The term Banshee has been translated as "the angel of
death or separation," or "the white lady of sorrow," and
some have called her the *madre di dolore* of Irish faith.
Maobh, the Mab of Shakespeare, or Maov, is the queen of
the Irish fairies, and the name of the O'Neill family's
Banshee is Maoveen, "the little Mab."

Whether conditioned by an environment where people
were extremely imaginative, or whether they inherited the
fey qualities of their ancestors is hard to say, but many
Irish Americans have had an uncanny ability to foresee
doom. Indeed, even in Irish families whose members were
not particularly given to flights of fancy, strange signs and
omens have been recorded. In a little village in Wisconsin
some years back, two sisters were awakened by a strange
sound and went to the window to see, outlined against the
black sky, three coffins surrounded by lighted candles. The
following day a cyclone ravaged the village killing their
two brothers, and in a brief space of time death also
claimed their mother.

An interesting superstition has become attached to the
yew tree. Anyone daring to pluck a branch from the tree or
injure it in any way could expect death to come a year from

that day. In certain respects, death, particularly that of an old person, was taken as a natural part of life. It was the custom for each old woman to have her habit or funeral shroud always ready in case she died suddenly. "I'll wear that hereafter," the grandmother might say. "It will quench the fire of hell for me." In the following ballad, "O'Reilly's Frolics," a man contemplates his last journey:

> When my corpse will be laid on a table along the room,
> With a white sheet on me down to my toes,
> My lawful wife by me, and she crying most bitterly,
> And my dear loving children making their moans!
> The night of my wake long streams of tobacco,
> Cut on a plate, on my navel for fashion's sake,
> Mould candles in rows, like torches, watching me,
> And I cold in my coffin by the dawn of day.

Many Irish people seemed to be able to foretell the exact day of their death. My grandfather, with no complaints beyond the inevitable symptoms stemming from aging arteries, foretold his death with an astonishing degree of accuracy. On the day before the event he called his youngest son to conference and with grace and dignity told him he would be dying on the morrow. Though grieved at the news, the son immediately made a trip downtown to accomplish the mission as dictated by his father.

"Get out my good black suit and have it cleaned and pressed," my grandfather had commanded. "And be sure to get in a good supply of whiskey. There'll be plenty of people coming in from the country and it will no doubt be a cold night so they will be needing a drop of something to warm them."

My grandfather preserved many of the old customs. In honor of the Crucifixion he would never shave on Good Friday or get his hair cut. Having a firm notion that one must have all his hair on the Day of Judgment, he always insisted the barber gather the hair clippings and slip them into an envelope, after which he took the clippings home and buried them in the flower garden. When we were frightened by a storm he would lead us out to the porch, shake his fist at the heavens, and swearing in his Moses voice, command the thunder and lightning to be gone.

"And it stopped — short — never to go again — when the old man died."

This line from an old verse can still send chills running down the spine of those who remember their Irish grandfathers, for the moment a person died in an Irish home the clock was stopped. This was done so that friends and neighbors would know, without having to inquire, the actual time of death.

"Keep the life in me till the priest comes" was the oft-heard plea of an Irishman who had come upon his last hours. To die without the consolation of a priest was considered a calamity. Of equal concern was the dying man's wish to be laid out in proper garments and to have a fine wake and a grand funeral. The Irishman's preoccupation with such matters stems partly from his true generosity and consideration of others, from his desire to see that neighbors and friends would enjoy "full and plenty" at his wake.

Traditional wakes still survive in Ireland, although in a somewhat modified form. The ceremony is usually held in a room off the kitchen, after the body has been prepared by local women. In former times, the body was laid out on a table or bed in the largest room of the house. Clay pipes were abundant, and it was the duty of a neighbor to see that every man who called at the house lit up and took a few puffs. A plate of tobacco along with a dish of snuff was placed beside the corpse, or, as in "O'Reilly's Frolics," sometimes on his chest.

The body is traditionally covered with white linen, and sometimes adorned with black ribbons for an adult, with white for the unmarried, or with flowers for a child. However, many of the old Irish wore a long brown garment similar to a Franciscan habit. The letters IHS were embroidered on the breastpiece of this garment. Some people thought the letters meant, "I have suffered," but they actually are a symbol of our Lord. Lighted candles surrounded the corpse, and in addition to the plates of snuff and tobacco, salt, an ancient emblem of friendship or welcome, might also be used.

When the preliminary rituals had been observed, the Caointhe, or leading keener, began the singing of the lamentation. During the course of the evening, and especially when a newcomer arrived, the women of the house gathered around the corpse, joining in with the wailing cries of the Caointhe. "O why did you leave us, Ochon," they would cry, for in spite of the celebrative aspects of the Irish wake it was only right and proper that grief be expressed at the passing of a loved one.

The custom of keening not only gave a relative or friend an opportunity to display her talent for poetry, but also provided a touch of drama. There are those who have suggested the keener was paid. It is possible this may have been true on occasion, and considering the Irishman's distaste for hypocrisy, the practice of paying the keener may have been one reason for abandoning the custom.

It is difficult to determine which aspects of Irish behavior have been most severely criticized, but it seems safe to say that their conduct at wakes would come close to the top of the complainer's list. Fun and games were a very definite part of the wake culture. They played Horse Fair, Hunt the Slipper, Fronsey Fronsey, Hot Hands. No doubt many of the wake games were leftovers from pagan times.

Certainly this was the opinion of the clergy, many of whom did their best to banish the practice. But when we consider that the wake sometimes lasted two or three nights and that the corpse was never to be left alone, it seems reasonable to assume the games might have been played partly for the purpose of keeping everyone awake.

We can be sure the Irish had good reason for holding so closely to the tradition of never leaving a corpse unguarded. The first consideration had to do with their reverence for the dead. Supernatural forces may have been at work, too. But there was a more basic reason for the vigilance. During a period that lasted well into the nineteenth century, body-snatchers were constantly on the prowl looking for corpses which they sold to medical schools. Since the Irish buried the dead only a few feet under the earth it was not uncommon to find that bodies were often stolen from the grave.

To make matters worse, scientists and doctors themselves often employed men to do their grave-digging for them. Indeed, grave-robbing became so prevalent that in country churchyards where the old church no longer stood, it was necessary to put up rude cabins and pay a man to watch the graves so that the dead might be allowed to rest in peace.

When Sir Walter Scott was touring Ireland in July of the year 1825, he made an entry in his journal remarking on the kindness of the Irish and their natural disposition to gaiety, and concluded with the comment: "While the Scotchman is thinking about term-day, if easy on the subject about hell in the next world — while an Englishman is making a little hell of his own in the present because his muffin is not well roasted — Pat's mind is always turned to fun and ridicule."

To pull the leg of an innocent bystander was something Irishmen simply could not resist. Usually the jest was accomplished in a subtle manner, but not always. Indeed, there were times when the process bordered on the slapstick. Consider the two English gentlemen who were once visiting a Killarney pub. Making a great fuss about the outlandish customs of the natives, they expressed a desire to attend an Irish wake, whereupon an eavesdropping carman said he knew just the place since a cousin of his had died that very morning.

Evening came and off went the Englishmen to the mountain wake. Sitting there in the humble abode of the carman's cousin's family, they thought what a good job it was they got in on the affair. It was all so jolly, the drinks, the games, and especially the plethora of wall-to-wall wit. But in the moment when some Irishman uttered a particularly amusing remark, there was a sudden twitching at the corner of the corpse's mouth.

"By Jove, the rascal is alive," exclaimed one of the Englishmen, and at that, up jumped the corpse and out the door and down the mountain road he ran, graveclothes and all. As anyone can plainly see, this was not the best way to win friends or influence Englishmen, especially since these two Englishmen had been persuaded to make liberal offerings to pay for the liquor and thus insure the success of the mock celebration.

Indeed, much bantering and exchanging of jokes did go on at a legitimate Irish wake. However, the main topics of conversation were much as they are now: prices, politics, priests, and parsons. Inevitably, subjects of this sort led to many heated discussions. The wake, in fact, offers the Irishman an excellent opportunity for indulging his passion for debate.

On the morning of the funeral, the coffin is taken outside and laid on chairs so that friends and relatives can say a last farewell. Before the lid is put on the coffin the mourners lean down to kiss the corpse. Now the procession begins with the four nearest of kin taking up the coffin. The procession is usually on foot, and the coffin is carried at a fast marching pace. The changing of bearers is done without breaking the steps. As the people approach the church a horseman rides ahead and begins to toll the bell. At the proper moment, a relative of the dead person hands out "crapes" to the mourners. Bands of black cloth are tied around the men's hats, while priests attending the funeral are given large pieces of white linen called "cypresses," which were folded and worn as sashes over the shoulder.

On the way to the graveyard, which could be of some distance, the marchers follow a prescribed traditional route. A circuit may be made around the site of an ancient cross. In Fethard, County Tipperary, there is a certain gate through which a corpse is never carried because it was through this same gate that Cromwell entered the town. Sometimes the journey is made over mountain paths. When a priest or prominent person is being carried on one of these winding roads, the sounds of a thousand or more voices lifted in keening lamentations and echoing among the mountains is truly magnificent.

Rain never interferes with a funeral procession, and in fact is considered a good omen. But no matter what the weather, when the coffin is lowered into the ground, clay is immediately shoveled over it, after which the spade and shovel are laid on top of the grave in the form of a cross. Following the recitation of the graveside prayers, the mourners wander off to say a prayer for other departed friends and relatives.

Epitaphs found on old tombstones in Ireland can be lengthy and sometimes poetic, but many of the inscriptions — of the type often found in village churchyards here in our own country where Irish Americans are buried —

most often tend to be short and of a moralizing nature:

> O Stranger pause when passing by
> As you are now so once was I
> As I am now so you shall be
> So be prepared and follow me.

It is curious to note that we rarely find an inscription in Irish. Many are in Latin, a few in French, but the majority are in English. There is an abundance of stones and carved crosses in the old Irish cemeteries, and tombstones engraved with interesting religious designs. One of these shows a cock rising from a pot, which is a representation of the old Irish legend: "Our Lord's enemies mocked him after his death, saying, 'He said He would rise again. He will as soon as that cock boiling in the pot rises,' whereupon the cock jumped up on the rim of the pot and began to crow."

Numerous, too, are the stones bearing the symbol of the trade of the deceased, a stone and hammer with tongs and anvil carved on it for the smith, a shepherd's crook and shears, the farmer's plough, or perhaps a figure from Euclid's geometry on the schoolmaster's monument.

It must be confessed that the ancient eemeteries of Ireland are not always given proper attention. In certain areas is is not uncommon to find a good many tombstones consigned to oblivion by encroaching weeds and nettles. But for all of that, the Irish, who worship not the great nor look down on the poor, still bury their dead with reverence and dignity. And although they may not have been successful in solving the mystery of death itself, they can at least, in contemplating their own inevitable demise, be consoled by the thought that all Irishmen — except perhaps the man who stole the goat to make a bodhran — will be judged on that last day by none other than St. Patrick.

CHAPTER 13

IRISH GHOSTS AND FAIRY RATHS

"EVERY CRADLE asks us 'whence' and every coffin 'whither.' The poor barbarian, weeping above his dead, can answer these questions as intelligently as the robed priest of the most authentic creed."

Significant indeed are these words of Robert Ingersoll, the eminent nineteenth century lawyer and speaker. Thousands of explanations having to do with the universe and with man's origin have been advanced, accepted, and then discarded. Ptolemy said the sun revolved around the earth. Here was a pronouncement not only accepted and taught by the Church, but held, with slight modification, up until the sixteenth century when Copernicus proved Ptolemy to be wrong.

But while the Church attempts to offer consoling concepts regarding human life and death, men of science have created a growing skepticism of any belief that cannot be proved in a laboratory. Nobody has ever seen a soul. Nobody — weil, at least we have no definite proof of it — has ever seen a spirit. But must one see in order to believe?

For all the remarkable strides made by science, we seem to be living in an era where there is a greater fear of the unknown than there has ever been in the past. Living as we do in a restless and rapidly changing world, we need more than ever to be furnished with some sort of satisfactory explanations concerning death, a subject that presents a thousand questions without evoking one single sensible answer. Are we destined to end up as powdered dust that feeds roots of weeds and wild flowers, or to become merely specks in a shaft of sunlight? A child, with his infinite capacity for wonder, sees miniature miracles in sun shafts. But time and science combine forces to murder a child's imagination.

In Ireland, however, a man's imagination never leaves him alone. Indeed, one cannot be truly Irish without being attuned to the vibrations of the "other world." The Irish, in fact, have always had a feeling for the supernatural, along with a firm belief in some form of immortality. Unfortunately, the tendency to equate superstition with ignorance has all but brought about the disappearance of the "little people." But ghosts still abound in Ireland and there are people still living — particularly in the remote areas — who are perfectly willing to regale visitors with tales of haunted houses and eerie encounters.

Growing up in the hills of West Limerick, the Irish writer and well-known lecturer Kevin Danaher can recall the terror and delight he felt upon listening to one such spinner of tales. He remembers once asking the sage, "Would you not be in dread of going into a haunted house?"

"In dread is it?" exclaimed the old man. "What would I be in dread of, and the souls of my own dead thick as bees around me?"

What of Irish ghosts? Are they more numerous than elsewhere? Many writers who have made a study of haunted houses all over the world have said that Irish ghosts are more immediate and have the sort of glowing intensity that cannot be found anywhere else.

Irish legends of ancient times were not only beautiful; they also indicated a belief in reincarnation. There were Midhir and Etain, for example, the immortal lovers who died and were born again. Meeting in the Great Hall of the King's Palace at Tara, they recognized one another and then, unable to come to terms with the changes wrought by civilization, they flew away together as swans.

With the coming of Christianity, stories of demons and spirits of evil who engaged in constant struggles with the powers of goodness and truth were quite common in Ireland. But long before that, at a time when the De Danann princes had defeated the Firbolgs at the Battle of Taillte, demons were already the order of the day. Following the battle, the De Dananns elected Bove Dearg as their king, and to conciliate the opposing forces Bove gave his daughter Eve to Lir of Shee Finnah in marriage. After bearing him two sets of twins, Eve died. Later on, Lir took in marriage another Eve who had been a sister to the first one. The second Eve became filled with hatred on observing the affection bestowed on her sister's children by both her husband and her father. Came a day when she took them to the shore of Lake Derravarragh in County Westmeath, and as soon as the children went in to bathe she struck out with her magic wand and turned them into four beautiful white swans.

After telling the children they must spend three hundred years on Lake Derravarragh, three hundred years on the Sea of Moyle, and three hundred years on Inis Glora, she granted them two favors. They would be allowed to retain their Gaelic speech, and would also be able to sing sweet music which would have the power to lull to sleep anyone who listened to it. In the end, Eve's father, Bove Dearg, employed his own druidical wand so that he might change his wicked daughter into a screaming demon of the air.

During the eighteenth century, the new English aristocracy built beautiful and stately mansions. Considering the manner in which these people obtained the means to live so extravagantly, and their conduct to those around them, it is not surprising to find that it is in these very houses that ghosts often go flitting about, destroying the tranquility of anyone who is venturesome enough to take up residence.

Several haunted houses still remain in the Dublin area, and though skeptics may scoff, it seems to have been definitely established that those relating the ghostly happenings have been perfectly sensible individuals. A haunting experienced by a woman we shall call Margaret supports the belief that the soul or spirit sometimes comes back in the form of an animal. Moving into a large and sunny old house with her two daughters, Margaret had no reason to believe it contained a ghost. But within two weeks the family had their first introduction to the unwanted visitor.

Sleeping in a room at the back of the house, the two little girls became frightened when they heard sounds that indicated something was jumping up and down. Margaret, going in to quiet them, heard the sounds too. When at last the girls had drifted off to sleep, she heard a strange sighing which at first seemed to be coming out of the wall, but then began creeping around the room until it reached the bed where her daughters lay sleeping. The creeping sounds continued and then touched the bed so that to Margaret's ears it seemed as if an invisible beetle were fluttering its wings against the quilt. Suddenly, a heavy object seemed to fall, then came footfalls and the pecular impression that a cat or animal was jumping up and down. The whole episode lasted no more than ten minutes, at which time the sounds died away near the door of the bedroom.

Except for a few odd whispers and heavy thuds, nothing particularly dramatic happened for the next week. Then one night she was sitting by the bed reading a story to her eldest daughter when she noticed the girl was staring in terror at the fireplace. Following her gaze, Margaret turned and saw a huge black animal sitting on the rug and gazing into the fire. Thinking, or rather hoping, it might be her daughter's pet, she asked cheerfully, "Well, have you come in for your supper?" At that, the creature lifted its head and stared at her with human eyes, revealing a face that was dark and terrible, and yet the face of a woman. As Margaret stared back, a sad and angry howl came from the animal and, in almost the same instant, it vanished.

Needless to say, the family felt compelled to give up the house. It was not until some time later that they discovered an explanation for the ghostly presence. Some fifty years earlier, a woman living in the house had been robbed and murdered by her son and buried by him under the hearth-stone. Plagued by the ghost, the new tenants searched the place until they found the woman's skeleton. After giving it a decent burial they were no longer troubled by the spirit who sat by the fireside howling, and who was, after all, only trying to get someone to take her bones from the place where she had met with such a tragic fate.

The more one studies the habits of ghosts, the more one is convinced it is primarily the troubled ghost that walks by night. Usually the sleepwalker from the spirit world has returned to tell of some injury visited on him, and oftener than not it involves murder. Recently, a story came to my attention that had a special impact because of its similarity to a ghostly happening in my own life. The Halls, whose interesting books on Irish scenery and character were published in 1842, heard this story from a woman who lived in Bantry Bay, County Cork.

"When I was a little girl, my uncle was a magistrate of the county of Cork during a period when he was often called upon because of the Irish troubles. He was a kind-hearted and vigilant man. Riding home from the town of

Bantry one evening about six o'clock, just before sunset, for it was summer, he saw a fine vessel of foreign build at anchor and nearer the shore than was to his liking. It was very calm that evening and no sound came from the sea which, with the rays of sun falling across it, was still as glass. My uncle took up his telescope and saw that the ship was indeed a foreign vessel and that it carried, as was the custom, a good quantity of guns. As he was about to turn away and was making a mental note to check the newspapers to see what manner of ship might be legally anchored off Bantry, he noticed a movement at the stern of the ship, then saw a tall thin figure rise out of the sea.

"Now, my uncle was not the slightest bit superstitious, yet upon observing this strange form which seemed to be shrouded in the garb of graveclothes, he was filled with terror. As he stood watching, the figure stretched clasped hands toward the ship several times, and after about four or five minutes, slowly descended back into the sea.

"After a sleepless night my uncle rode into Bantry and, accompanied by a force of men, boarded the ship in his capacity of magistrate. Embarrassed at the seeming poise of the skipper and at the proferred papers so perfectly in order, he knew not what to say. But on impulse, he told of what he had witnessed the previous evening. As he recounted the experience the skipper began to tremble and sank into a chair, covering his face with his hand.

" 'All is in vain,' he cried out. 'The vengeance of God is everywhere.'

"At that he confessed that he had murdered the captain on the high seas; had led, in fact, a mutiny. Then he ended his confession with these words: 'Sir, *that* wraith or ghost has followed me from sea to sea, from harbor to harbor, in storm and calm, everywhere.' "

Subsequent evidence bore out the truth of the skipper's

confession and, according to the Halls, one or two of his associates were executed in Cork.

Not so with my own ghostly captain.

It happened while on a cruise to the Outer Islands of Hawaii, and after we had been at sea for several days. The voyage had been pleasant and relaxing, although at the outset we had been favored with a simply magnificent sea storm. On this particular night we had retired early. Shortly after midnight I was visited with the sort of dream that seems to be made up of both fantasy and reality.

I was standing on the deck of the ship and someone was calling my name. It was dark and it was light, the waters of the sea calm, and at the same time turbulent. Standing but a few feet away from me was a man dressed in the uniform of a ship's captain. For an instant I saw his face, and his hand clinging to the rail. Then, a man came up from the prow of the ship and flung the captain into the now turbulent waters of the sea.

It was then I must have awakened, the terror still upon me, the feeling that someone had been murdered so strong that I found myself moving toward the phone. I picked up the receiver and put it down again. I tried to tell myself it was only a dream. But I knew it was more than that. Finally, I woke my husband who, skeptic that he is, tried to lure me back to normalcy by asking me the color of the captain's eyes.

When morning came the mood was still with me to such an extent that I had breakfast in the stateroom. The truth is, I could not bring myself to move out of the cabin for the entire day. By evening, I had only partially recovered and as we went in to dinner, my husband, with his usual tendency toward levity, suggested I seek a remedy for my ailment from the ship's doctor who always dined with us. Not wishing to cast gloom on the rest of our table partners,

I asked him not to speak of the incident. But it was obvious that he had no intention of honoring my request.

As I might have known, his account of my encounter with a ghost brought laughter from everyone but myself, and oddly enough, the doctor. A witty and interesting man, he himself had experienced a close brush with death, and was, in fact, a real-life character from the book, *The Great Escape*. Now, he sat perfectly still, as if he were taking a long look into the past. When the laughter had subsided, he said thoughtfully, "That's very strange."

By this time the others had noticed his sober expression and the slight paleness of his face. They stared at him, waiting for him to go on. At last he spoke again.

"Last year," he said slowly, "only a year ago, actually — the captain of this ship died at sea." He paused for a moment. "He was thought to have fallen overboard, and as near as anyone can figure out, it happened about the time you mentioned, just past midnight."

"He was murdered," I said.

"There are those who suggested just such a possibility," he admitted. "As a matter of fact, the authorities made quite an extensive investigation."

The doctor went on to say that since there was little specific evidence to support the theory of murder, the investigation came to naught. But he was murdered. Of that I feel certain.

Because my sea ghost never came back, I managed to convince myself that the spirit of the dead captain, having accomplished its mission, that of letting someone know he had met with foul play, could at last rest in peace. Now and then, I say a prayer for him. For that is what the Irish have been taught, that whenever a departed friend or relative comes back to invade their dreams, it is a sign they are in need of prayer.

It is not only victims of wrongdoing, however, who are compelled to return to former habitats. One old Irishman had loved his earthly home so much that he would, on occasion, return to it so that he might sit by the fireside rocking in his favorite chair. Then there was the man from Limerick who told of seeing corpse candles walking the banks of the Shannon, which were, he believed, the holy ones returning to former habitats. "It's no wonder Ireland should be more haunted, more visited by holy things than other lands," he once remarked. "Blessed be the saints who made it their dwelling place for years."

In Ireland there are also numerous tales of legendary and ancestral ghosts. Such is the story of the Bridal Barge of Aran Roe, which tells of Mourne O'Glanny, an Irish beauty of the eleventh century who set forth in her bridal barge to meet her prospective bridegroom. She received in the midst of her journey a message from him that read:

> Fair Mourne O'Glanny —
> Come no further towards Ballyliffin.
> Turn and make with all speed to Sligo Rock.
> The O'Flaherty are abroad again,
> Pillaging the North Coast. In a battle
> On the Mainland at Dunluce Castle I
> Was wounded. Soon I will come to Sligo.

Putting in at Sligo Rock, Mourne spent the next weeks pacing back and forth, searching in vain for a sign of Aran Roe. Then, one night, awakened by strange sounds, she went rushing down to the landing barge where Aran and his fifty men, all in chains, lay dead on the deck of a barge that was carpeted with blood. Wrapping Aran in the red cloak she had made for their wedding day, she brought him into the house and for seven days kept constant vigil at his bier. When the mourning period was over, she had his body placed on the dais high in the stern of the barge and surrounded him with all her bridal finery.

With the help of an old Warn Woman from Mayo, Mourne had the faces and bodies of Aran and his men gilded with the dust of mountain gold so that the elements would never have the power to destroy their appearance of youth. The fifty men were propped up in the prow in such a way that it appeared they were guarding their master. A bronze shield and the O'Glanny sword were placed upon Aran's breast, and the barge was piled with bundles of wood and dry rushes. When the new moon could be seen in the sky, Mourne commanded her servants to cut the ropes and send forth the bridegroom's barge. Then, standing on the parapet, she lifted a goblet of poisoned wine and drank it long and deeply.

"A portent to you, Aran Roe," she cried out, flinging the golden goblet into the bay. "Sail ever through the years, a symbol of my everlasting love, and to the Black O'Flahertys the curses of all women ring with mine, the women you have robbed of all they love."

Mourne watched the ship glide slowly out to sea. Then, looking at the weeping women around her, she asked them to light her funeral pyre, after which she lay down on the bier and closed her eyes.

There are many who have told of seeing the scarlet bridal barge with its fifty golden warriors who must forever guard the corpse of Aran Roe. Among the witnesses was a man who was once a professor of history at Notre Dame. James Reynolds, whose *Ghosts in Irish Houses* contains the tragic tale of Mourne O'Glanny, has also seen the bridal barge. In fact, Reynolds has thrice seen the ghost ship, two times near Rathlin Island, and once at dawn just off the coast of Galway.

A haunting that favors neither night nor day is called

the legend of the Hungry Grass. Recently, a man living in
the Dublin hills gave an account of his reactions when he
came upon such a patch of grass, which is supposed to
mark the spot where someone had died of starvation during
the tragic famine days.

"Suddenly, without a moment's warning, a terrible feeling
took hold of me. My stomach fell in as if with the most
awful hunger, my knees trembled and the sight left my
eyes. A sweat, so cold it froze my blood, broke out on me.
I fell on my hands and knees and knew I would die in a
few minutes."

Fortunately for Malachy Horan, a companion walking
ahead of him noticed his plight and, getting a morsel of
bread out of his pocket, forced it into his mouth, at the
same time admonishing him never to cross the hills without
a piece of bread in his pocket.

Those familiar with the grass describe it as being white
and herb-like. "Like keeb it lies lank in Autumn and mostly
grows by sheep-walks." A district nurse once came upon
the grass when on her way to a maternity case, and stumb-
ling into her patient's house she was barely able to whisper,
"Bread."

The Hungry Grass hauntings seem once more to give
credence to a belief that ghosts often need our help. Those
who have studied the habits of such restless spirits tell us
that if we give the ghost a friendly blessing it will likely
as not go on its way. Nevertheless, it is not particularly
reassuring to find that there are certain persistent spirits
who do not know they are dead and are trying to reach
earth again so they might possess a mortal.

And what about the fairies?

It has been said, and even by the English, that Irish
fairies are, like the natives over whom they watch, essen-
tially poetic in nature. It has also been said that they are at

times inclined to be a bit vindictive. Even so, the old countrymen insist the fairies will leave us alone if we don't get in their way. In fact, their attitude toward fairies gives further evidence of that innate quality of courtesy which is so much a part of the Irish people.

"If we knew how to be neighborly with them," said an Irishman of long ago, "they would be neighborly and friendly with us."

But how can anyone be neighborly with a fairy? "Leave food and water out for them" is what the old people would have told us. At night, of course, for that is the time when they are abroad. On the other hand, if one wished to invite disaster, all he had to do was throw out the water used for washing feet without giving the fairies a warning.

There are a good many taboos in Ireland relating to feet water. During a period when there were no high rubber boots, people always washed their feet before going to bed at night. After the feet-washing ritual was over, it was customary to take the vessel of water outside and empty it into a channel. If anyone were so careless as to leave the water in the house overnight, it would be the same as giving the outsiders a key to the house. For had not the fairies power over the feet water?

Long ago in Ireland, a man walking the road one night came upon the figure of a woman who had been dead for ten years. As he stood there unable to speak, she began complaining about how she was soaked and scalded with dirty water and the dregs of the teapot. She ended her litany of complaints by admitting she had in life said unkind things about a certain woman in the townland, and that as a part of her purgatory she was to stand outside the woman's house from nightfall to dawn. "Tell her, for the love of God," she concluded, "to give me a warning." And from that time on, the housewife made certain to call

out, *"Seachain —* Watch out!" or *"Chughaibh an t-uiscei
—* Watch out for the water!" in the instant before she threw
out the water.

Irish fairies fall into so many different categories it would
be impossible to deal with them all in such limited space.
There are the trooping fairies and the Merrows and the
solitary fairies. The leprechaun or fairy shoemaker belongs
to the latter group. *Daoine sidhe* is the Irish word for fairy
people. In certain respects fairies seem to behave pretty
much like human beings. Most of them live in large
societies, they love to feast and dance, and they are given to
faction fighting and to playing the ancient game of hurling.
It is only on November Eve that they have a tendency to
gloom, and it is on this night that they sometimes dance
with ghosts.

The country people considered the fairies to be fallen
angels, but Irish antiquarians tell us they are the Tuatha De
Danann who, having dwindled away in popular imagination, are now only a few spans high. As to their fondness
for music and their ability to produce the most profoundly
beautiful sounds ever heard by mortals, there seems to be
no dispute whatsoever. The same man who saw corpse
candles walking the banks of the Shannon often heard the
voices of what he referred to as the "gentle people," and
felt their music ringing in his ears.

"Bewildered I was by them," he said, "like a goose in a
fog, until I could not so much as see my own hand. Yet,
there are many who would think I was no better than a
romancer if I told them I believed."

Many there are indeed who would consider him to be a
romancer. Yet that last great Irish bard, Carolan, once slept
on a fairy rath and forever after had fairy tunes running
around in his head. Raths or *Cusheen Loo* are circular
ditches enclosing a little field. Anyone digging down into

them will find stone chambers with beehive roofs and walls made of unmortared stone. Sometimes they are mistakenly called "Dane's forts" from a misunderstanding of the word Danann. It was in such forts the ancient Celts fortified themselves. Flint arrowheads are often found near these raths. These are called "fairy darts" which are said to have been flung at men or cattle by the fairies when they were angry.

Thousands of these raths and forts and fairy paths and trees can be found in Ireland, and there are people who still believe horrors and curses will fall on anyone who disturbs them. Back in the nineteenth century the Halls spoke with regret of the unprofitable waste of fertile land that prevailed because of the Irishman's reluctance to put a spade into the earth of a rath. And even in 1969 when it was discovered an earth ring lay across the path of Shannon airport, not one workman could be found to take part in such folly, so that there had to be an immediate replanning of the runway.

Crofton Croker, who made quite a study of fairies and fairy raths in the eighteenth century, describes the "gentle people" as being a few inches high and having an airy, almost transparent body so delicately wrought it could dance on a dewdrop without breaking it. Their garments, he said, are white as snow and shine like silver, and their hats or caps have been selected from the red flowers of the foxglove. But for all of their delight in feasting — a Donegal girl who lived with the fairies for a spell told of dining on white bread, fresh butter, and cream — it would seem that they are quite capable of surviving on a liquid diet. So if anyone should wonder why morning dew vanishes so swiftly, it is easily explained. The dew is, in fact, collected from leaves and grass blades by the hungry fairies.

Of all the fairy tribes, the leprechaun is the luckiest one

to meet. He not only cobbles shoes but is the only fairy who knows where crocks of gold are hidden. If you keep your eyes on a leprechaun you can prevent him from vanishing, and who knows, he might even tell you where the pot of gold is hidden. However, leprechauns are very clever and inclined to resort to many tricks. A man named Owen a-Kieran once got one of these little people to tell him where the crock of gold was hidden. It was buried beneath a tall *bouchaillin-buidhe,* or Benweed, the leprechaun told him. At that Owen let him go and he then proceeded to tie his red handkerchief on the bouchaillin-buidhe so he would be able to tell it from the thousands of other bouchaillin-buidhe that were growing in the field. Then off he went for help and shovels. But when he returned he found that the leprechaun had outwitted him once more, for there wasn't a single bouchaillin-buidhe in the field that didn't have a red handkerchief on it.

In truth, Ireland possesses an unbelievably rich store of fairy tales. There is, for example, the legend of the Soul Cages, which tells of a male Merrow who kept the souls of shipwrecked victims in lobster pots in his comfortable house at the bottom of the sea — "So as to keep them warm and snug," he explained to an earthman who came to have dinner with him.

It is a pity few writers have seen fit to let Irish American children in on some of these tales, for they reveal in an interesting and unique manner certain enchanting beliefs of the past. Children should be encouraged to read these fairy tales, not just for the sake of sharing a richness that was a part of their ancestors' literature, but for the sheer joy of being temporarily transported to another time, another place. For as Yeats so aptly put it in his poem, *The Stolen Child,* "The world's more full of weeping than we can understand."

CHAPTER 14

A LAND OF MUSIC-MAKERS

THAT GREAT IRISH bard Carolan who sat on a rath and forever after heard fairy music running around in his head once wrote in a poem, "I spent a time in Ireland happy and contented, drinking with every strong man who was a real lover of music."

Since the Irish from earliest times were known to be great lovers of music, Carolan would have had very little trouble meeting up with numerous kindred spirits as he journeyed about the countryside pleasuring the populace with his harp-playing and singing. Not only was the music of the harp appreciated, but also the music of the Uileann pipes, the fiddle, and a variety of trumpets. In fact, supernatural effects were once attributed to the sound of trumpets, and it was said that the horn of Finn MacCool could in an instant throw all his warriors into a deep slumber.

Even in our own times, it would be difficult to find an Irish man or woman, or a child for that matter, who is not a real lover of music. One of the greatest riches for an Irish child is to have a parent who makes a habit of singing a song or reciting a poem. Indeed, it has often been said in Ireland that if a child were deprived of such a glory, all the wealth of the world could not compensate for the loss.

Few people realize the exquisite beauty and variety of Irish folk songs, which are said to be unsurpassed by those of any other country. Folk music, properly defined, consists of a body of traditional music and song that is an expression of a country's people; thus, the folk music of Ireland would be that which was created by the men and women of Irish-speaking Ireland. During the years when Irish was the spoken language of the majority of the natives, they created an impressive variety of music and poetry, much of it still unedited and uncatalogued today.

According to Edward Bunting, an early preserver and guardian of native Irish music, the musical modes of Irish folk music generally fell into four classes. There was music of a graceful and expressive nature; melancholy music; soothing or sleep-composing strains; and, of course, the merry or sprightly tunes. Probably the most ancient airs existing in Ireland are the "Lamentations of Deirdre," the music to which Fenian poems of Ossian and Fergus were sung, and the songs of the Banshee. Some scholars, including Bunting, hold that the Caoinan, or keening music, had its origin in the song of the Banshee. In any case, Caoinans, dirges, and the airs to which Ossianic poems are sung, are all part of the most ancient tradition of Irish music.

A typical song of sorrow was sung by Cuchullain, who lived during the same period as Deirdre. Forced into combat with his close friend, Ferdia, Cuchullain overthrew and killed him. The following is the last verse of the lamentation composed by Cuchullain as he mourned for his friend:

> Wars were shared and gay for each
> Until Ferdia faced the breach;
> Gentle Ferdia; dear to me,
> Always shall his image be —
> Yesterday a mountain looming,
> Now a shadow in the gloaming.

Donal O'Sullivan, who holds the post of Research Lec-

turer in Irish Traditional Music at Trinity College, Dublin,
has become a leading authority on Irish folk music. In his
book, *Irish Folk Music, Song, and Dance,* he states that
one finds in the best of Irish folk songs "a beauty and
tenderness beyond the ordinary; a deep and passionate
sincerity; a naturalness which disdains all artifice; a feeling
for poetical expression unusual in folk songs: all combined
with a mellifluous assonance which renders them eminently
singable." Although the songs may suffer somewhat in
translation, the following lines still manage to convey a
certain beauty that is so often evident in the love songs of
the Irish:

> The white blossom is on the moorland and autumn is
>   returning,
> And although marriage is a pleasant, pleasant thing,
>   sad and tearful it has left me.

Dr. Douglas Hyde's translations of "The Love Songs of
Connacht" provide us with another example of the type of
songs that found favor with the Irish. Like most Irish love
songs, they are sad, with an intensity of emotion that is
apparent in these lines:

> I thought, O my love, you were so —
> As the sun or the moon on a fountain,
> And I thought after that you were snow,
> The cold snow on top of the mountain.
> And I thought after that you were more
> Like God's lamp shining to find me,
> Or the bright star of knowledge before,
> Or the star of knowledge behind me.

There is another interesting old song, "Cusheen Loo,"
that has been translated from the Irish. It is hard to tell
how old it is, but this is true of many of the old songs, the

majority of which were anonymous. The song "Cusheen Loo" was supposed to have been sung by a young bride who was captured and held in one of the fairy forts. Wishing to escape, the young woman manages to get slightly outside the margin of the fort, while pretending to be hushing her child to rest. Combining a lullaby with a plea to be rescued, she addresses the song to a woman she sees in the distance. These are two of the verses:

> Sleep, my child! for the rustling trees,
> Stirr'd by the breath of summer breeze,
> And fairy songs of sweetest note,
> Around us gently float.

> Oh, thou who hearest this song of fear,
> To the mourner's home these tidings bear.
> Bid him bring the knife of the magic blade,
> At whose lightning-flash the charm will fade.
> > Sleep, my child!

It is said that some of the old Irish families had fairies for their ancestors. Perhaps the harper Carrol (or Gerald) O'Daly of County Wexford was one of these. If not, he must have surely sat on a rath and heard fairy tunes going round in his head, for it was O'Daly who wrote the song, "Eileen Aroon." So beautiful is this song that Handel, who heard it when he was in Dublin, once said he would sooner have written it than all his oratories. This celebrated song has been sometimes claimed by the Scottish, who adapted it and changed the rhythm. As a result, "Eileen Aroon" is almost universally known as "Robin Adair":

> White stars of Bethlehem
> Bloom in the meadow grass,
> Where you were wont to pass,
> Eileen Aroon!

> Birds sing your requiem
> While by yon rippling stream
> Softly you sleep and dream,
> Eileen Aroon!

It is only because of the constant dedication of men like Edward Bunting that so much of Ireland's beautiful folk music has survived. Other guardians of Irish folk music include Henry Hudson, William Forde, John Edward Pigot, James Goodman, Patric Weston Joyce, and William Petrie, who founded the Society for the Publication of Irish Melodies around the middle of the nineteenth century.

"Let me write a country's songs, and I care not who makes its laws," said the Scottish philosopher, Fletcher of Saltoun.

In Ireland, the lawmakers knew full well the power of the poet. Hadn't they back in 1366 initiated the Statutes of Kilkenny, which forbade singers, poets, storytellers, rhymers, harpers, or any other Irish minstrels to ply their trade, and warned the English settlers not to harbor these poets and singers or make gifts to them?

There was even a time back in the sixth century A.D. when the Irish themselves decided the poet had too much power. At this time, all Irish lords kept poets, who earned their daily bread by composing verses praising the lord and his family. But the poet was as capable of damning as he was of praising, and on occasion resorted to blackmailing a man who feared the mockery of his pen. There were so many of these poets, each with his band of attendants, that their support became too great a burden for their lords. The poets, in fact, came close to being banished from the country, but were saved by another poet, St. Colmcille, who managed to exact a promise of restraint and good behavior from the culprits.

Later on, the Normans adopted the Irish custom of employing court poets, and also composed poetry of their own in Irish. Some of the earliest writings about Normans include a long poem that praises Dermot MacMurrough and the first Norman invaders. In camps and castles the minstrels sang their litany of praises, commending Dermot for his nobility, bravery, generosity, and wealth. Throughout the late night hours they raised their voices while their pouches filled with coins. The Normans and their minstrels also composed love songs such as the following written in Norman-French:

> *Harrow! jeo soy trahy*
> *Par fol amour de mal amy!*

> Woe is me! I am undone
> by foolish love for a faithless one!

During the eighteenth and nineteenth century there was a marked change in Irish songs, brought about by the introduction of English and Lowland Scottish songs. The result of this mingling of traditions was the carrying over of Irish forms of verse and metre into the English language. There are many nineteenth century songs that have been translated into English, yet have kept the last line of each verse in Irish, possibly to confound the oppressor, as in "The Groves of Blarney":

> I would climb the high hills of the land,
> I would swim to the depths of the sea,
> For one touch of her lily-white hand,
> *Ach ar Eirinn ni neosainn ce h-i.*
>   ("Ireland over all")

With the decline of the Irish language, Irish songs began to be written in English. These songs, usually adapted to the old native airs, were printed on broadsheets. Thus began the era of the ballad singer.

A professional ballad singer needed to have a broad repertoire, since it was necessary for him to be able to sing not only songs familiar' to the local parish, but also songs that would draw crowds to fairs and races. To catch the attention of a crowd, the street singer began with the lines, "Come all ye lads and lasses," or "Come all ye faithful Irishmen," so that eventually "Come-all-ye" became the name for a street ballad. A street singer might begin his description of a boxing match in the words of the following verse, then go on to describe every round of the fight in at least fifty successive verses:

Come all ye sporting heroes and listen unto me,
I pray you give attention, whoever you may be,
Till I sing about a boxing-match that was held the other
    day
Between a Russian sailor and the gallant Morrissey.

"Buy the new ballad!" the street singer would call out, as he went about the crowd waving the broadsheets. "Only a penny each the ballads!" The Irish people loved to sing and dance and since this was the only way they could get a copy of the new songs, the street singer could usually depend on a complete sellout.

Unfortunately, few songs of the true ballad singers have ever been copied down. The blind ballad singer Zozimus, whose real name was Michael Moran, was once a lively part of the Dublin scene. Taking a stand on one of the bridges over the River Liffey, he would sing songs like the following:

In Aygipt's land, contagious to the Nile
Ould Pharo's daughter went to bathe in style.

She took a dip and came into the land,
And for dry her royal pelt she ran along the strand.

She tripped upon a bulrush and she saw
An infant lying on a wad of straw,
She gazed upon it, and in accents mild
Said, "Tar an' ages, gerrils, which of yiz owns the child?"

Gone are those old ballad singers like Michael Moran
who used to lighten our great-grandfathers' days with their
songs. Only the first part of Moran's "Finding of Moses"
is remembered, but though we regret the loss of subsequent
verses, it is remarkable to think that even this small portion
of the song has survived. Indeed, it is remarkable that
ballads were even written in those days. Certainly, it must
have been difficult for these ballad composers, most of
whom were attempting to express themselves in a language
they had not yet mastered.

In the light of Ireland's history, it is not surprising to
find many Irish ballads proclaiming the country's sorrows
rather than its joys. The insurrections of 1798 and 1803
inspired numerous ballads, including "The Boys of Wexford," "The Croppy Boys," "Bold Robert Emmet," "The
Shan Van Vocht," in which Ireland is portrayed as a dis-
crowned queen, "The Rising of the Moon," and "The
Wearing of the Green." The Fenian, Leo Casey of County
Longford, was imprisoned for his views. He was only
fifteen years old when he wrote "The Rising of the Moon."
Here is a verse from this rallying song:

Out from many a mud-wall cabin eyes were watching
   thro' the night.
Many a manly heart was throbbing for that blessed
   warning light;

Murmurs passed along the valley, like the banshee's
lonesome croon,
And a thousand blades were flashing at the rising of
the moon.

Death, graves, and prisons were often subjects for Irish
ballads. The Tipperary writer Charles Joseph Kickham is
best known for his novel, *Knocknagow,* but he is also
remembered for his patriotic ballad, "Patrick Sheehan."
A member of the Fenian Brotherhood, Kickham was sentenced in 1865 to serve fourteen years' imprisonment. In
his famous ballad, he expresses a longing to go back to
Tipperary, to the Glen of Aherlow.

Although "The Wearing of the Green" is no longer
Ireland's national anthem, the following lines from this
blood-stirring ballad are still sung by Irish Americans on
St. Patrick's Day:

O Paddy dear, an' did ye hear the news that's goin'
round?
The shamrock is by law forbid to grow on Irish
ground!
No more St. Patrick's Day we'll keep, his colour can't
be seen,
For there's a cruel law agin the wearin' o' the Green!
I met wid Napper Tandy, and he took me by the hand,
And he said, "How's poor ould Ireland, and how does
she stand?"
She's the most distressful country that ever yet was
seen,
For they're hangin' men and women there for wearin'
o' the Green!

So if the colour we must wear be England's cruel red,
Let it remind us of the blood that Irishmen have shed;

And pull the shamrock from your hat, and throw it on
the sod,
But never fear, 'twill take root there, though underfoot
when trod.
When law can stop the blades of grass from growin'
as they grow,
And when the leaves in summer-time their colour dare
not show,
Then I will change the colour too I wear in my
caubeen (*plush hat*);
But till that day, please God, I'll stick to the wearin'
o' the Green.

Blood-stirring the words may be, but they are also sad.
Even Thomas Moore's songs dealing with love and Ireland
— "The Harp That Once through Tara's Halls" and "Oft
in the Stilly Night" are his best known — have a touch of
sadness.

Many of the old Irish ballads have found their way into
American folk music. Murphy's "Connemara Cradle Song,"
for example, has as its chorus, "Hear the wind blow, dear,
hear the wind blow; lean your head over, and hear the wind
blow." Irish emigrants to America preserved another ballad,
"The Blackbird and the Thrush." This ballad has in its
last verse words that are almost identical to the words of a
popular American song:

Oh meeting's a pleasure, but parting's a grief,
And an unconstant lover is worse than a thief,
For a thief can but rob you, steal all that you have,
But an unconstant lover would send you to your grave!

On the other hand, the sentimental ballads often associated with Ireland bear little resemblance to the true Irish
ballad. Very few of these songs were even written by an

Irishman. Indeed, the majority of them came out of Tin Pan Alley following World War I. The lyrics of "When Irish Eyes Are Smiling," for example, were written by George Graff, who was of Dutch and German descent.

Undoubtedly, it was just this sort of ballad that helped the homesick Irish immigrant preserve a sense of his own identity. Nevertheless, while the Irish American was watering the garden of his soul with the "Come Back to Erin" sort of melody, many of the ballads being sung in Ireland were charged with a bitter and mocking humor that has always served as a defense against a history of oppression and adversity.

From just such a song came the title for a biography of the late John F. Kennedy. Popular in Dublin in the early part of the twentieth century, this ballad, supposedly sung by a woman whose husband has run off to war, provides an excellent, if chilling, example of the satirical qualities that are often found in Eire's song and poetry. The following lines are taken from this anonymous ballad, titled "Johnny, I Hardly Knew Ye":

> With drums and guns, and guns and drums
> The enemy nearly slew ye;
> My darling dear, you look so queer,
>   Och, Johnny, I hardly knew ye!

> You haven't an arm and you haven't a leg,
>   Hurro! Hurro!

> You haven't an arm and you haven't a leg,
>   Hurro! Hurro!

> You haven't an arm and you haven't a leg,
> You're an eyeless, noseless, chickenless egg;
> You'll have to be put with a bowl to beg.
>   Och, Johnny, I hardly knew ye!

But at the same time such ballads as "Johnny, I Hardly Knew Ye" and "The Night before Larry Was Stretched" were being sung, so too were "The Love Songs of Connacht." The Irish can show an appreciation for both the satirical and the gentle.

Jonathan Swift, that master of satire, in *An Examination of Certain Abuses,* rails at the lawmakers for allowing Dublin street peddlers to misrepresent their wares. He calls attention to one such offender who went about crying "Salmon, alive, alive" without even trying to hide the fact that the fish was cut into a dozen or more pieces. Similarly, there is a bit of humor in that somewhat sad ballad of sweet Molly Malone. For as the fishmonger's daughter wheeled her barrow down streets broad and narrow, the cockles and mussels she sang of as being "alive, alive, oh!" were actually as dead as stones.

Very little was written during the post-famine days. The Irish language, of course, was close to extinction in many parts of the country, and now Ireland, once known for its poets and singers and storytellers, had a new generation growing up who hardly knew their country ever owned a poet until Thomas Moore began composing lyrics in English. However, due to the efforts of the Ossianic Society, and the works of men like O'Donovan Rossa, O'Curry, and Standish Hayes O'Grady, much of history and song has survived that might have been lost forever. From old Gaelic manuscripts came half-forgotten legends and ballads. As people once again began singing these ballads and telling the old tales, that national spirit so necessary to the survival of a country was reborn.

Let no Irishman doubt that Gaelic was a forceful factor in the long, sad struggle for independence. Douglas Hyde, one of the founders of the Gaelic League, said the League was the only body in Ireland which appeared to realize that Ireland had a past, a history, and a literature, and the only body which sought to render the present a continuation of the past. Patrick Pearse referred to the League as the most revolutionary influence in Ireland. Later on, when the dream of independence was close to becoming a reality, Michael Collins, the Sinn Fein military leader, had this to say about the League: "We only succeeded after we had began to get back our Irish ways, after we had made a serious effort to speak our own language."

It was singularly appropriate that the movement to which Michael belonged was called Sinn Fein ("Ourselves Alone"). The emergence of the movement owed its inspiration to Arthur Griffith, whose newspaper, the *United Irishman,* spoke out for a separate parliament and an intensive program of industrialization.

There were those who had no faith in the ability of the Sinn Feiners to gain freedom for Ireland. But with the Sinn Fein Rising and Roger Casement's execution, the old faded ballads again had the power to cause deep feeling in the most dispirited Irish heart. Writing a poem about the 1916 Easter Rising, Yeats ends each verse with the words, "A terrible beauty is born." It was a beauty that was to manifest itself in a great many Irish ballads, as in James Stephen's "Spring," the second verse of which begins with a plea,

> Be green upon their graves, O happy Spring!
> For they are young and eager who are dead.

Many of the leaders of the 1916 Rising had been poets. Among them was Patrick Pearse who, on the night before he was to be executed, wrote these lines:

> The beauty of this world hath made me sad,
> This beauty that will pass,
> Sometimes my heart hath shaken with great joy

To see a leaping squirrel in a tree,
Or a red ladybird upon a stalk . . .

Was Pearse reflecting on the beauty of the world when
he, along with Thomas J. Clarke, Sean MacDiarmada,
Thomas MacDonagh, Eamon Ceannt, James Connolly,
and Joseph Plunkett, signed the Easter Proclamation of
1916? Perhaps the first and last paragraphs of the Proclamation issued by the Provisional Government of the Irish
Republic will best serve to convey the philosophy of these
men:

IRISHMEN AND IRISHWOMEN: In the name of
God and of the dead generations from which she received her old tradition of nationhood, Ireland, through
us, summons her children to her flag and strikes for
her freedom . . . .

We place the cause of the Irish Republic under the
protection of the Most High God, Whose blessing we
invoke upon our arms, and we pray that no one who
serves that cause will dishonour it by cowardice, in-
humanity, or rapine. In this supreme hour the Irish
nation must, by its valour and discipline and by the
readiness of its children to sacrifice themselves for the
common good, prove itself worthy of the august destiny
to which it is called.

All who signed the Proclamation were executed, as
were many of their followers.

Before the 1916 Rising, the writer Sean O'Faolain had
not been sympathetic to the Fenian cause. He admitted his
own inability to come to terms with so seemingly swift a
return to freedom:

We are blinded and dazzled by our icons, caught in a
labyrinth of our dearest symbols — our Ancient Past,

our Broken Chains, our Seven Centuries of Slavery, the Silenced Harp, the Glorious Dead, the Tears of Dark Rosaleen, the miseries of the Poor Old Woman, the Sunburst of Freedom that we had always believed would end our Long Night and solve all our problems with the descent of a heavenly human order which we would immediately recognize as the reality of our never-articulated dreams.

But when, watching from his window, he saw the British take out the leaders of the uprising and shoot them in ones and twos and threes, he knelt and wept.

O'Faolain and others who rallied to the cause after the Rising were determined to prove the truth of the words spoken by Pearse at the graveside of O'Donovan Rossa: "Life springs from death; and from the graves of patriot men and women spring living nations."

Numerous ballads have been written about these heroic men, including "A Lament for Patrick Pearse," "Rossa's Farewell," "Wrap the Green Flag Round Me," and "The Little White Cross." Two verses from "Kevin Barry," which found favor among Irish Americans, are typical of ballads from that era:

> In Mountjoy Jail one Monday morning
> High upon the gallows tree,
> Kevin Barry gave his young life
> In the cause of liberty.
> Just a lad of eighteen summers,
> Yet no one can deny,
> As he walked to death that morning,
> Proud he held his head on high.
>
> Calmly standing to attention,
> While he bade his last farewell
> To his broken-hearted mother

Whose grief no one can tell.
For the cause he proudly cherished,
This sad parting had to be.
Then to death, walked softly smiling,
That old Ireland might be free.

Sad songs of souls and prisons are still heard in Ireland. Time was when the singing of these patriotic ballads helped create sympathy for the Fenian cause, particularly in America. Today they serve an even greater purpose, that of perpetuating an appreciation for a literature that belongs to "ourselves alone."

And if the "come-all-ye" street singer seems to have vanished into the past, it is heartening to note the work being accomplished by the Comhaltas Ce Ceoltoiri Eireann. Founded in 1951, this society has not only developed the Fleadh Ceoil, or Feast of Music, into a major competitive activity, but has brought music to the towns and villages. Held in a different town each year on Whit weekend, the Fleadh Ceoil brings thousands of musicians into the area. For three days every street and lane is alive with singing and dancing and the playing of fiddles, flutes, pipes, and bodhrans, the goatskin tambourines that are said to be capable of making the dead rise up and dance when played properly.

During the rest of the year, strains of harp music rise up in the musty air of castles where beautiful Irish colleens in fifteenth century costumes offer the "bread of friendship," serve a medieval banquet, and sing songs of the heroes of the past. Songs are also sung at pubs, cabarets, wedding parties, hurling matches, and football games. "Singing Pubs" have always been popular in Ireland. However, today's singing sessions are often apt to be of a more organized nature, with special artists being engaged for the evening. There is a spirit of hope in the air during these gatherings, as a hail of Irish voices join in singing such ballads as this old-time favorite:

> Ireland is Ireland through joy and through tears,
> Hope never dies through the long weary years.
> Each age has seen countless brave hearts pass away,
> But their spirit still lives on in the men of today.

CHAPTER 15

GAELIC STORYTELLERS

"A TUNE IS MORE LASTING than the song of the birds," says
an old Irish proverb, "and a word more lasting than the
wealth of the world."

It is not surprising that the Irish country people should
have had such a magic way with the spoken word, as well
as with the written word. They were, after all, an imaginative and impressionable people, and the carriers of an oral
literature since ages past. Most of them had no access to
books. There were no radios, movies, and few forms of
organized entertainment. As a result, they were more
inclined to observe the small beauties around them — to
instantly respond to the sight of a cloud crowning a moun-
taintop, or golden gorse spilling out over the hills like
melted sun, or even so simple a thing as the beginning
of a new day.

Some fifty years ago, storytelling was still a familiar
feature of the social life of the Irish people. In those days,
one could not go into an Irish house, particularly along
the western coast of Ireland, without being regaled with
tales of long ago. The tales might be as much as a thousand
years old, or they might only be as old as the memory of
the man or woman who told them. Any child fortunate
enough to be living then stored up rich memories from a
very early age. The writer, Seumas MacManus, who loved
to sit around neighbors' firesides listening to old men tell

old tales, learned over a hundred of these stories by the time he had reached the age of seven.

Unfortunately, the art of storytelling, cultivated in Ireland by successive generations from earliest times, is in danger of becoming a thing of the past. These days, the rich folklife of the Irish is more likely to be preserved between the covers of a book. The tape recorder is all but taking the place of the Seanchai, the man or woman whose specialty was recounting local tales, family sagas, genealogies, and tales of the supernatural.

There were other storytellers in Ireland, too, who were not classified as Seanchais. A storyteller had to possess an extremely good memory; his mind was a storehouse of traditions. He knew the old hero tales, at least a few of them, was familiar with the Irish proverbs, and could give, at the drop of a hat, a humorous, or chilling, or even poignant account of an incident that had touched his listeners' lives in some way. Usually, his stories were told to a group of people who gathered around the fireside on any ordinary night of the week. But there was one man from Connemara who often found his audience at an Irish wake.

Actually, the Connemara man felt the need to put words together, not necessarily to recapture a scene from his own past, but to recreate a memory passed on to him by his beloved grandfather. "It stuck in my mind all these years," he would say by way of beginning. Then he was off, recreating a happening that took place in the Connemara hills in the days when the saying of the Mass was forbidden.

"It was an old ruin where the Mass was held in those days," he began. "Indeed, it was one of the oldest ruins in the western part of the country in which the Mass was held that my grandfather told me about. There were neither walls nor a roof on it then, though long in the past it had been a great hall where bardic meetings were held. There had been a chapel in the hall, too. But of course, in my grandfather's time, there were only the ruins poking up from the mound and looking at themselves in the little stream that ran alongside the bottom of the hill.

"Hundreds of people had come down from the mountains to hear the Mass that day — word had somehow got to them that the priest would be there — hundreds of them, the women all dressed in their purple and scarlet dresses, standing along the sides of the mound where the cross from the old chapel still stood. The day was a quiet one. There wasn't so much as the stir of a breeze, so that the lighted candles the priest had set up on an old stone slab looked as if they'd been painted on a great piece of green canvas.

"The people were saying their prayers, softly, more or less to themselves. But as the priest raised the consecrated wafer, those hundreds of people bowed to the earth and cried loudly and in unison, *'Mile Failte Crois na Slanaightheoir* — a thousand welcomes, Christ our Savior!' "

When the old man had finished describing the scene, there was a single instant pause. Then the listeners at the wake murmured in one voice, *"Mile Failte Crois na Slanaightheoir!"*

"It is a pity that this form of outdoor worship has passed away from us," the old man said with a sigh. "As my grandfather said, 'It was like a picture.' But isn't it a blessing that he was of a mind to leave the picture with me."

The Irish indeed have a talent for leaving pictures in the minds of those around them. Somehow, they seem to know instinctively that the spoken word, especially when accompanied by the appropriate gestures, is capable of leaving an indelible imprint on another's mind. Peig Sayers, one of the most celebrated of the latter-day storytellers, knew full well that the carrier of an oral tradition had to be an actor, as well as a teller of tales.

Born in the parish of Baile Viocaire, Dunquin, County Kerry, in 1873, Peig married at a very early age and went off to live on the Blasket Island. Unlettered but not unlearned, a natural orator with a keen sense for the turn of a phrase and the lifting rhythm so appropriate to the Irish language, she was, without a doubt, Queen of the Gaelic Storytellers.

Peig's own father was a well-known Seanchai. A master of storytelling in his native Kerry, he was, astonishingly enough, still at it when he was ninety-eight. When he stopped in the middle of a story one night, Peig knew the end was near, for he had never before been afflicted with a lapse of memory. He died nine days later without having finished the story.

The telling of the great Finn-tales, or hero stories, is traditionally restricted to men. The gift of poetry is said to pass from father to daughter, the gift of storytelling from father to son. But Peig was an exception to this rule, for she not only possessed a retentive memory, but had a talent for drinking in life as if it were a cup that would soon be empty.

When Peig was a little girl in Kerry, the bacach would sometimes call at the house. Many were the tales exchanged between the bacach and Peig's father. But though she welcomed the intermittent visits of the bacach, they often caused her to indulge in one of the seven deadly sins, the sin of impatience. In truth, there were times when she feared the night would vanish before the storytelling session ever got under way. While the supper dishes were being stacked away in the cupboard, her brother was carrying in a fresh armful of turf. After that, the hearth had to be swept and tidied, the proper number of chairs arranged around the fireplace. Then everyone knelt to say "Mary's Crown" — as the rosary was called in those days.

On the nights when the bacach led the rosary, it seemed to Peig that he elected to include everyone who had ever died in Ireland, and in all other parts of the world. Indeed, it was a mystery to her how the old people ever managed to stay on their knees for so long a time. But even after the prayers were over, she was subjected to further delays, for the bacach was determined to pay for his bed and board with more than a story or two. He was also a sort of wandering newspaper, bringing with him bits of news and gossip from other counties that seemed as far away from Peig's own Kerry as Australia or America. After the gossip was shared, and before he so much as considered getting on with the story hour, he spent a great deal of time enumerating and interpreting the prophecies of St. Colmcille, often finalizing them with a prophecy of his own.

"As sure as I'm sitting here," he said on one particular night, "a sign will precede the last act in poor old Ireland's tragedy." At that, he leaned forward to redden his pipe at the fire, and it was a good five minutes before he settled back in his chair, a signal that he was ready to continue. "Several counties away from here, at the Rosses up in Donegal, there lives a red-headed miller with two thumbs on one hand. The wheel of his mill will turn three times with blood — this has been foretold, mind you — before our freedom will be completely won." Having created the appropriate mood in his listeners, he was ready to get on with his entertainment.

"You've all heard of Finn MacCool." He looked around the dimly lit room, his gaze stopping for a moment to rest on the bright burning coals of the turf fire. "Indeed, with your father such a teller of tales, there may be little in the way of stories I could be telling you that you haven't heard before. But there's always something new to be learned about Finn MacCool, the most remarkable of all the

Fenians." Again, the bacach delayed getting into the story, as he briefly reviewed the history of the Fian, or Fenians, the highly trained, daring warriors that figure so importantly in Irish legend.

"They had to master twelve books of poetry. A Fenian also had to be skillful in wood-running, and without stopping in flight, be able to remove a thorn from his foot. I only bring up the wood-running because it's an important part of the story."

This last assured the listeners that he was not about to drift off into further digressions before he got into the mainstream of the story.

"It was in the third century that this great man lived. He was the son of Cumal, Chief of the Fian, was Finn MacCool. The Fian, as you know, was of Munster and Leinster origin, not of Ulster, as was the Red Branch. Other remarkable men amongst the Fenians, besides Finn himself, were Finn's son, Ossian, and the chief bards Oscar of the Sharp Swords, who was the son of Ossian, and brown-haired Diarmuid, of whom you'll be hearing much more.

"In those days, there was a great deal of hunting, fighting, and feasting, with many warrior-poets on hand to record all the glorious deeds of the Fian. And there were storytellers like ourselves, to entertain them when the feast was over. As some of you may know, Ossian had a strange experience when he was living no more than a stone's throw away from where we're sitting this very minute. On many an occasion, he saw a sea of strange white horses riding through his fields. As time went on, he was determined to capture one of these beautiful white steeds. True to his desire, he managed to catch and mount one of the horses, and lo and behold, the white steed took him off to a place called Tir na nOg, the "Country of the Young," where it is said you'll get happiness for a penny. It was a pleasant place all around, for, as Ossian said, 'There were plenty of beautiful ladies who were free and fair as a May morning.'

"There came a day, however, when Ossian was suddenly overcome by a longing to go home and visit with his friends. The king of Tir na nOg tried to talk him out of this notion. He told Ossian that all his friends were dead, and had been for a long time, fifteen hundred years, in fact. But Ossian refused to believe him. Indeed, he was as determined to go back as he had been determined to capture the white steed back in County Kerry. The king finally gave him another white horse which he assured him would take him safely home. But he also gave Ossian a warning. 'Do not, under any circumstances, dismount from your horse,' he said, 'for if you do, you will become old, shriveled, and withered.'

"It wasn't long before the horse had brought Ossian back to Kerry. But he could scarcely recognize the place. It was as if some black arts man had touched the landscape with a magic wand, causing everything to become old and ugly. Where there had once been beautiful and stately castles, there were now only crumbled rocks. Where there had been grass of a rich velvety green, there was now only blackness. As Ossian turned the horse onto a narrow dirt road, he saw an elderly priest attempting to lift a sack of corn on his back. When the priest saw Ossian, he cried out, 'For the love of the Virgin Mary, would you help me with the sack?' Although Ossian had never heard of the Virgin Mary, he made haste to help the poor old priest. But in the instant he leaped off his horse, didn't he become old and more withered than the man who sought his help?

"He helped the priest get the sack of grain up on his back. Then he told him what had happened. 'And now I can never go back to Tir na nOg,' he said finally, 'for my horse has galloped off without me.'

" 'Perhaps it's better if you don't go there,' said the old priest. He persuaded Ossian to go home with him, and in no time at all, he had converted him to Christianity. 'Now you'll be going to a much better place,' he told Ossian after he had baptized him, at which Ossian answered, 'But not for a while, I hope.'

"No one seems to know exactly how long Ossian stayed in Ireland after he came back from the Country of the Young. It has been definitely established, however, that poor brown-haired Diarmuid was allowed to spend but a brief time here on this island.

"It all began with Finn MacCool. The time had come when he decided to take a wife. Therefore, he sent out a message asking that all the beautiful young women in the land assemble at the foot of Slievenamon, one of the enchanted mountains of Ireland, indeed, one of the places where the Tuatha De Danann went to dwell when they were defeated by the Gaels. Appropriately enough, its ancient name means 'Mountain of the Fair Women of Ireland.' At any rate, on the day of the great event, Finn MacCool climbed to the summit of Slievenamon and took his seat on a huge stone dolmen, having previously announced that whoever was the first to reach the top of the mountain would be his bride. And who should win but the fair Grania, daughter of Cormac, who was then king of Ireland?

"It was a joyous day for Grania, and for Finn too, for Grania was not only fleet of foot, but as fresh and beautiful as a newly opened rose. As it turned out, her talent for wood-running proved to be a necessary skill in the days to come. What happened was that Grania chanced to meet the fair brown-haired Diarmuid.

"The meeting took place at Tara. It seems there was a great feast going on in the palace of Grania's father,

Cormac, and on this particular night, the women were allowed to mingle with the warriors. At the height of the feast, a fight commenced between the hounds of King Cormac and the hounds of the Fenians. In his haste to run outside to quiet the hounds, Diarmuid let his cap fall, revealing a face which, it had always been said, no woman could look upon without half going out of her mind with the beauty of it. Of course, Finn, Grania's betrothed, was a handsome man too, but Diarmuid had him beat altogether, and the moment Grania set her eyes on him, she knew that no one else would do for her. Diarmuid, fool that he was, fell in love with her, too. One needs give the man credit. It is a fact that he had no desire to be disloyal to his leader, Finn MacCool. In truth, he did his best to evade the advances of the girl. But in the end the two of them eloped.

"For almost two years Diarmuid and Grania traveled all over Ireland, pursued all the while by Finn MacCool and his men. *M'anam le Dhia* ('My soul to God'), how they must have run! There's probably not a place in Ireland where they have not left their footprints. Each night they slept on one of the dolmens you see all around you — God knows there are some 336 of them scattered over the land. Some think these great unhewn stones, supporting a flat horizontally placed stone, were Druid altars. But from all indications, it is more likely they were tombstones. At any rate, they are now commonly called 'the beds of Diarmuid and Grania.'

"It was Diarmuid who prepared the beds each night, carefully covering the top flat stone with mosses or ferns, or sometimes heather. It was not an easy life they had. Yet despite their many hardships, and the fact that they knew they were being constantly pursued, they remained as much in love as ever. But their happiness was brief, the ending as sudden as the onset of a storm out on the bay beyond us. And strange it is, too, that the ending should have come about on the summit of another mountain. Beauty did not triumph in this case, I'll have you know! On the top of Benbulben, brown-haired Diarmuid was slain by the warriors of Finn MacCool. *'Gonadh e sin mo sgeal-sa go nuige sin* — And that is my tale up to now.' "

Stories such as the ones told by the bacach could not fail to entrance the young Peig Sayers. Always after, she remembered them. Later on, when she lived on the Blaskets, stories from her own new life became a part of her vast repertoire of verse, proverb, and story. On the islands, life had an almost medieval simplicity. The people were not only close to the earth, but to each other. At the end of the day, after the evening meal was over and the family rosary had been said, the neighbors often gathered around Peig's fireplace for a long night of storytelling. Although some of the stories told at these gatherings were woven from the threads of her own life on the Blasket Islands, every now and then she would include a story told to her by the bacach or by her father. It was then she would entrance the people of the island, many of whom had never heard the old Finn-tales.

On the night she related the story of Deirdre, she did not employ the customary dramatic devices, such as flashing her thumb over her shoulder to indicate a mystery, or putting a hand to her mouth to suggest secrecy or mischief. But often during the recital of the story, she would clasp her hands together in such a manner as to suggest she was saying a prayer for the two lovers whose sorrows she seemed to understand completely.

"Long ago, around the time of Christ, a great king noted for song and story ruled over Ulster in the beautiful and ancient country of Ireland. The name of the king was

Conor MacNessa. Conor was the grandson of Rory Mor, a powerful ruler of Ulster who had become monarch of Ireland and was founder of the Rudrician line of Ulster kings.

"Although Conor was a great king in many ways, he was human and thus a prey to human frailties. To look at him, one would think he could do no wrong, for he was a singularly handsome man. His eyes were the blue of the Irish sea, his hair thick and curly, the color of ripening wheat. As with all kings of those days, he had a storyteller of his own, whose name was Feidlimid. When Feidlimid told the king that there would soon be a child in Feidlimid's house, the king was overjoyed. Indeed, he awaited the birth with almost as much joyful anticipation as the father himself.

"On the night when the child was born, Conor happened to be at Feidlimid's house, or rather, made a point of being there when it was announced that the baby's birth was imminent. That night, Conor wore a crimson, deep-bordered, five-folding tunic. His shirt was a brilliant white interwoven with threads of red gold, and fastened in the tunic over his bosom was a gold pin. As Conor awaited the birth of Feidlimid's child, there sat beside him his favorite Druid, who always accompanied the king to important functions, political or social, to inform him of any significant signs or omens which might be inherent in each event. That night, the Druid appeared to be in a strange mood. When the woman who had been assisting the birth came into the room crying out, 'It's a girl child,' the king was so relieved that all was well, he almost cried himself. But no sooner had the rejoicing begun than the Druid arose and, with lifted hand, began speaking in a low and ominous voice.

" 'This babe,' said the Druid, 'will be the cause of misfortunes untold coming upon Ulster.'

" 'No!' said Feidlimid, the father of the infant. 'That cannot be.'

" 'No,' groaned the king, clutching at the gold pin on his bosom. 'We must not let such a terrible thing happen. Not to the daughter of Feidlimid! And not to the land of our fathers!'

"But the heartbroken Feidlimid was not to be consoled, no matter how much the king tried to comfort him. In the end, the king, not so much to prevent anything happening to the daughter of his storyteller, but more to prevent disaster coming to Ulster, decided to take charge of the infant himself. Calling the servants around him, he commanded them to prepare the infant for a journey, and after he managed to convince Feidlimid that this was the only sensible thing to do, off he went with the servants and the child. At the end of a long journey, they finally arrived at a secluded fort where Conor made arrangements to have the infant confined until she reached the age of maturity, after which he would make her his wife.

"During the years when the child, whose name was Deirdre, was growing up, she saw no one except her nurse, her tutor, Conor's spokesman, and sometimes Conor himself. In time, she grew to be a very beautiful young woman, and because she was so loved by the few who knew her, they trusted her completely. Never once did they entertain the slightest notion that she would do anything rash or foolish.

"But one day Deirdre, enchanted by the splendor of the summer season, chanced to wander further away from her sheltered home than usual. And there in the woods beside a lovely stream she met a handsome young man whose name was Naisi. The eldest of the three sons of Usnach, Naisi was so overcome by the mere sight of Deirdre that he could scarcely speak. At the same time, he had the strange feeling, as he slowly began walking towards her, that the meeting had been ordained from the very beginning of time.

"As for Deirdre, in spite of the sheltered life she had led, she immediately fell in love with Naisi. Her love for him was so strong that she met him several times, and even though she knew by this time that it would be wrong and dangerous to go against the wishes of the king, she pleaded with Naisi to elope with her. So in love was Naisi that he enlisted the aid of his two brothers, Ainle and Ardan. The arrangements were made, and Deirdre embarked with Naisi on a strange and adventurous journey. Crossing the plains of northern Ireland, they eventually fled to Alba, a place which is now called Scotland. All was well for a short while. But such a beautiful woman as Deirdre was hardly likely to escape attention. When the king of Alba became aware of her rare beauty and began showing signs of coveting her, Naisi and his brothers whisked her off to another island.

"Meanwhile, back in Ireland the nobles in Conor Mac-Nessa's court could not help but pity the wandering lovers. 'Let them return,' they begged their king. 'After all, they are very young. Let them have peace in their own country.'

"Conor considered the matter, making every attempt to hide his anger from the nobles. Finally he agreed to absolve the young lovers and allow them to return. But no sooner had Deirdre and the three sons of Usnach returned to the green fields of Emania than a body of Conor's friends led by Eogan fell upon the three sons and slew them. Conor took the brokenhearted Deirdre for himself, after he had convinced his nobles that it was not out of malice but out of concern for his beloved Ulster that he had perpetrated such a horrible deed. But as the king might have known, many of the nobles, and especially Fergus MacRigh, whose honor Conor had pledged for the safety of the sons of Usnach, were shocked at his betrayal. It was not long before

Fergus led an assault on Emania. In the battle, Conor's
son, along with three hundred of his people, were slain,
and the town of Emania was pillaged and burned.

"For a year following the burning of Emania, Deirdre
continued to live with Conor. But all during this time, she
never once smiled or raised her head or engaged in conversation. So incensed was the king at her attitude that, at the
end of the year, he was compelled to indulge in a last act
of cruelty. He gave her to Eogan, the chief of Fernmach,
the very one who had slain her husband and his two
brothers. As Deirdre was being taken from Conor's house
to the house of Eogan, she sat in the chariot praying that
something would happen to prevent her from ever arriving
at the house of her husband's murderer. Then, in despera-
tion, she leaped from the chariot, and as she landed on the
ground her head struck a sharp rock. In that instant death
claimed her.

"After her death, Fergus MacRigh, along with his companions and three thousand followers, left Ulster, going
into Connacht where they took service in the army of
Medb. Indeed, following her death, the sorrows of Deirdre
became the sorrows of Eire. *A Dhia Saor Eire* — God save
Ireland!

"As for Deirdre, her story is not likely to be for-
gotten. Even now, we weep with her as she weeps over the
graveside of Naisi, and sings her freshly composed lamentation:

> The lions of the hill are gone
> And I am left to weep alone.
> Without my love I can't abide,
> So dig the grave both deep and wide."

On those nights when Peig Sayers included Deirdre in
her repertoire, her visitors were not likely to linger. No

sooner had the story been completed than they all began to "scatter homeward to the white gable," which was the islanders' way of saying they were off to bed. Although they loved to hear about Deirdre of the Sorrows, it is the sort of story that leaves its listeners feeling sad and a bit lonely.

After the visitors were gone, Peig, as was customary, drew ashes over the peat embers while she recited the prayer, "I preserve the fire as Christ preserves all. Bridget at the two ends of the house, and Mary in the center. The three angels and the three apostles who are highest in the Kingdom of Grace, guarding this house and its contents till day."

Despite the fact that sorrow was a frequent visitor at Peig's house, she herself was not given to thoughts of loneliness. Her husband met death at an early age. And when her son Tom fell from a cliff, it was Peig who had to postpone tears while she tried to smooth the damaged skull back into shape. Of this sorrow she would say, "Let everyone carry his cross." In the days following the boy's death, she often recited a lament of the Virgin Mary for her Son, and there were many who said it was the most moving thing they ever heard in their lives.

During the years when Peig lived on the Great Blasket, few visitors came to the island. Then, in 1930, there began a steady flow of people in search of Irish lore and language. Among the visitors were Dr. Robin Flower from the British Museum in London, and Kenneth Jackson of Britain. Following Jackson's published collection of Peig's stories in the journal of the Irish Folklore Society in 1938, many Irish people, as well as foreigners, were drawn to the cultural riches of the Blaskets. It was an island that also produced such talented writers as Maurice O'Sullivan and Tomas O'Crohan, who wrote *The Islandman*. One of the visitors to the island was Maire Ni Chinneide, a woman

who was instrumental in having Peig dictate her life story
to her son, Michael. This resulted in the publication of *An
Old Woman's Reflections,* a book that was subsequently
translated from the Irish by Seamus Ennis.

During the last years of Peig's life, Seosamh O'Dalaigh,
a collector of the Irish Folklore Commission, visited Peig
on numerous occasions. In the midst of her household
chores, Peig dictated her store of traditional folklore to
Seosamh. Her patient cooperation enabled O'Dalaigh to
fill some six thousand pages of manuscript. In the end, he
managed to obtain 375 tales from Peig, including forty
long folk tales and as many songs, and an abundance of
folk prayers, proverbs, and riddles.

Shortly before her death, loneliness came at last to this
indomitable woman. The loneliness had already begun to
set in when she realized she had to leave her beloved island.
By 1950, she was blind. "Dark, dark, dark," she said,
describing her condition to Seosamh O'Dalaigh, who was
still gathering material from her as she lay ill.

In the last chapter of *An Old Woman's Reflections,* Peig
mentions her neighbors and tells of how the people on the
islands lived in the shelter of each other. "Everything that
was coming dark upon us," she wrote, "we would disclose
to each other. And that would give us consolation of mind.
Friendship was the fastest root in our hearts."

Toward the last, she seemed to be of the opinion that
she would not be remembered for long. But she was wrong
about that. Peig Sayers died in 1958. On August 3, 1969,
a memorial stone sculpted by Dr. Seamus Murphy of Cork
was unveiled by the Chief Justice, Cearbhall O'Dalaigh.

"I'll be talking after my death," she once said.

And so she will. Her grave looks out over the sea toward
the Blaskets. But the soft lilting tones of her voice have
been captured on tape, her words and the unique shape of

her mind preserved between the covers of a book. Although she may be gone on the way of the truth, she has left a great deal of truth in the place of herself. She has also left her son, Michael O'Guithin, who is still alive and composing poetry in Dunquin. Because of Peig, the female Irish storyteller will occupy her rightful place in Irish history.

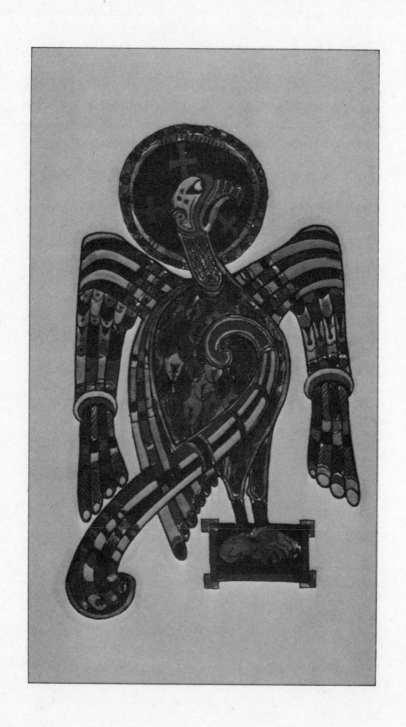

CHAPTER 16

LANGUAGE AND LITERATURE

"IN A LAND WHERE time seems to stand still, the past and the present are apt to fuse," wrote Devin Garrity in his introduction to *The Mentor Book of Irish Poetry.* "Thus the sagas of the ancient Celts are as real and useful to the Irish poets as are yesterday's episodes in the fight for liberation; the Irish memory is long."

The land Devin Garrity spoke of, known for centuries as an island of poets, saints, and scholars, has also been referred to as a "wallflower of the western world." But her somewhat isolated geographical position has helped enhance Ireland's individuality. When the Roman legions, sweeping out over Europe, superimposed their own culture on that of other nations, the native customs and language of the conquered people were often lost. Roman legions never reached Irish shores, and Ireland became the first country north of the Alps to produce a body of literature in its own language.

The earliest system of writing in Ireland was called Ogham, a system found only where the Irish Gael had lived. From Ogham developed the early Irish alphabet, two copies of which are extant, that of Forchern, who lived in the first century, and that used in the Book of Leacan.

Before parchment or paper were available, the ancient Irish used beechen tablets called *Taibhle Fileadh,* philosophic tablets, or "tablets of the sages." The alphabet was, appropriately enough, referred to as *Faiodh,* "a voice."

A distinctively Irish literature existed long before the coming of Christianity in the fifth century brought the Latin alphabet to Ireland. Then, when churches and monasteries became the nucleus of Irish learning, Latin was studied right alongside Irish. The monks produced not only religious verses, but poems of a more personal nature that reflect two outstanding qualities of Irish literature, the clear eye and flawless feeling for words. The following quatrain illustrates this well:

> *Tanic sam slan soer*
> *dia mbi cloen caill chiar;*
> *lingid ag seng sneid*
> *dia mbi reid ron rian.*

> Summer's come, healthy free,
> That bows down the dark wood;
> The slim, spry deer jumps
> And the seals' path is smooth.

The earliest examples of Irish literature are found in the Ossianic poems. Reputed to have been written by Ossian, son of Finn MacCool, the poems tell of the adventures of the Fenians and contain passages of exquisite beauty such as this lovely nature-picture:

"A tale for you: oxen lowing, winter snowing; summer passed away. Wind from the north, high and cold; low the sun and short his course; wildly towing the waves of the sea. The fern burns deep red; men wrap themselves closely; the wild goose raises her wonted cry; cold seizes the wing of the bird: 'tis the season of ice, sad my tale."

An Ossianic poem that describes Irish scenery and also pictures the Fenian warriors as they set forth on a deer-hunting expedition, accompanied by their three thousand hounds with golden chains, contains these verses:

Thus we were arrayed and armed
When we went to pursue the deer.
No Fenian warrior went forth
Without a shirt of satin and two hounds,

A garment of smooth silk,
A coat of mail, a sharp blue glittering dart,
A helmet set in stones of gold,
And two spears in the hand of each hero.

A green shield that oft was upreared in victory,
And well-tempered sword that scattered heads.
Thou might wander o'er the white-foaming bays of ocean
Without beholding a man like Finn.

We came to a green mount above a valley,
Where the trees were leafy and pleasant,
Where the joyful birds made music,
And the sound of the cuckoo resounded
From the top of the cliff.

The ancient Irish kept all important records, such as history, laws, and genealogy, in verse. Even St. Patrick, after he had systematically arranged the ancient laws, asked a bard to put a thread of poetry around them. It is not surprising, then, to find that in very early times it was only Greece and Rome who could be said to excel Ireland in the area of poets and poetry. Numerous Continental scholars, including Zeuss and Constantine Nigra, maintain that it was the ancient Irish who were the inventors of rhyme. Already in the sixth century the Irish not only rhymed but had the ability to make intricate rhyming metres, and they exhibited a fineness of execution and technique which was not approached by the English until the sixteenth century.

"After the seventh century," wrote Dr. Douglas Hyde in his *Literary History of Ireland,* "the Irish brought the rhyming system to a perfection undreamt of even to this day, by other nations."

The first English poet to use rhyme was none other than Aldhelm, a pupil of the eighth century Irish monk, Maeldubh, whose school was on the site of the present English city of Malmesbury. Otfried, who was educated at the Irish monastery of St. Gall in Switzerland, was the first poet to introduce rhyme to the German people. Indeed, the first poets to sing in the Icelandic language bore the Irish names of Kormach and Sighvat, and were descended from an Irish ancestress.

In his *Literary History,* Hyde makes still another significant statement: "Perhaps by no people on the globe at any period of the world's history was poetry so cultivated, and better still, so remunerated as in Ireland."

One of the early masterpieces in which we can take pride is the Book of Kells, lauded by Joyce as the "fountainhead of Irish inspiration." Thought to be the greatest achievement in Irish manuscript illumination, the Book of Kells was probably written between A.D. 760 and 820, though it may possibly have been much earlier. Some scholars suggest the book may have been planned and begun in Iona, and that it was later taken to the Columban monastery at Kells after Iona was sacked by the Vikings. By the beginning of the eleventh century, when the book belonged to the church of Kells in County Meath, it was called "the great gospel of Colum Cille," either because St. Colmcille was supposed to have written it, or because it belonged to a principle monastic establishment of his order in Ireland.

Originally contained in a cover of gold, a custom of the times indicating the preciousness of the enclosed material, the Book of Kells is now quite modestly displayed in the old library of Trinity College, Dublin. It is written on thick vellum, and despite its misadventures, is in relatively good condition. From its 340 pages, 5 are missing, and some of its margins have been cut away by an insensitive book-binder. But it is astonishing to think the manuscript managed to survive at all. A passage in the Annals of Ulster, for example, tells us, "The great gospel of Colum Cille, the chief relic of the western world, on account of its wrought shrine, was wickedly stolen in the night." Filched from the western sacristy of the great stone church of Ceannus (Kells), the book, sans golden cover, was found under a sod only a few months later.

Because Oriental and especially Coptic influence is evident in the art work of the manuscript, it is thought that there must have been a direct connection between early Irish Christianity and the monasteries of Egypt, and with the Greek Christianity of the southeast Mediterranean. After all, the old records show that Egyptian monks came to Ireland, and it is also known that Irish monks spent some time in Egypt. The varying styles indicate that at least four Irish monk-artists took part in the painting of the book. The penmanship itself is remarkable: the capitals at the beginning of paragraphs are made up of brightly colored entwinements of birds, snakes, and distorted men and animals engaging in combat or performing acrobatic feats. Illuminated in colors that seem to defy the breath of time, blazing with intricate, elaborate windings and ribbon patterns, the book has caused more than one observer to suggest it must have been the work of angels, and not of men.

Other early Christian illuminated manuscripts include the Book of Durrow, the Book of Armagh, and the Book of the Dun Cow, all of which exhibit a richness of color and fantasy, furnishing us with striking examples of the elegance of Irish penmanship. Leabhar na hUidhre, the Book of the Dun Cow, is actually the oldest manuscript of Gaelic literature. Such manuscripts, along with the Book of Leinster, the Book of Ballymote, and of course, the Annals of the Four Masters, still provide inspiration for Irish poets and storytellers.

Considering the circumstances under which Irish people lived during the many war-riddled centuries, it is astonishing that literature of any sort could have been written, much less survived. It is even more remarkable to find that the poets were so well-known and poetry so universally memorized and recited by all classes of people as it is in Ireland. The fact that literature did survive can be attributed, at least in some measure, not only to those early chroniclers, but to the works of such men as Geoffrey Keating.

At a time when the Irish were deprived of the power of printing, Keating (1570-1644) dedicated himself to the task of preserving the ancient records. Hundreds of manuscript copies were made of Keating's *History of Ireland.* He also composed religious work, such as *Three Shafts of Death,* and wrote poetry. A product of some of the last Bardic Schools, Keating made a conscious effort to write in a style that would be understood by the people. As a result, he became one of the first eminent popular writers.

It was not until the seventeenth and eighteenth centuries that Anglo-Irish poets, that is, Irish poets writing in English, began to emerge. Out of this period came Swift, Sterne, Berkeley, Congreve, Burke, Sheridan, and Goldsmith. Swift, of course, made his contributions to nationalism under the sheltering wings of the church; the latter four chose to live in England where they might enjoy the financial security unknown to other writers.

What is most important about this period is that Ireland's

literature, concerning itself as it did with a sense of a proud past, and of injustices done, brought about a sense of national unity that had never been known in the past. This, of course, did not happen overnight. In the beginning, the changeover from the Irish language to the English seemed to have a paralyzing effect on the imagination of many native Irish writers. As time went on, however, Irishmen who had been singing of the faded glories of Ireland began to realize just how little they actually knew about their country's past.

During the nineteenth century, O'Curry, O'Donovan Rossa, O'Grady, and others made haste to remedy the deficiency. Other writers, such as Moore, Mangan, Ferguson, and Allingham also took part in the rediscovery of their Irish past, translating their findings into English and paving the way for the tremendous outpourings of literature that were to come out of Ireland.

Oddly enough, the dawning of the twentieth century found the younger generation almost totally devoid of any interest in Ireland's past. Naturally, they had heard of such patriots as Sarsfield, Tone, and Robert Emmet. These were names that were spoken of in their homes with the same reverence as that accorded the saints. They were familiar with the verse about bold Robert Emmet, "the darling of Erin," who had laid down his life for Ireland — he had been hanged after the rising of 1803. But they simply could not identify with him.

Then they began to interest themselves in new translations of Irish literature, such as Standish Hayes O'Grady's English versions of the old hero tales. Eventually, such works, along with the research of other scholars, like Kuno Meyer and Douglas Hyde, caused the Irish people to make friends, not just with the heroes of Cuchullain's day, but with the heroes of more recent times. And so it was that

the words of Robert Emmet's speech, delivered from the
dock shortly before he was put to death — "When my
country takes her place among the nations of the earth,
then, and not till then, let my epitaph be written" — began
to have meaning for them at last.

This period of Ireland's awakening, which took place in
the early part of the twentieth century, was an exciting era
for the young. Those coming to Dublin for their college
education stepped right into the Irish Revival, which was
already showing itself in billboards sporting such soul-
stirring announcements as:

Irish Plays for One Week.
Riders to the Sea, by J. M. Synge
Kathleen ni Houhilan, by W. B. Yeats
Spreading the News, by Lady Gregory

Many of the young people would make significant contributions to the Irish Literary Revival, and some of them,
Patrick Pearse for one, would lose their lives in the
struggle for Ireland's freedom.

And so it was that, for a period which lasted some
twenty-five years, Ireland produced more literary names of
note than any other country in the world. Would that there
were space allowed so that we might fit into these pages
the long litany of Irish poets and writers. Or that this writer
had such a way with words as to be capable of encouraging
Irish Americans to search out for themselves the words of
these wondrous writers. Perhaps these lines from Padraic
Colum's *A Cradle Song* will give some idea as to the lyrical
beauty of poems written during this era:

O, men from the fields!
Come gently within,
Tread softly, softly,
O! men coming in.

Mavourneen is going
From me and from you,
Where Mary will fold him
With mantle of blue.

From reek of the smoke
And cold of the floor,
And the peering of things
Across the half-door.

O, men from the fields!
Softy, softly come through;
Mary puts round him
Her mantle of blue.

Bearer of two great Irish saint names, Padraic Colum is one of Ireland's great poets. Born in Ireland in 1881, he heard stories at his grandmother's house before he could read, and learned songs and poems before he went to school. He received his education at Dunleary and later moved to Dublin where he founded the *Irish Review* and played an important role in the struggle for Irish freedom.

An early associate of the Irish Literary Revival, also called the Irish Literary Renaissance, Colum was formerly president of the Joyce Society. When the National Theatre Society merged with Yeats' Irish Literary Theatre to form the Abbey Theatre, he was one of the original signers of the pact. His play, *The Land,* was the Abbey's first popular success. In 1914 he came to the United States and became editor of a literary magazine, *Forum*. He and his wife Mary Colum taught comparative literature at Columbia University. Both of these talented people were prominent literary figures in America.

Besides being famous for his lyric poems, Padraic Colum wrote plays, essays, short stories, and also prepared Homer's masterpieces for young readers in *The Adventures of Odysseus* and *The Tales of Troy*. He also wrote children's stories, translating from the Irish, and at the request of the Hawaiian legislature made a survey of Polynesian folklore which he subsequently published in two volumes.

One of the more recent outstanding Irish poets is Patrick Kavanagh, who was born in County Monaghan in 1904. "That a poet is born, not made, is well known," Mr. Kavanagh once said. At the same time, he said that he himself was not born as a writer until 1955, the "birth" taking place on the banks of Dublin's Grand Canal. He died in 1967, after which, in response to his poem, "O commemorate me where there is water, canal water preferably," his friends erected a memorial seat on the Grand Canal in Dublin. His autobiography *The Green Fool* ran into libel difficulties at the outset, but has recently been published in London, while two posthumous collections of his work, *Lapped Furrows* and *November Haggard,* have been published in New York by the poet's brother.

An Irish poet who died at the height of his powers was William Butler Yeats. Someone who knew him once said that his whole being was so charged with pyschic energy that one became aware of his presence on the street or in a room before one actually saw him. Yeats had a long memory. He never forgot a kindness done him or a wrong done him. He also had a great passion for fairies and ghosts. Indeed, his three great passions were love of country, love of the unseen life, and love of a beautiful woman named Maude Gonne. In the beginning, his imagination was set on fire by Standish Hayes O'Grady's translations of the old Irish hero tales. Yeats, along with George Moore, was one of the great stars of the Irish Literary Renaissance, the period that brought forth not only Padraic Colum, but such writers as Stephens, Gogarty, and

Campbell. During his literary career, he edited several volumes of Irish poetry and fairy tales, wrote poetry of his own — "Murmur, a little sadly, how Love fled" he wrote in his poem, *When You Are Old*— and also played a major role in the founding of the Abbey Theatre.

Yeats won the Nobel Prize for Literature. So too did another Irishman by the name of George Bernard Shaw. Referred to by "innocents" as a British playwright, this Irishman offers the following somewhat flippant advice to aspiring authors: "My method is to take the utmost trouble to find the right thing to say, and then say it with the utmost levity."

Irish writers seem to have had little difficulty finding the right things to say, and have always possessed a talent for squeezing laughter out of an existence from which they could extract little else. Often, in the Irish short story, humor romps right alongside tragedy. In Liam Flaherty's *A Red Petticoat,* for example, a poor widow and her family, after weathering a bad winter, have had their only pig taken from them by the grocer in payment of a debt. Although they are too hungry, as the eldest son put it, to make any plans for the future, they sit around the dwindling turf fire singing and composing poems and satires on their enemies. When the mother at last decides to go out and use her wits to get her hands on some food, she does it with grace, putting on her shawl and her new checked apron, and making her exit with dancing steps, singing as she dances, "There was an old peddler in love with a nun God forgive him."

It is quite natural that the Irish short story should have stayed closer to its folk roots than any other national or ethnic school of fiction, except perhaps the Jewish. After all, it sprang out of an oral literature that came from the lips of farmers and fishermen and their wives, from such storytellers as Maurice O'Sullivan and Peig Sayers, whose dove-tailed talk revealed an instinctive knowledge of writing techniques.

"The essence of a great short story," said Yeats, "is character isolated by a deed, to engross the present and dominate memory."

It would be difficult not to be engrossed by Seamus O'Kelly's *The Weaver's Grave,* for it is one of the most engaging short stories to appear in this century. Throughout its sixty some pages the author so successfully sustains a single effect — the pervasive impression that the dead are more alive than the living — that the reader, returning from the ancient burial ground where "the whispered scandals of Cloon na Morav ("Meadow of the Dead") were seen by the gravediggers and the widow of the weaver through such a haze of antiquity that they were no longer scandals, but romances," will be afflicted for days after by the moribund mood of the story.

A writer who contributed richly to Irish literature, not only through his short stories, but also through his novels and plays, is Daniel Corkery. His book *The Hidden Ireland* became a classic. Padraic O'Conaire made his contribution to the development of literature through the medium of the Irish language. In fact, O'Conaire was the first man for centuries to try to make a living by writing in Irish. Frank O'Connor, author of *My Oedipus Complex,* became such a complete master of the Irish short story that his works seem more truth than fiction. Mary Lavin, who was born of Irish immigrants in America but whose home has been Ireland since she was ten, has had her sensitively written short stories published in the *New Yorker.* Sean O'Faolain's polished writing has often found its way into print. Other Irish writers who had a special gift for the short story include Samuel Beckett, James Plunkett, Bryan MacMahon, and, of course, James Joyce, whose short story *The Dead* is a masterpiece.

Eire also boasts an abundance of playwrights. Often the dialogue in Irish plays is of such excellence that the voices of the characters have a way of rising from the printed page. In John Millington Synge's *Riders to the Sea,* Maurya, the central character in the play, has lost her husband, her father-in-law, and four sons to the sea. As the play opens, she is waiting to hear if a fifth son, Michael, has drowned, while her sixth son Bartley is even now preparing to go to sea.

Shortly after Bartley rides off on his red mare, Maurya learns from her two daughters that Michael has indeed drowned. But tragedy hasn't yet finished with Maurya, for neighbors are carrying Bartley's body in — his horse plunged and threw him into the sea. As the women keen softly in the background, Maurya speaks out loud as if she were alone:

> They're all gone now, and there isn't anything
> more the sea can do to me . . . . It isn't that I
> haven't said prayers in the dark night till you
> wouldn't know what I'd be saying; but it's a great
> rest I'll have now, and it's time surely.

Another famous dramatist, Sean O'Casey, though tormented with eye afflictions almost from cradle to grave, was nevertheless quite capable of watching the world from the bridge of vision. *An Intimate Portrait of Sean O'Casey* written by his wife, Eileen, tells of the other afflictions that plagued him, her brief affair with another man, the tragic death of their son, and those wild and terrible periods of despair that are a part of every writer's life. O'Casey spent the first twelve years of his life in the Dublin slums and his later years in England.

In *Purple Dust,* the O'Casey play that enchanted New

York playgoers, two English plutocrats seek the simple country life in a remote Irish village, bent on rejuvenating a crumbling Tudor mansion. They have the misfortune to hire Irish laborers who for obvious reasons are over-anxious to expose the mansion's lack of solidity. In the course of the constant conflicts, one of the workmen, responding to a burst of sarcasm on the part of his pompous employer, indulges in the following soliloquy:

There is sweet music in the land, but not for the deaf; there is wisdom too, but it is not in a desk it is, but out in th' hills, an' in the life of all things roving around under th' blue sky.

All things "roving around" under the blue sky of Ireland did not always meet with James Joyce's approval. But although he left his homeland when only twenty-two, he brought a part of it with him. Indeed, the three things he was supposed to have rejected, family, church, and country, were the very themes that supplied him with subject matter for his poems, short stories, and novels. Joyce was a very lonely man. Publication was not easily achieved, even after he became famous. Whenever life saw fit to deal him a slice of happiness, it often followed up by dealing him an equal portion of pain. At a time when he was rejoicing over the birth of a grandson, his daughter went through a nervous breakdown. Like O'Casey, his eyes began to fail him fairly early in life. So close to blindness was he during the writing of *Finnegan's Wake* that he had to have help, not only with putting it together, but with the research.

Although that much celebrated novel, *Ulysses,* has provided a veritable treasure trove for those who seek out hidden meanings, it is possible that Joyce, if he has some-how managed to accomplish his ascent to Paradise, may be inclined to chuckle at some of their discoveries. That America should have become a chief "diagnostic clinic" for Joyceans is thought by the author's cynical friend, Oliver Gogarty, to have come about because of the country's preoccupation with detective stories, crossword puzzles, and smoke signals. In fact, there are many who feel that the Joyce worshippers have become the victims of one of the most enormous leg-pulls in history.

Perhaps it may be closer to the truth to merely point out that Joyce, who so desperately wished to have control over all things, had not the power to control *Ulysses*. Jung once said he read it from the end backwards, adding that it was as good a way as any since the novel had no forwards or backwards or top or bottom. But for all the difficulties encountered in pursuing *Ulysses,* one cannot but be aware of the flashes of genius that come and go like heat lightning, and which on occasion have the impact of a thousand Roman candles exploding in the dark of a long night.

A candle that burned all too briefly burned in the person of Brendan Behan, who, looking out the window of his prison cell one February morning shortly before his seventeenth birthday, pondered on the old Irish saying, "If we live through the winter the devil wouldn't kill us in summer."

For Brendan Behan, death came on March 20, 1964, when he was only forty-one. The philosophy of this fiery Irish rebel is reflected, at least to some extent, in these lines: "I have a total irreverence for anything connected with society, except that which makes the roads safer, the beer stronger, the old men and women warmer in the winter and happier in the summer."

As regards drinking, which had a great deal to do with his early demise, he had this to say: "I can only say that in Dublin during the depression when I was growing up, drunkenness was not regarded as a social disgrace. To get enough to eat was regarded as an achievement. To get drunk was a victory."

In Behan's autobiography, *Borstal Boy,* we are offered a vivid account of his youthful experiences in a British prison and reformatory. The story of this legendary conversationalist's early life has been adapted for the theatre by the Irish writer, Frank McMahon. *Borstal Boy* was first presented in Dublin's Abbey Theatre under the direction of Tomas MacAnna, who also directed the play when it was staged in New York and won the Tony and the New York Drama Critics Circle Award.

Many were the distinguished performances offered the American public by the Abbey Theatre, which toured the United States during the early part of the century and introduced actors and actresses of extraordinary talent, among them Barry Fitzgerald and Sara Allgood. The famous American designer, Robert Edmond Jones, recollecting his reaction to the Abbey players' first appearance in this country in 1911, paid the actors the following tribute:

> I kept saying to myself on that first evening: Who are these rare beings? Where did they come from? How have they spent their lives? What music they must have heard, what books they must have read, what emotions they must have felt! They literally enchanted me. They put me under a spell. And when the curtain came down at the end of the play, they had become necessary to me. I have often asked myself since that time how it was that the actors could make me feel such strange emotions of trouble and wonder; and I find the answer now, curiously enough, in an adddress spoken by a modern Irish poet to the youth of Ireland: "Keep in your souls some images of magnificence." These Irish players have kept in their souls some images of magnificence.

During the days of its flowering, the Abbey Theatre

experienced many setbacks, stemming largely from a lack of funds, public criticism, and the threat of censorship. Consequently, it was often difficult for actors and actresses to keep in their souls "some images of magnificence." Following the birth of the Irish Free State in 1922, the Abbey Theatre was granted an annual state subsidy, one of the first of its kind in the English-speaking world. In 1951 the theatre burned down, and it was not until July of 1966 that the company was able to move from its temporary home to the new theatre which was built on the old site. The Abbey Theatre has contributed a unique style of acting, along with plays of lasting value, and is considered to be one of the world's outstanding dramatic centers. Interestingly enough, numerous non-native actors of distinction, Orson Welles among them, received their early training in Irish companies.

Other important centers of drama in Ireland which have also been given subsidies are the Gate, Pike, Studio, Garrick, the '37', Globe, Lantern, Gas Company Theatres, and Gemini Productions. Gaelic theatre also thrives. Recent productions at the Gate Theatre have included the Irish play *Have Mercy on Young Priests* by Eoin O Tuairisc. Among the new crop of Irish dramatists are John B. Keane, Brian Friel, Tom Coffey, and Hugh Leonard, all of whom write for an international audience. A new group of younger poets in Ireland includes Kinsella, Clarke, Murphy, Kell, and John Montague.

If that great poet and playwright William Butler Yeats were still around to give one of his famous lectures, he might very well give these young writers the same advice he gave the poets in his own time. Bidding them to be mindful of their heritage and write about their country, he concluded: "Cast your eyes on other days, that we in days to come may be, still the indomitable Irishry."

CHAPTER 17

FAMOUS WOMEN OF EIRE

THAT WOMEN OF Ireland have traditionally been accorded much respect is indicated in the old Book of Ballymote, which contains a history of famous women down to the time of the English invasion. A woman in those days was close to being on equal terms with a man, for the records show references to druidesses, poetesses, physicians, and lawmakers such as Bridget Brethra, who lived about the time of Christ and practiced law at Conor MacNessa's court. This famous and learned woman gave the legal decision which made it possible for the daughter in a family to receive a *coibche,* or marriage portion from the estate, and also made provisions for her to inherit the land in the event there was no son in the family.

In ancient Irish law, a woman retained certain property rights after marriage. Although the husband was the leading partner in the matrimonial venture, a wife was not her husband's chattel, but rather his partner. Women of Eire were also allowed to retain their maiden names after marriage. In case of legal separations — at least those showing just cause for separation — a wife could take all her marriage portion, her marriage gifts, and receive a certain amount of damage money.

Although a wife's contributions to the household generally included such implements of industry as the spinning wheel, spindle, and loom, it would appear that the women of Ireland were by no means devoid of vanity. Well-kept fingernails, which were often dyed crimson, were the mark of a well-bred woman. Eyebrows were dyed with berry juice and faces often tinted with vegetable dye, while a woman's hair, her crowning vanity, was worn in spiral curls, or braided down the back and fastened at the ends with golden rings or hollow golden balls.

In his beautiful poem, *Lament for Erin,* Colmcille speaks of Erin's women as being "illustrious for fond espousal." In those days, as in ancient times, the six maidenly gifts were considered to be "beauty of person, beauty of voice, the gift of music, knowledge of fine needlework, the gift of wisdom, and virtuous chastity." Cuchullain's wife Emer was said to have possessed all of these maidenly gifts, and was modest and shy besides.

All ancient Irishwomen, however, were not like Emer. Many of them were much too spirited to be satisfied with their needlework. When Canair the Pious, a holy maiden of the Benntraighe, went to Inish-Cathaig in response to a vision, she was met on the shore by St. Senan, who had earlier forbade any woman to come upon the island where he had his monastery and school.

"Go to thy sister on yon island east," he commanded Canair. "No woman shall enter here!"

Canair did not hesitate to point out to Senan that it was not only men who had given service to Christ and his apostles, but women as well. Concluding her case, she reminded him of the fact that women were not excluded from heaven. "Why then shouldst thou not allow women to come to this island?" she asked, whereupon St. Senan was at last convinced of the reasonableness of her request.

Despite the tendency of certain saintly Irish women to withdraw from the world — Canair was a hermit saint — and the tendency of others toward vanity, there was one characteristic that nearly all famous Irishwomen had in common, and that was their concern for other human beings. One who exemplifies this characteristic is Ireland's "Mary of the Gael," St. Bridget. Also referred to as queen of the Irish race, and in more recent times as the standard-bearer of the Women's Liberation movement, the beloved Irish saint established a foundation at Kildare unique for sixth century Ireland. It was a monastery for both men and women, and was governed jointly by an Abbess and a Bishop-Abbot.

Born of a bondswoman in the year 450, Bridget was the daughter of the Irish chieftain Dubtactius. A shepherdess and dairymaid during her early years, she went about her churning singing happily:

> Mary's Son, my Friend cometh
> To bless my kitchen.
> The Prince of the world to the border
> May we have abundance with Him.

During those early years, Bridget learned to love all living things, and by the time she returned to her father's house she had become exceptionally beautiful. Determined to be a "bride of Christ," she turned away the many young men who sought her hand in marriage. In the ensuing years her impulsive and charitable acts were often to lead her into trouble.

Even as a child her generous nature showed itself. When she was nine years old the king of Leinster gave her father a rich sword garnished with costly jewels. Distressed at the poverty-stricken conditions of sick neighbors, and with no one to turn to for help, Bridget removed the jewels of the sword and gave them to the needy family. Hearing the news of her theft, the king of Leinster stormed into her father's house, calling Bridget into his presence.

"How dare you presume to deface the gift of a king?"
he demanded.

Calmly, Bridget reminded him that the gift had been
bestowed on a much better king than he was, whom she
found in such extremity that "I would have given all that
my father hath and all that you have, yes, yourselves too
and all, were ye in my power to give, rather than Christ
should starve."

Bridget is also a perfect example of Irish hospitality,
since by some miracle she managed to milk her cows three
times in one day to provide a meal for unexpected visitors.
Symbol of eternal light, she founded four monasteries, the
most famous one founded with Bishop Conlaeth in Kildare.
It is here that St. Bridget established a nunnery. Her nuns
were celebrated as the guardians of the "Fire of St. Bridget."
The fire was fed diligently by the religious women, and remained unextinguished through long ages of invasions, yet
despite the vast quantities of wood consumed there was
never an increase of ashes.

Although Bridget ruled the monks of Kildare as well as
the nuns, and was in charge of thirty religious houses, she
still found time to travel about Ireland helping the poor
and healing the sick. She died in 525 and is thought to be
interred in County Down, in the same tomb with St. Patrick and Colmcille. The widespread belief in the healing
powers of Bridget's cloak probably stemmed from the fact
that the people of a later era had heard about the numerous
miracles she accomplished in her lifetime. Indeed, it was
thought that anyone who touched Bridget's shadow was
instantly healed. One of the many legends concerning Ireland's "Mary of the Gael" tells us that she was once seen
hanging her wet cloak, for drying, on a ray of sunshine.

Ireland can claim as many women poets as women saints.
In fact, Ireland has the only literature in Europe, and per-

haps the world, where one finds a succession of women poets. One of the last of the great classic poems written by Irish women was composed by the wife of Art O'Leary during the eighteenth century. This gifted poetess was an O'Connell of Derrynane, County Kerry, and in the custom of the times, she kept her own name, Eibhlin Dubh, or Black Eileen, after marriage.

Actually, the marriage of Art and Eibhlin was short-lived. What happened was that one of Art O'Leary's horses ran in a race with a horse belonging to a man named Mr. Morris, and Art's horse won. Since no Catholic was supposed to own a mount worth more than five pounds, Morris went to O'Leary and said, "Papist, five pounds for your horse." O'Leary refused the insulting offer. A quarrel ensued and a magistrate plucked from the crowd declared O'Leary an outlaw. As he rode off, a band of soldiers followed him and no sooner was O'Leary in sight of his house than he was felled by the musket of a raw recruit.

Following the death of her husband, Eibhlin Dubh composed a *Keen for Art O'Leary*. The poem is in the great Irish tradition of keens, or laments for the dead. The following verse taken from the lament has been translated by the Irish poet, John Montague:

> Swiftly I clapped my hands
> And best as I could read
> Followed in your tracks
> Till under a stunted furze
> I found you before me dead.
> Without pope, without bishop,
> Without monk, without priest,
> To say a psalm over you
> But a crooked old crone
> Who tucked her cloak-end

Over your streaming blood.
I did not wait to wipe it
But drank with cupped hands.

An Irishwoman who lived a century earlier reacted to her husband's death somewhat differently. Her picture still hangs in the hall of beautiful Dromoland Castle, along with the old paintings of the famous O'Brien lords, and an oil portrait of Brian Boru, the first Christian High King of Ireland. Her name was Mary Mahon O'Brien, though she was more properly referred to as Moira Ruadh, or "Red Mary." In a battle against Cromwell's invaders in 1651, Red Mary's husband was slain. Attempting to save her son's estates from being confiscated by the Cromwellians, this shrewd woman claimed that Conor was not her husband, and that she was not actually married, which was true to a certain extent since she was, in fact, a widow. To prove she was indeed single, and to provide further protection for her son's property, she drove into Limerick and agreed to marry any Cromwellian officer selected by the commander of the garrison.

No sooner had she stated her purpose than a captain named John Cooper, captivated by the beauty of this spirited red-haired Irishwoman, volunteered to marry her. Thus was Red Mary able to save the O'Brien land holdings. Of the husband acquired by her trickery, it is said she treated him in such a way as to cause him to often reflect that marriage was a bed of thorns rather than a bed of roses.

A woman who achieved fame in Ireland as a teller of tales, though not of the Gaelic variety, was Maria Edgeworth. Born in England January 1, 1767, Maria was most famous for her regional novels, in which she used rural Ireland for the setting of her stories, calling attention to such evils as the absentee landlord and showing the effects of this practice on the lives of the Irish country people. In pioneering this particular type of novel, she exerted considerable influence on other nineteenth century writers.

The Edgeworths, of English origin, had settled in Edgeworthstown, County Longford, as early as the sixteenth century. It was Edgeworthstown House where Maria's father Richard Lovell Edgeworth spent his childhood and where Maria pursued her literary career. Situated nearby as part of the property of the Edgeworthstown House was the old vicarage of Firmont, where lived a cousin of Maria's father, Robert Edgeworth. Robert had four sons, among them the famous Abbé de Firmont who, at the risk of his own life, attended Louis XVI when he went to his death on the scaffold.

The Edgeworth family was known for its unconventionality, and Robert Edgeworth was no exception. He was the great-grandson of Archbishop Ussher, the scholar and writer, who is buried at Westminster Abbey. Loved and respected as a Protestant rector, he shocked his friends and relatives in the year of 1749 by suddenly announcing his intention to embrace the Catholic religion. That he should have seen fit to embrace a religion which would cause him such a loss of prestige — as a member of the Catholic Church he would not be allowed to vote, nor would his sons be allowed to attend the university — was too much to be borne even by the members of the ordinarily liberal-minded Edgeworth family. There was nothing to be done but forbid him to ever again enter Edgeworthstown House.

The hapless Edgeworth cousin, now practically an outlaw, took his family to Toulouse, France, where there was not only a colony of other Irish exiles, but an Irish college as well. In spite of his banishment from Edgeworthstown House, two of Robert's sons, who later returned to Ireland to find out if their property had been confiscated, were welcomed by Maria's father. Maria's half-brother, Sneyd Edgeworth, only twenty-one at the time of the Abbé Edgeworth's death in 1807, wrote a biography of the Abbé. Two copies of the book, dedicated to Maria and printed in London in 1815, are in the Bodleian Library at Oxford.

It was not until Maria was fifteen years old that she went to live permanently in Ireland. By that time, she had attended Mrs. Lataffiere's school in Derby and completed a two-year course at a finishing school in Wimpole Street, where among other methods used to help her become a poised young woman, she was swung by the neck to increase her height.

In her attempts to stretch her mind she was to undergo further torment, for she could scarcely write a paragraph but what her father did not either cut it to ribbons or refashion it to suit his own tastes. Admittedly, Richard Lovell Edgeworth was a great help to Maria in the beginning. But his constant surveillance was bound to have an effect on her writing. There has been much disagreement concerning the extent of Edgeworth's influence on his daughter's literary development. There are a few who do not favor the opinion that the influence was necessarily pernicious. Nevertheless, what Maria referred to as "the crooked marks of Papa's critical indignation" would have inevitably caused some damage to the author's spontaneity. In spite of that, she was able to produce seventeen works of an extraordinary variety and at a time when the writing of novels was strictly a man's field.

The Russian writer Ivan Turgeniev has been quoted as saying that, but for Miss Edgeworth's stories of the poor in Ireland and of the squires and squireens, he would probably not have written of the comparable Russian classes. Sir Walter Scott also found inspiration in her work, including in the preface to *Waverly*: "To emulate Miss Edgeworth's admirable Irish portraits."

Still, it is difficult to evaluate her work. Often her characters, particularly in the novels with an English setting, lack depth and have a kind of artificiality about them. But though it might be said that honest Thady, the viewpoint character in *Castle Rackrent,* seems more an English servant than an Irish one, the novel does acquaint us with the manners and eccentricities of eighteenth century landlords. If Maria, lacking the touch of the poet, fails to capture the vitality and richness of the Irish peasant, she is to be admired for her intent, that is, for attempting at a time when prejudice was at its height to reveal the beauty and generosity of the Irish character.

"She never had to write for bread," said a friend, counting this as one of the author's many blessings. Yet despite the fact that Maria had never known want, one of her outstanding virtues was a willingness to administer to the needs of others. Richard Lovell Edgeworth, that celebrated inventor of turnip-cutters, self-winding clocks, the tellograph — a means of transmitting messages — and numerous other devices, was married four times, and Maria served as a nurse and governess to her nineteen younger stepbrothers and stepsisters. Often, too, she was called upon to preside over the house, a center of intellectual pursuits that attracted such luminaries as the Swiss scientist, M. Picet, Dr. Erasmus Darwin, and Sir Walter Scott.

During the famine in Ireland, Maria used her talents to obtain food and clothing for the poor and starving people of Ireland. Her program of soliciting care packages extended to America, and was so well-known that gifts coming from as far away as Boston reached her even though inscribed with the insufficient address, "To Miss Edgeworth for her poor."

In a letter to her stepsister shortly before her death in 1849, Maria included lines from a poem she had composed. In the poem she expresses the conflicting emotions that were all part of her love for Ireland:

> Ireland, with all thy faults, thy follies, too,
> I love thee still, still with a candid eye must view
> Thy wit too quick, still blundering into sense,
> And even what soberer judges folly call,
> I, looking at the Heart, forget them all.

Maria lived to the age of eighty-two and is buried in Edgeworthstown, in the Protestant cemetery that also contains the grave of Oscar Wilde's sister.

No impressive monument graces the grave of Ellen Hanley who, living in the tiny village of Ballycahane, County Limerick, had no way of knowing her short life would furnish inspiration for the Gerald Griffin novel, *The Tragic Story of the Colleen Bawn.*

It all began in the summer of 1819. At the time of the tragedy, Ellen, fresh and beautiful as a clump of spring violets, and not yet sixteen, was already being described as "a regular colleen bawn from head to toe." Her mother died when she was a child of six and when her father married again, a kindly old uncle by the name of Connery took her to live with him. In the modest little house the two of them lived quietly, and Ellen was the apple of the old man's eye.

But someone else had his eye on Ellen. As a matter of fact, the handsome young man who cut such a fine figure on horseback and looked so magnificent in his hunting clothes had not completely escaped Ellen's attention. Feeling certain the dashing young man, whose family lived in Ballycahane Castle, and who was himself a lieutenant in the Royal Marines, would not so much as look at the side of the road a poor girl like herself walked on, Ellen was content to watch from afar.

Young John Scanlan had other ideas in mind. Bold and reckless, and considered by the Irish country people to possess the two qualifications the devil likes best — money in his pocket and nothing to do — Scanlan had as his constant companion a servant named Stephen Sullivan, who was to help him carry out his dark deeds.

The first meeting with Ellen was cleverly arranged, master and manservant managing to get caught in the rain near Ellen's house and being subsequently offered — as they had anticipated — the hospitality of kindly Mr. Connery. Things happened fast after that. Secret meetings were arranged, and eventually there was even a promise of marriage, but only in the event that Ellen agreed to borrow — without consent — the meager savings her uncle had tucked away. There followed an elopement and a mock wedding, Ellen having no thought but that the priest was authentic.

The elopement took place June 29. On September 6, Ellen's body was washed ashore at Moneypoint on the River Shannon. All indications bore evidence that she had been brutally murdered. John Scanlan was tried for murder, and though he was defended by the famous lawyer and liberator, Daniel O'Connell, he was convicted and sentenced to be hanged at Gallows Green. To the last he protested his innocence, insisting it was Sullivan who had committed the murder. On the day he was to be hanged, the horses drawing the carriage he rode in refused to cross the bridge that linked the city of Limerick with Gallows Green, all of which led the people to believe he was indeed innocent.

It was not until some four months later that the authorities caught up with Sullivan. At the trial he also pleaded not guilty. But just before he was hanged he made a full con-

fession, telling in a rush of words how he took Ellen out
in a boat, beat her about the head with a gun, and then,
trussing her up with a rope, flung her body into the
Shannon. In the end he cried out, "I declare before the
Almighty that I am guilty of the murder. But it was Mr.
Scanlan who put me up to it."

Ellen Hanley was buried in Burrane churchyard, County
Clare. On her grave is a flat tombstone to which a concrete
edging has been added to keep morbid souvenir hunters
from chipping away the stone. Because of her extreme youth
and innocence, and because such a crime was a rarity in
Ireland, she has achieved a kind of immortality. At the age
of twenty-five, Gerald Griffin, who covered the murder
trials as a young reporter, wrote a novel based on Ellen's
tragic love affair, and as a result he became the toast of
London's literary gatherings. Later on, Dion Boucicault
staged it as a play titled *Colleen Bawn,* while Benedict
used the material for an opera, *The Lily of Killarney.*

A woman who grew up in an entirely different environment was Maude Gonne, who achieved fame through the
roles she played on the stage of the Abbey Theatre and
because of her passionate involvement in the struggle to
free Ireland from English domination. Many considered
Maude Gonne the most beautiful Irishwoman of her generation. She came from a wealthy and socially prominent
family; her father was an Irish officer in the British army.
But she rebelled against her parents' way of life at an early
age and thenceforth devoted her own life to the Irish cause.
When she was seventeen, she was presented at the Viceregal
Court in Dublin Castle, which was then presided over by
Albert Edward, Prince of Wales. At the Court Ball, the
Prince was so struck by Maude's beauty that he escorted
her to the royal platform, where it is said she entertained
the royal party by singing "The Wearing of the Green."

Maude Gonne not only took part in political activities, but also fought against poverty and illness in the Dublin slums. In 1900 this spirited woman, who would later play the title role in Yeat's revolutionary play *Kathleen ni Houlihan,* founded the Daughters of Erin, a group of activists bent on expressing their dissatisfaction at being excluded from Ireland's nationalist societies.

"Who dreamed that beauty passes like a dream?" asked Yeats in a poem inspired by Maude. So in love with her was he that he became involved in her rebel activities, but his love was never returned in full measure.

Another woman who had a significant influence on Yeats was Lady Gregory. Lady Gregory had been the wife of a distinguished British colonial administrator. Following his death she went to the trouble of learning the Irish language so that she might collect folklore from the country people who lived in the vicinity of her home at Coole Park in County Galway. Having learned the language of the people, she set about paying a visit to each humble cabin, where she sat listening to their tales of fairies and demons, often trading sorrows with the native Irish even as she shared the warmth of the turf fire. During the period when she allowed Yeats to share her quest for hidden wisdom, she introduced certain gracious elements into his life that had been lacking in the past. Eventually, her home at Coole Park, which had known such guests as Guy de Maupassant, provided a refuge for the poet.

With Yeats, she founded the Abbey Theatre, remaining one of its directors until the time of her death. Indeed, Lady Gregory wrote many plays of her own and on occasion collaborated with the poet. Two of her most important works were *Cuchulain of Muirthemne* and *Gods and Fighting Men,* in which she retold the classic tales of early Irish literature. The story of the son of Aoife, taken from

Cuchulain of Muirthemne, furnished the basis for Yeats' verse tragedy, *On Baile's Strand.*

It was St. Patrick himself who once said there were three orders of saints, those who are a glory on the mountaintops, those who are gleams on the sides of the hills, and those who are just a few faint lights down in the valley. Sinead Bean de Valera may belong to the latter category. Although Ireland's beloved first lady has for the most part chosen to remain a faint light down in the valley, even a brief glimpse into the life of this remarkable woman is enough to convince one that she has shed a considerable amount of light on the lives of those around her.

Mrs. Eamon de Valera, who was born in Dublin to Laurence Flanagan and Margaret Byrne, celebrated her ninety-fourth birthday June 1, 1972. Of her it can be truly said that age has failed to wither her, nor has custom had the power to stale her infinite variety. Even in her most recent photographs one still sees traces of a lovely Irish colleen, along with that odd combination of saint and pixie so often apparent in the faces of women of Eire.

Qualifying as a primary school teacher at the age of twenty-one, she taught at the National School before she returned to St. Xavier's where she had received her earlier education. She continued to teach there until her marriage to Eamon de Valera. While at St. Xavier's she became an enthusiastic student of the Irish language. In her spare time she taught Gaelic to voluntary classes, attracting such students as Sean T. O'Ceallaigh, president of Ireland from 1945 to 1959, and also Eamon de Valera.

Although Sinead de Valera has often been described as a woman of gentle beauty, she is nevertheless no stranger to sorrow. She was close to thirty-two when she married. Only six years later, following the Easter Rising, her husband was imprisoned in England and held there until

June of 1917. One can imagine the anguish and loneliness that came to this woman during the years when her husband was so often away from her and she had to look after their seven children, one of whom died in 1936.

But, as is the case with all first ladies, there were many high points in her life, too. When the president was conducting his campaign of 1919-1920 on behalf of the Irish Republic, she came to the United States to join him. In more recent times, when she accompanied him on his official visit to the Holy Father, she received the Grand Cross in Gold of the Papal Distinction from Pope John II. On the occasion of the state visit of the King and Queen of Belgium to Ireland in 1968, she was honored with the civil decoration of the Grand Cordon of the Order of Leopold.

Hostess to many distinguished visitors during her years at Aras an Uachtarain, her guests included the late President John F. Kennedy, President Radhakrishnan of India, Prince Ranier and Princess Grace of Monaco, General and Madame Charles de Gaulle, Cardinals Cushing and Spellman, and many other leaders of church and state. But what is most remarkable about Sinead de Valera has to do with a facet of her life little known to most Irish Americans. She embarked on a literary career at the age of fifty-seven and began writing a series of children's plays in Irish, then went on to write books of fairy tales in English as well as stories and poems in Irish. Even today she keeps up her interest in storywriting, in the Irish language, and in other cultural activities.

The Irish poet James Stephens, who once expressed a belief that "Women are wiser than men because they know less and understand more," might have changed his views had he been acquainted with so knowledgeable a female as Miss Devlin. As an Irish television personality remarked, "Anyone tangling with Bernadette better know their facts."

On May 30, 1431, Joan of Arc was burned at the stake in Rouen, France, at the age of nineteen, after being found guilty of sorcery. On February 17 in the year 1972, Ireland's Joan of Arc was sentenced to six months in jail for defying a government ban on parades. Two years previously, at the age of twenty-four, she served four months of a six-month sentence after having been accused of provoking riots during the bloody street battle in Derry. A Marxist Joan of Arc she may well be, or even a "Spitfire" as she was called by certain individuals following the famous hair-pulling incident in the House of Parliament. She is also a truly dedicated young woman.

Born in Cookstown, County Tyrone, Bernadette Devlin has written an autobiography titled *The Price of My Soul.* In it she furnishes a vivid description of an Ulster childhood, giving the reader a good idea of the struggle a Catholic family had to go through in order to make ends meet and uphold some degree of family pride. She was only nine at the time of her father's death. When she was nineteen and had to face the loss of her mother, a kindly Protestant neighbor came in to clean the house and prepare a hot meal for the bereaved family. Two years later when Bernadette was fighting the Mid-Ulster by-election, that same neighbor stood in the street and shrieked, "You Fenian scum!" Such was the background that provided the motivation for the Irishwoman who was to become the youngest member of the House of Parliament in Westminster.

Although Miss Devlin is not considered to be the leader of all the Catholics in Northern Ireland, it would appear that she has the respect of the majority of them. One cannot but admire her for her honesty and the fact that she has not let success go to her head. She has sense enough to know, especially since she has had to suffer the arrows of a somewhat hostile press, that there is a time to be silent.

She probably will not accomplish all her aims. Yet it seems safe to say that there would still be a Stormont Government had it not been for the intellectual capacities of such Irish leaders as Bernadette Devlin. Indeed, the words Yeats once used to explain Maude Gonne's rebel tendencies — she who lived in "storm and strife" — might also be used to describe this modern rebel:

> What could have made her peaceful with a mind
> That nobleness made simple as a fire?

CHAPTER 18

SONS AND DAUGHTERS

NOT LONG AGO, a third-generation Irish American named Bernard P. McDonough made the following statement: "The good Lord and the United States have been mighty good to me. But after all, I'm Irish."

Bernard McDonough was born May 25, 1903, in San Antonio, Texas. His mother died when he was not yet five years old and he was sent with his two sisters to live in Belpre, Ohio, just across the river from Parkersburg, West Virginia, where he was reared by his Grandmother McDonough and a maiden aunt. At a very early age he worked in the oil fields and on the railroad. When he was sixteen he was working in the forge room of a Parkersburg shovel factory. By the time he reached the age of fifty-two he had made that same shovel factory, the largest one in the world, a part of the McDonough Company.

Mr. McDonough's first job after his graduation from Georgetown University was in the admissions office of a small business college. Finding this type of work a bit too confining for his volatile nature, he turned to selling insurance. Later on he began investing in real estate, purchasing several plots of land on corner locations. Five years after his graduation from Georgetown he had built about thirty service stations and a dozen supermarkets on this property. Although his holdings now include marine equipment businesses and the Endicott Johnson Shoe Company, his fortune came primarily from the construction business.

During the years when he was expanding his operations, his thoughts often turned to his grandfather, Patrick Mc-Donough, whose story had been told to him when he was a child. Back in 1862 the grandfather, making his way from his family's home in Galway to the ship that would carry him to America as an emigrant, chanced to walk by Dromoland Castle in County Clare. Gazing wistfully at the magnificent stone structure, he said to himself, "After I've made my fortune in America I'll come back to Ireland and have as fine a home as that castle. I may even buy Dromoland."

Patrick McDonough never did make a fortune in America. It was his grandson who was to fulfill his dream. But although the knowledge of his grandfather's wish encouraged his interest in his Irish ancestry, Bernard Mc-Donough's reasons for buying Dromoland Castle were of a somewhat different nature. Shocked to find that during the 1950s four hundred thousand young people had to leave Ireland to seek their fortunes in other countries, he tried to think of a way he might help them out. In 1962 he bought the castle of his grandfather's dreams for the sum of $200,000 with the idea of converting it into a resort hotel for tourists.

In the process of turning the old Irish castle, which had no adequate heating system and only eight bathrooms, into a modern hotel with central heating and sixty-seven new bathrooms for each of the sixty-seven guest rooms, the industrialist spent more than $1,500,000. Directing the work himself, he was to find the unraveling of Dromoland's structural mysteries both frustrating and fascinating. But what brought him the greatest satisfaction was the fact that this project provided employment for a force of 485 skilled workers for a period of at least six months.

Finding there was no place in Ireland to train hotel workers, McDonough built the Shannon International Hotel at nearby Shannon airport for that very purpose. In the following years Clare Inn, on the grounds of Dromoland, and Limerick Inn, on the road between Limerick and Shannon airport, were constructed, giving further employment to approximately four hundred Irish men and women.

"Even if I never make any profit out of all this," Mr. McDonough once remarked, "I'm glad to be doing something for Ireland."

Providing a refuge for the self-made millionaire when, as he says, "his blood pressure begins to pop," Dromoland Castle flies both the flag of the United States and that of the Republic of Ireland. And although it gives Bernard McDonough considerable satisfaction to know he has managed to keep a number of Ireland's young people from leaving their native land, like so many other successful Irish Americans he has shown his gratitude to the land of his birth with his numerous philanthropies. Only recently, in 1971, he gave one million dollars to Georgetown University for its new law center.

The story of one millionaire's dream is significant because it points up a certain characteristic of the Irish immigrant, that ingredient called grit. And millionaires or not, many Irish immigrants have at one time or another cherished a similar dream. For many have heard the same wistful words that were spoken by Patrick McDonough some hundred years ago, falling like an echo from the lips of another son of the old sod, or listened with a mingling of dismay and disbelief while an Irishman, totally ignorant of the history of the land of his ancestors, tells how his grandfather no doubt once owned a castle in some remote corner of the Emerald Isle. The mind sometimes takes strange, off-trail journeys in its efforts to cast off sadness, and this

is particularly true if the mind happens to belong to an
Irishman. And perhaps, for Irish immigrants, the castle
was, like Kathleen ni Houlihan in Yeats' allegory, a symbol
of the land they were leaving and had little hope of ever
gazing upon again.

It would be hard to find a sadder episode in the history
of the world than the story of the Irish exodus. Lured by
glowing accounts of ship travel given on billboards posted
near their chapel gates, more than three million Irish came
to America as immigrants between 1845 and 1891. They
were victimized people in their own country and they would
be victimized again. Indeed, many of them bought tickets
to America only to find they were worthless.

A mention has already been made of the hardships encountered by passengers traveling on the coffin ships.
While other ethnic groups suffered similar hardships, statistics bear out the fact that deaths on board British ships
exceeded the mortality rate on board ships of other countries. In the records of the Commissioner of Immigration for
the State of New York, the quota of sick per thousand in
1847 and 1848 shows British vessels with 30 as compared
to American vessels with 9-3/5 and German vessels with
8-3/5.

Passengers who managed to survive the long and hazard-
out journey by sea were to encounter on arrival in America
another type of enemy — agents, runners, or brokers, all
of whom were bent on separating the newly arrived Irishman from his few cherished possessions. Confidence men
of the cleverest sort, they knew full well the wisdom of
wearing a bright green neck tie and of further gaining the
trust of a greenhorn by speaking in a cultivated accent of
the glories of the "ould counthry."

Many were the high-spirited boys and innocent young
girls who became the prey of these sharks of the land. In

fact, such were the conditions existing in 1850 that Mr. Vere Foster, offering testimony in favor of an official landing-place so that passengers arriving in New York would be protected from those who regarded them as lawful prey, described conditions thus: "A few of the passengers were taken ashore to the hospital at Staten Island and we arrived alongside the quay in New York this afternoon. The 900 passengers dispersed as usual among the various fleecing houses, to be partially or entirely disabled for pursuing their travels into the interior in search of employment."

It was the Irish immigrants of the peasant and laboring classes who were most often the victims of land sharks, a fact which made it impossible for them to push their way into the country where they might have sought a type of employment more suited to their inclinations and abilities. Many of them, forced to stay in New York, ended up living in the basements of tenement houses, which were frequently flooded to the depth of several inches with stagnant water. During the year 1864 in certain portions of the Fourth Ward of New York, the tenement house population was packed at the rate of about 290 thousand inhabitants to the square mile.

Unable to find employment, the tenement Irish were in some instances driven to begging in the streets, and since the streets were fringed with groggeries, intemperance was often added to the other evils. The fatal tendency toward overindulgence on the part of some of these immigrants may account for the fact that the Irish element in the nineteenth century figures unenviably in New York police records, though it must be pointed out that their offences were primarily related to rows or riots and that crimes of deliberate murder or frauds were not common to the Irish.

Although the vast majority of immigrants were temperate in their habits, the tendency to overindulgence on the part of a small minority cast discredit on the entire Irish population. For some reason, perhaps because of his mercurial disposition and the fact that he preferred indulging in public in the company of fellow imbibers rather than at home, liquor was more injurious to the Irishman's image than to that of other ethnic groups. Aware of the seriousness of the problem, one Irishman wrote to his people in Ireland imploring them to advise their friends and relatives to leave off the use of intoxicating drinks before they ever so much as thought of coming to America.

"Otherwise, they are not wanted here," he wrote. "Let them stay home, where, even if of dissipated habits, they can meet some good Samaritan who will extend to them the hand of friendship in distress; for here the man inclined to drink will meet with nothing but bad whiskey and a pauper's grave, and not one to say, 'Lord have mercy on him!' "

Needless to say, the overindulging Irishman was not granted mercy by the tenants of the New World, and inevitably he had to face prejudice not only among Americans but among his own people as well. But even the soberminded and law-abiding Irish were the victims of prejudice. Strange as it may seem, the Irish were the first people to be called foreigners in America. The trouble was, they were Roman Catholic, and in America as in the old world, a number of people, unable to shed an inherited prejudice which their ancestors had brought into the country, hated and feared the Catholic Church.

Religious persecution was often directed specifically against the Irish. New Hampshire made its Irish residents swear an oath against the Pope. Pennsylvania taxed them for being Irish. New York State forbade them to carry arms. Until 1836, to be an elector in the state of North Carolina it was necessary to swear a belief in the Protestant religion. And even as late as 1856 New Hampshire still excluded Catholics from every office.

To make matters worse, Orangeism, the principles and practices of a secret society organized in Northern Ireland in 1795 to support Protestantism, cast its dark shadow on the progress of the Catholic Irish. In 1844 the American Protestant Association, many of whose members were exponents of Orangeism, embarked on a crusade against the "foreigner" which led to the Philadelphia riots of 1844. During these riots, the Orange air, "The Boyne Water," was played at the same time flames were consuming St. Michael's Church. Forty deaths resulted from the riots, and two rectories and a Catholic seminary were put to the torch.

In 1850 there began a "Know-Nothing" movement which was again directed specifically against the Catholic Irish. The constitution of Know-Nothingism, also called Native Americanism, was adopted on June 17, 1845, the anniversary of the Battle of Bunker Hill. It was dedicated to resisting the policy of the Church of Rome, and other foreign influence, by placing in all offices none but native-born Protestant citizens. At the height of this movement, a Philadelphia businessman wrote his sister in Ireland telling her the people better stay where they were since they were at least safe from murders in Ireland. The falsehoods then being circulated about Irish Catholics are similar to those being circulated in Northern Ireland today, and so successful was the propaganda that it aroused hostility even among Protestants who were ordinarily mild and tolerant men. As might well be imagined, religious prejudice added bitterness to national prejudice, and to such a degree that there were Irishmen who felt compelled to deny their Irish origins.

During this period, and for a long time after, the Irish

were divided into three general classes. Those who now boast of falling into the category "lace curtain" Irish may be surprised to find that members of this class were not necessarily affluent, but were so-called because they were sympathetic to Anglo-Saxon sentiment and perhaps even a little ashamed of their Celtic background. Cherishing a devout wish to be accepted by the old established families of Boston, Irishmen belonging to this group went over to the Protestant religion, some of them even going so far as to disguise their names, so that an O'Brien might become a Bryant, or an O'Reilly a Ripley. Another category, the "shanty" Irish, were generally found among the poorer classes, but the term actually referred to a type of immigrant who showed no interest in anything that did not pertain to Ireland and who often never even bothered to become an American citizen.

It must be said that these two extremes comprised a very small segment of the Irish in America. It is the middle group, properly referred to as the Irish American, that were in the majority. These people were primarily interested in doing something about the prejudice that existed against them, and were convinced that the best way to do so was to become good Americans. John Boyle O'Reilly was one of these Irish Americans.

Arriving on American shores November 28, 1869, this Fenian hero had already survived the horrors of four prisons, including Mountjoy. He had been transported to Australia but managed to carry out a daring escape from the penal colony of Bunbury. A student of Irish history and a poet as well, he was to carve an auspicious career for himself during the next twenty-one years and to become known in America as one of the most outstanding journalists of the nineteenth century.

O'Reilly possessed a talent for putting things in their

proper perspective. "Plain talk is like spring medicine —
unpalatable, but necessary," he once remarked. In his
attempts to elevate the Irish socially, materially, and
morally, he was as quick to point out their faults as he was
to call attention to their virtues. On those occasions when
the Orangemen saw fit to commemorate the Battle of the
Boyne victory, O'Reilly appealed to both the Orange and
the Green factions in an effort to make them realize that
the blatant display of the prejudice they felt toward each
other was not only harming themselves but making all
things Irish seem ridiculous.

Shortly after his arrival in America he settled in Boston
and began writing for the *Pilot,* a newspaper that was the
voice of the Irish in America. Aware of the frequent notices
appearing in the want ad columns which stated "No Irish
Need Apply" or "No Catholics Need Apply," he began
giving the offending firm free advertising, by informing
his readers that "The firm which advertises itself as wanting
neither Irish help nor Irish trade is, from its own letterhead,
George Frost and Co." Aided by such leading Protestants
as Oliver Wendell Holmes and Wendell Phillips, he continued his fight against bigotry, exposing prejudice when
it showed up in such periodicals as *Scribners, Harper's
Weekly,* and the *Atlantic Monthly.* Upon his death in 1890
the editors of these same magazines paid tribute to him in
words like the following, taken from the obituary in *Harper's
Weekly*:

> Boyle O'Reilly . . . was easily the most distinguished
> Irishman in America. He was one of the country's fore-
> most poets, one of its influential journalists, an orator
> of unusual power, and he was endowed with such a gift
> of friendship as few men are blessed with . . . .

Probably the most touching eulogy offered in memory of
this remarkable man were the words spoken by the Irish

patriot, Patrick A. Collins, who had fought with O'Reilly for Irish freedom:

Here was a branded outcast some twenty years ago, stranded in a strange land, friendless and penniless; today wept for all over the world where men are free and seeking to be free, for his large heart went out to all in trouble, and his soul was the soul of a freeman; all he had he gave to humanity and asked no return. He was born without an atom of prejudice, and he lived and died without an evil or ungenerous thought.

O'Reilly's poem *Wendell Phillips* contains the line, "A sower of the infinite seed was he, a woodsman that hewed toward the light," which description can be appropriately applied to the poet himself, a man who advocated civil rights not just for Irishmen but for men of all races.

In the struggle to achieve civil rights, for their own people and for people of all ethnic groups, we find a number of other Irishmen, some long before the time of John Boyle O'Reilly. There was Bishop Dr. Carroll, and the Bishops Spaulding, Connolly, and Cullen. And there was Bishop England. Having received a communication from his superiors in July of 1820 advising him that he had been appointed Bishop of Charleston, South Carolina, the Reverend John England, reluctant to leave his home in Bandon, County Cork, made the following entry in his diary some three months later:

This day was the anniversary — twelve years — of my ordination to the priesthood. On this day I parted with my family to go whither I thought God had called me, but whither I had no desire to go. Should this be read by a stranger, let him pardon that weakness of our common nature which then affected me, and does now after the lapse of three months.

Actually, the Catholics of Ireland had never been close

to the hierarchy of the Church, whom they had reason to believe were inclined to favor the rich and who often appeared to be insensitive to the basic needs of the ordinary man. But Bishop England was not one of those who hid behind a polished desk in some inaccessible office. Arriving in Charleston with little enthusiasm for his mission, it was not long before he was rambling about the countryside preaching open air sermons and making friends with the Cherokee Indians and Negroes. Though plagued with frequent bouts of rheumatism, he traveled from place to place in the manner of a country doctor. On quite a number of occasions he was turned away from an inn because of his religion, and many were the nights he spent in the forest or in some lonely glen.

Along with his other labors he published a catechism, established the Book Society, preached before the State Legislature, and, oddly enough, was instrumental in the forming of an anti-duelling association. Referred to in Rome as the "Steam Bishop," he made numerous trips to the Vatican, and in spite of his wide range of interests, found time to promote the spread of literary and scientific knowledge in the city of Charleston. A man not lacking in humor, and admired for his intelligence, he was eventually able to win the respect of the Protestant clergy.

So respected was Bishop England that the Protestants often gave him the loan of their churches. People of every creed came to listen to this famous preacher, and indeed, there were occasions when a minister might even ask Bishop England to give a sermon to his own parishioners. In this way, he helped to expose the falseness of the prejudice against the Catholic Irish.

As time went on, it was not only the members of the clergy who embarked on a campaign to combat bigotry, but Protestant politicians as well. Henry A. Wise, campaigning for the office of Governor of Virginia, took the members of the Know-Nothing movement to task for proclaiming their slogans of "No Popery" and "Save the Bible from the Papists," chiding them for what apparently appeared to be their new-found interest in the Bible. Senator R. M. T. Hunter, delivering a speech at Richmond, suggested that there were certainly some offices which the sons and daughters of the Catholic Church were still considered competent to discharge, and he then called attention to the works being done by the Sisters of Charity, whose members, he pointed out, "may enter yonder pest-houses, from whose dread portals the bravest and strongest man quails and shrinks."

The Sisters of Charity, established under the episcopacy of Bishop Carroll, was founded in Emmitsburg, Maryland, by a convert to Catholicism, Elizabeth Seton. From its earliest days the order included many nuns of Irish birth. By 1867 the number of sisters living in the community amounted to 410. The most prosperous branch of the order in the state of New York numbered several hundred sisters, the majority of whom were Irish.

Caring for the poor, the sick, and the aged, those who were orphans and those who were in prison, and even the insane, these generous and selfless women made the name of Sister a name of honor throughout America. During the Battle of Gettysburg when Sisters of Charity, along with Sisters of Mercy and of the Holy Cross, went to the battlefield to tender their services to the injured and the dying, so impressed was one Protestant preacher that he made the following comment which was subsequently published in the newspapers of the time: "Although I hate their religion and despise their sectarianism, I must do justice to the self-sacrificing devotion of those pale unmated flowers, that never ripen with fruit."

Surely such pale unmated flowers, a grandaunt of mine among them, deserve to occupy a place in that impressive litany of famous Irish Americans. It is because of them, and men like Bishop England and the priests who followed after him, that so many Irishmen were able to keep their faith, and at the same time make many significant contributions to the American way of life. These dedicated nuns and priests managed to lift themselves up, and their own people with them, to such an extent that not much more than a century later the grandson of an Irish immigrant would become the first Catholic to be elected President of the United States.

Few people realize that the Irish landed on the shores of America with less capital than the English, the Scottish, or the Germans, and in many respects, under less favorable circumstances than the people of any other country. The fact that they managed to accomplish so much in their adopted land gives proof of the inherent vigor and vitality of their race. The Irish in America have made their mark in almost every walk of life: as merchants, bankers, manufacturers, athletes, lawyers, physicians, statesmen, men of science, scholars, nurses, teachers, and as soldiers "wise in council," as one Irishman put it, and "terrible in battle."

It would be impossible to list all the Irish who distinguished themselves in the American Revolutionary War. There was the famous General Edward Hand who numbered among his troops Irishmen from all four provinces of Ireland. There were many other officers, including General John Sullivan of Limerick and Colonel Stephen Moylan of Cork. Indeed, so great in number were the Irishmen committed to helping win the War of Independence that two witnesses testifying before a committee in the British House of Commons claimed that half the Continental Army was from Ireland. And while the House of Commons was contemplating this startling revelation, in the House of Parliament Lord Mountjoy was moaning, "We have lost America to the Irish."

Four of the signers of the Declaration of Independence were Irish-born and five of Irish descent. At least twenty-two sons of Erin sat in the first Continental Congress. When Charles Carroll signed his name to the Declaration of Independence, and added, "Of Carrollton" to his signature, Benjamin Franklin exclaimed, "There goes a cool million!" Captain John Barry, an Irishman by birth and a resident of Philadelphia, was in command of the *Lexington* when he made one of the first important captures of the Revolutionary War by taking the British ship *Edward*. Fighting Jack Barry achieved his most famous victory in 1777 when he captured five British ships, and received the following word from George Washington: "I congratulate you on the success that has crowned your gallantry — accept my wishes that suitable success may always attend your bravery."

What was particularly commendable about the fighting Irish was their conduct toward the enemy. During the Civil War it was often said that the Irishman showed an infinite amount of compassion for the prisoner-of-war, often assisting in the care of the wounded and even going so far as to divide rations with an enemy when necessary. One of the most noble soldiers of the Confederacy was Patrick Cleburne. Born near the city of Cork, he referred to his native land as the "old country" and always in the same manner as a son might speak of his mother. In battle he preferred the Irish soldier, not just because of his courage but because of other qualities, such as endurance, cleanliness, cheerfulness, and, surprisingly enough, because he was more amenable to discipline.

In the nation's capital there stands a statue of General Shields. A close friend of Abraham Lincoln's, this famous

Irish American was the only man in history to have been a United States senator from three states — Illinois, Minnesota, and Missouri. Both Lincoln and Ulysses Grant were hopeful that he might become President of the United States, and he might well have fulfilled their desire had it not been for his Irish birth.

An Irishman who had his beginnings in County Waterford was Thomas Francis Meagher, leader of the much celebrated Fighting 69th New York Volunteers under the command of Michael Corcoran. Once condemned to death by the English, and, like his fellow countryman John Boyle O'Reilly sentenced to life imprisonment in Australia in 1849, he escaped to New York where he became a lawyer, lecturer, and editor. In 1866 he became governor of Montana.

So numerous are the Irish Americans who have achieved fame of one sort or another that one hesitates to make mention of a few for fear of doing disservice to the others. But mention ought to be made of the Irishman whose fame has been perpetuated with a statue in Duffy Square in midtown Manhattan. A priest of the New York Archdiocese and a scholar of note, Father Francis P. Duffy is best remembered for his heroic conduct while serving as an Army chaplain in World War I. And let us not forget Father Flanagan. Emigrating from Ireland when he was but eighteen, he managed, in the course of establishing his famous Boy's Town in Omaha, Nebraska, to prove the truth of his conviction that "There is no such thing as a bad boy."

An Irish American who was to achieve fame in an entirely different area sounded the keynote for his future life when he uttered this first bright saying, "Mother, when I get to be a big boy can I have all the things I oughtn't to have?" Born in St. Paul, Minnesota, on September 24, 1896, F. Scott Fitzgerald could trace his ancestry right back to Francis Scott Key. But although his maternal grandfather, P. F. McQuillan, passed "by his own unaided exertions from the humblest beginnings to a place among the merchant princes of the country," F. Scott was more impressed with the advantages that came from his father's old Maryland family, and was always a bit skeptical, even ashamed, of his mother's side of the family. The resulting conflict was to provide a theme that would be implicit in many of his novels and short stories.

"*Gatsby* was good enough — a classic now," wrote an acquaintance of Fitzgerald's who wished to express her reaction to his novel, *Tender is the Night*. "But this is superlative. And you might be a hundred years old in your wisdom and knowledge of the hearts of men and women!"

Perhaps it was his insight into the hearts of men and women that caused Fitzgerald to be the unhappy person he was. Even in death he was surrounded by unhappy circumstances. Like most Irish he had a devout desire to be buried among his own relatives, a request that was denied by the Catholic Church, just as his books had been proscribed by them. Probably no more than thirty or forty people gathered around the famous author's grave, and the services were, as his biographer Andrew Turnbull put it, "a meaningless occasion having no apparent connection with the man, save as one of life's grim jokes designed to make us think." Ironically, the day F. Scott's Grandfather McQuillan was buried, thirty-nine firms shut down their doors and his funeral was attended not only by leading citizens of the day, but by men and women from all walks of life, including the children of the Catholic Orphan's Home which had so often benefited from his generosity.

But on a quiet street in St. Paul, a certain brownstone house has been recently designated a National Historic Landmark. It was here that Fitzgerald, in the summer of

1919, wrote his first novel, *This Side of Paradise,* and it is more than likely the works of this talented and sensitive Irish American author will survive long after the brownstone house on Summit Avenue has fallen into decay.

Fitzgerald, and many of his fellows, had little or no knowledge of the land their grandfathers were forced to leave behind when they came to America. Even today, the average Irish American knows so little about the land of his ancestors. This unfortunate state of affairs is being rapidly remedied by Minnesota's Dr. Eoin McKiernan. Growing up in rural Cold Springs, New York, and listening to tales told him by his mother, Eoin McKiernan developed an interest in Irish culture at a very early age. When he was twelve, the family moved to New York City. During his high school years he was already taking part in the cultural and social activities of the Gaelic Society, an organization founded in New York City in 1884, some nine years before the Gaelic League of Ireland was founded by Douglas Hyde. By the time he had completed the greater part of his formal education and spent a year in Ireland on a research project made possible by the Hill Family Foundation, he had become committed to spreading the news of Irish culture to his fellow Irish Americans.

He is well qualified to accomplish his objective. Author, lecturer, and television personality, and formerly chairman of the English Department at the College of St. Thomas in St. Paul, he keeps in close touch with the land of his ancestors and was recently awarded Ireland's highest literary honor, D.Litt., an award bestowed previously on only two other Americans, John F. Kennedy and Robert Frost.

Attempting to establish an institute devoted to Irish civilization, McKiernan encountered many obstacles. Through the efforts of another American of Irish descent, Dr. John Schwarzwalder of the Twin Cities Educational Television

Corporation, a series of television programs on Ireland was inaugurated in 1963. Financed by the Patrick and Aimee Butler Family Foundation, the programs were entitled "Ireland Rediscovered" and "Irish Diary." They were conducted by Dr. Eoin McKiernan, and included a vast amount of information relating to Irish history, literature, art, music, and architecture. It was shortly before the launching of "Irish Diary" that Patrick Butler and Dr. and Mrs. McKiernan co-founded the Irish American Cultural Institute, whose original directors also included Senator Eugene McCarthy, Bishop James P. Shannon, Dr. Charles E. Rea, and Al Muellerliele.

In the process of furnishing Irish Americans with information on the various aspects of Irish culture, publication of a quarterly journal, *Eire-Ireland,* was undertaken by McKiernan. Later on, aware of the need to supplement the scholarly magazine with one which would have a more general appeal, this tireless and dedicated man began publishing a monthly periodical called *Ducas.* While the word Ducas is more or less untranslatable, it does refer to tradition, heritage, breeding, and all the other elements of Gaelic culture that have shaped the Irish Americans into the people they are today. Dr. Eoin McKiernan hopes that *Ducas* will serve a worthwhile purpose, that of instilling in its readers some degree of filial gratitude.

The Irish American Cultural Institute has taken another long step forward by promoting an interrelationship between the cultures of Ireland and the cultures of America. The Institute's Artists and Lecturers Series has brought such Irish specialists as Eoin O'Mahoney, an authority on genealogy, Ruaidhri de Valera, one of Ireland's most prominent archaeologists, George Morrison, Ireland's leading film historian, the novelist Benedict Kiely, and Kevin Danaher of the Irish Folklore Commission, to the Twin Cities. In

1972, a series of programs called "Irish Fortnight" sponsored jointly by the College of St. Thomas and the Institute, held in the auditorium of the O'Shaughnessy Education Center at the College, included a number of distinguished lecturers, among them Anthony Butler, who spoke on Irish humor, Alec Reid, an authority on Anglo-Irish authors, and the internationally famous theatre director, Tomas MacAnna.

It is Ignatius A. O'Shaughnessy who helped make possible the 300 million dollar Educational Center at the College of St. Thomas. Mr. O'Shaugnessy's paternal grandfather came from Gort in County Galway. A long-time benefactor of St. Thomas, and also of St. Catherine's College and Notre Dame, he has extended his philanthropies to include other ethnic groups, such as the Jewish community.

Irish people of lesser means shared in the development of the country by working on railroads, laboring in the mines, and toiling in the steel mills. Others heeded the admonition to "Go West," making their way across the country in wagons drawn by horses and oxen. "To a land of prairie, wood and water," said one of these settlers who, after arriving in Erin Prairie, Wisconsin, in June of 1858, set to building a house and planting his crops. In time he donated land for a church and cemetery. His wife was the first to be buried in St. Patrick's cemetery, and when her coffin was brought from the church to the grave a little white dove flew straight up to the sky, at which an Irishman attending the burial service remarked, "Tis her soul going to heaven."

During the latter part of the nineteenth century Archbishop Ireland, having worked on numerous projects for the good of Minnesota with the famous empire builder, James J. Hill, organized many Irish settlements in the state, Clontarf, Graceville, and Jessenland among them. Of the people who settled in the latter community the Honorary Secretary of the Irish Emigrant Society in St. Paul wrote: "Its people are what the Irish peasant can become even in this generation — intelligent, industrious, open-hearted, generous, brave and independent."

Adventure-loving Irishmen had made themselves known in California long before the onset of the Gold Rush in 1848. They were welcomed there by the Spanish. Captain J. S. Smith, who came from what was then known as King's County in Ireland, led the first party of white men overland to California. Heading a band of some forty trappers in the services of the American Fur Company, he crossed the lofty ridges and formidable barriers of the Sierra Nevada. A number of those early Irish settlers became extensive landowners and raisers of stock. A man by the name of Murphy who came from Wexford County, the home of John F. Kennedy's ancestors, imported the first greyhounds to California.

Since there are those who say the Irish are fond of boasting, one might as well have the game as the name, and indeed it is true that a list of famous Irish Americans would fill a thousand pages or more. There are, after all, quite a lot of Irish in America. In fact, more than 22 million Americans have Irish ancestors. Chicago alone is blessed with a million and a quarter people of Irish extraction.

An energetic Irish American sometimes referred to as that "awful but awfully effective mayor of Chicago" bears the name of Richard Daley. There is also John McCormack, World War I veteran and former Speaker of the House, who retired in 1970 at the age of seventy-eight and whose fifty-year-old romance with his late wife, Harriet Joyce, caught the imagination of an entire nation. When John McCormack was thirteen his father died and it was up to John to become the family breadwinner. Yet despite the fact that he had to leave school for a while, he was able to pass the bar examinations when he was only twenty-one years old. A chaplain of the House of Representatives once said of John McCormack, "I think if all of us lived the kind of life John McCormack lives, there wouldn't be any need for a chaplain."

Of Irish descent were twelve presidents of the United States, among them John F. Kennedy, William McKinley (whose ancestral home still stands in Dervock, County Antrim), Andrew Jackson, Woodrow Wilson, Calvin Coolidge, Harry Truman, and Richard Nixon. The governor of Nevada, Mike O'Callaghan, is Irish. So, too, is Ronald Reagan, governor of California.

Other notable sons of Erin include Guglielmo Marconi, the Italian physicist who invented the wireless — his mother came from Wexford County in Ireland; William Grace, founder of the Grace Steamship Lines, and the first Catholic to become mayor of New York City; Henry Ford, whose father was born in County Cork; and Eugene O'Neill, one of America's finest dramatists, whose father James O'Neill was born on a farm just outside Tipperary. John P. Holland, inventor of the submarine, was born in Liscannor, County Clare. Financed by Fenian funds, Holland came to the United States as a Christian brother. He wanted to break the power of the British fleet so that Ireland might be liberated. Thus he invented what was then called the "Fenian Ram" which was successfully tried out in the New York harbor.

The entertainment world virtually sparkles with Irish names and faces. In April of 1972 Pat O'Brien was honored by the American Academy of Dramatic Arts in New York with the Academy's Achievement Award. There is the late Tyrone Power, Jimmy Cagney, Errol Flynn, Bing Crosby, George Cohan, Victor Herbert, and Walt Disney. Carroll

O'Connor, a former editor of an Irish American newspaper,
the *Advocate,* is an actor who has helped bridge the generation gap by bringing the family together on Saturday
nights to watch the popular television series "All in The
Family."

Among the famous daughters of Erin there is "America's
Sweetheart," Mary Pickford, whose mother Charlotte, ever
retaining an echo of her Irish brogue, often addressed her
actress-daughter as "Mary me darlin'." Maureen O'Hara,
Maureen O'Sullivan, and Mia Farrow are others. Then
there is Ruth McKenney, known before her death in July of
1972 for her humorous portrayals of her Irish relatives.
Her stories about "My Sister Eileen" became a best-selling
book, a play, a movie, and a Broadway musical. When
the winners of the 23rd National Book Awards were announced in 1972, the prize for fiction went to *The Complete
Storie by Flannery O'Connor,* while *The Collected Poems
of Frank O'Hara* shared in the poetry prize.

Few Irish Americans have realized their dream of owning
a castle in the Emerald Isle. On the other hand, the son
of an Irish immigrant was successful in producing a daughter who later became a princess. Tracing her Irish ancestry
right back to County Mayo, the former actress Grace Kelly,
now H. S. H. Princess of Monaco, is at present the International Chairman of the Irish American Cultural Institute.

Pat Nixon, first lady of the land, a woman whose inex-
haustible good humor has enabled her to win friends and
influence people not only in our own country but in other
countries as well, is of Irish descent. Jacqueline Onassis,
America's former first lady, furnishes us with another
striking example of a daughter of Erin's ability to influence
people. There are those who may say that Jacqueline's love
of beauty, her sense of drama and style, come from her
father. But the Irish know better. Her mother Janet Lee

was, after all, a second-generation member of an Irish family.

If there seems a dearth of famous females, let us remember that it is only relatively recently that the Irish American female has been allowed to come out of the kitchen. Besides, in the past, Irish American women have chosen for the most part to bloom unseen.

The Irish American lady who probably best exemplifies the virtues admired in our grandfather's day is Rose Kennedy. A woman of grace and beauty, she is possessed of that unfailing sense of devotion and loyalty which no doubt came to her from an Irish heritage. Her relentless faith and her burning love for her children and her country are revealed in her many kind actions and in the significant contributions she has made on behalf of retarded children, one of her own among them. Perhaps the philosophy of this courageous woman reveals itself in a poem by an Irish poet, which she recently had framed:

Lord, I do not grudge
my two sons that I have seen go out to break their
strength and die, they and a few, in bloody protest
for a glorious thing.
They shall be spoken of among their people. The
generations shall remember them and call them
blessed.
But I will speak their names to my heart in
the long nights, the little names that were familiar
once round my dead hearth.
Though I grudge them not, I weary, weary of the
long sorrow.
And yet I have my joy.
They were faithful and they fought.

CHAPTER 19

THE SIX SORROWFUL COUNTIES

DURING ONE OF the many periods when the authorities considered it treason for anyone to sing of Ireland, and poets had to use figurative titles in speaking of their country, Eire's beloved Queen of Song, Ethna Carbery, wrote a poem that ends with these lines:

There shall be peace and plenty — the kindly open door,
Blessings on all who come and go — the prosperous
    or the poor.
The misty glens and purple hills a fairer tint shall show,
When your splendid Sun shall ride the skies again —
        Mo Chraoibhin Cno!
    (My brown-haired girl! My Ireland!)

This poem, composed by Ethna Carbery shortly before her death, also contains a promise that "The silver speech our fathers knew shall once again be heard." Yet even today the singing of songs containing the slightest tinge of nationalism is considered close to treason in the six separated counties. When "Come-all-ye" singers in Northern Ireland still sing, on occasion, of their "four green fields and one of them bondaged," they might even be interrupted by a band of British soldiers.

For those who think that the counties in question have been engaged in religious controversy from the beginning of time, it may prove enlightening to learn that during the eighteenth century both Catholics and Presbyterians were united in a common cause in an effort to free themselves from the bonds of the Penal Laws. They worked side by side in the interests of religious, political, and economic freedom, and eventually their combined efforts led them into a cultural revival. So successful was the revival that in the late eighteenth and early nineteenth centuries Belfast came to be known as the "Athens of the North."

One of the most outstanding cultural events of this period was the Harp Festival. This was initiated mainly for the purpose of preserving the music, poetry, and oral traditions from the old harpers. Six of the ten harpers who took part in the festival, which began on July 11, 1792, and continued for three days, were blind, and the oldest harper was ninety-seven. Edward Bunting, only twenty-one at the time, went from harper to harper copying down the airs of old Irish melodies in his little penny notebook.

It was in Belfast only a year previous to the Harp Festival that the Society of the United Irishmen was founded. The Society's motto, suggested by the harp, was "It is new strung and shall be heard." Its worthy aims were to "found a brotherhood of affection, a communion of right, and a union of power among Irishmen of every religious persuasion, and thereby to obtain a complete reform of the legislature founded on the principles of civil, political and religious liberty."

In 1795, just outside the city of Belfast on Cave Hill, five of the founders of the Society of the United Irishmen, Wolfe Tone, Thomas Russell, Henry Joy McCracken, Samuel Neilson, and Henry Spiers climbed to MacArt's Fort and made a vow they would never cease their efforts until Ireland's independence was accomplished. Following the rising of 1798, Henry Joy McCracken was hanged at Corn

Market in Belfast's High Street only a short distance from his home.

The prosperous industrial city of Belfast, occupying a portion of both County Down and County Antrim, became the administrative center of the six-county area in 1920 when, by an Act of the British Parliament, the six counties were separated from the rest of Ireland. Belfast is a populous city — over 400,000 in the 1960s, from about 8,000 in the 1700s — that has risen quickly to its present importance. Except for its growth in population, Belfast is much the same today as it was at the beginning of the century when the writer William Bulfin described it as a very rich and very busy city. Observing the huge shipbuilding yards and watching its huge columns of smoke rise up to insult the landscape, Mr. Bulfin had to ask himself if he could possibly be in Ireland.

A town in County Down not given to manufacturing is Downpatrick. Famous long before the time of Ireland's patron saint, Downpatrick is said to have been the residence of the native kings of Ulidia. Its ancient name was, according to the old Down Survey, Rath Keltair MacDuach, or "the fortification of Keltair the son of Duach." When St. Patrick landed in nearby Saul in A.D. 432, he converted the chieftain, Dichu, and may possibly have founded the original church at Downpatrick.

Two miles northeast of Downpatrick are the remains of the twelfth century Saul Abbey, founded by St. Patrick in 440. The abbey marks the very spot where he landed on his first missionary tour in 432 and the place where he died in 461. According to the old Down Survey, there were at one time in the vicinity of Downpatrick no less than five religious houses, including convents of the Benedictines, Augustines, and Cistercian monks, friars, and nuns. Nothing is left of these old centers of piety. Nor does there remain

so much as a trace of the old monkish verse that once
graced the hallowed place of Downpatrick's cathedral to
indicate the bones that were said to have reposed beneath
the altar. So writ the monk:

> One tomb three saints contains, one vault below
> Does Bridget, Patrick, and Columba show.

But in the churchyard of the cathedral is a large granite
boulder inscribed with a cross and the name PATRIC.

Farther to the north is Holywood, originally called Ard
Mhic Nasca, "the height of the son of Nasca"; later, the
Normans changed the name to Sanctus Boscus. Here in
1572 the Irishman Sir Brian O'Neill burned down the
sixteenth century Franciscan monastery to prevent Queen
Elizabeth's troops from establishing a garrison there. The
ancestors of General Stonewall Jackson of Civil War fame
lived in Holywood before emigrating to America in 1748.

Not far out of Holywood is Crawfordsburn, the picturesque village which takes its name from the Crawfords.
One of the members of this illustrious family, William Sher-
man Crawford, though a landlord and a member of the
British Parliament, was nevertheless a staunch supporter
of the Catholic cause. Not only did this champion of civil
rights advocate Home Rule for Ireland, but he also did
much to improve the conditions of the Irish tenant farmers.

Nearby is Clandeboye, the seat of the Marquis of Dufferin and Ava. An interesting landmark of the town is
Helen's Tower, erected by the first Marquis in memory of
his mother, the poetess and author Lady Helen Dufferin.
Of particular interest is the tower's reception room where,
inscribed on the walls, are verses relating to Lady Helen's
sons, along with various verses written in dedication to her
by such poets as Kipling, Browning, and Tennyson. Lady
Helen, a granddaughter of the dramatist Richard Brinsley

Sheridan, wrote the well-known ballad "The Irish Emigrant," which begins, "I'm sitting on the stile, Mary. . . ."

The father of the famous Brontë sisters was born in the village of Emdale in County Down, a county also celebrated for the "Mountains of Mourne that sweep down to the sea." Further up on the coast and still in the county of Down is Bangor. Founded in 555 by St. Domhgall, Bangor's fame as a center of learning spread throughout Europe. Under the direction of St. Carthagus, the school attracted scholars from all over the world. Among the pupils of the school were St. Columbanus and St. Gall, pioneer missionaries to the tribes of central Europe. When England's King Alfred wanted professors for Oxford University, he recruited them from Bangor.

Across the bay from Bangor is Carrickfergus, one of the oldest towns in Ireland. Situated in Antrim, the "county of the nine glens," the town holds many ancient fortifications and is supposed to have derived its name from *carrig*, a rock, and Feargus, an Irish king. Fergus MacErc was the first Irish king of Scotland and is thought to have been drowned off the Irish coast some three hundred years after the birth of Christ. In the time of Elizabeth, Carrickfergus was a strategic location in the British campaign to curb the Irish. It was in this harbor that William III, Prince of Orange, landed in 1690 to take control of Ireland. Here too, in 1778, Paul Jones, commanding the American ship *Ranger,* defeated the English naval vessel *Drake.*

Now famous for its salt mines, Carrickfergus also has many romantic associations. Carrickfergus Castle, the first real castle to be built in Ireland, is one of the finest examples surviving in the country. It stands on a rocky spur above the harbor, with a double-towered entrance building, a castle well, and a dungeon thick with ghosts. One of the prisoners held there was Con O'Neill of Castlereagh, head

of the O'Neill clan of Ulster. He managed to escape with
the aid of a rope concealed in a cheese sent him by his
loyal wife. Con was the father of Shane O'Neill. Still
preserved in Randalstown, County Antrim, are the ruins
of the sixteenth century castle that was once the stronghold
of Shane.

Farther to the northeast and about forty miles from
Shane's Castle is Maghera in County Derry. Maghera was
the birthplace of Charles Thomson, secretary to the first
United States Congress in 1774 who wrote out the Declaration of Independence. The city of Derry in County Derry
is not properly called Londonderry. The prefix was added
in 1609 when the city was burnt by the English and placed
under the jurisdiction of London. Derry is built on a steep
hill rising from the River Foyle and it contains the best-
preserved walls of any medieval town in either England or
Ireland. Founded by St. Colmcille, this second largest city
in the province of Ulster was originally called Derry-
Colmcille, Derry meaning "oak grove" and Colmcille sig-
nifying Colum, or Dove, of the Church. Although the
saint expressed his affection for Derry in verses containing
such lines as "Derry, my own oak grove, little cell, my
home," it is now often described as a city that started life
with a hot temper which has never cooled down.

Five of the six separated counties, Antrim, Down, Derry,
Tyrone, and Armagh, touch the shores of Lough Neagh,
the largest lake in the British Isles. Because it is the chief
fruit-growing district in Ulster, County Armagh is known
as the Garden of Ulster. This county also holds many
reminders of Ireland's past glories. Its very name, Armagh
or Ard Macha ("Macha's Height") suggests it was named
after the warrior-queen Macha, while its principle city,
bearing the same name, is reputed to have been founded by
St. Patrick in 432.

Some two miles out of Armagh is Eamhain Macha, or Navan Fort, founded by Queen Macha in 300 B.C. For six hundred years Eamhain was the seat of the kings of Ulster, and in the first century A.D., under the reign of Conor MacNessa, it was the headquarters and training school of the Red Branch Knights. Many of the place-names in this area have associations with history from the pre-Christian era. Creeve Roe, for example, expresses in English letters the sound of the Irish words *Craobh Ruadh,* meaning the Red Branch.

Fermanagh, which occupies the valley of the Erne — the Erne River winds through the center of the county — also contains many interesting landmarks. The capital of this county, Enniskillen, is delightfully situated on the exact place where the river connects Upper and Lower Lough Erne. Just west of the town is the Portora Royal School which has had among its pupils Oscar Wilde and the Reverend H. F. Lyte, author of "Abide With Me." On a peninsula of Lough Erne stands Castle Caldwell, with the famous "Fiddle Stone" at its gate. The inscription on the stone gives warning to all fiddlers even as it refers to the fate of a particular fiddler back in 1770:

> On firm land only exercise your skill
> That you may play and safely drink your fill.

The area around Enniskillen was once the stronghold of the Maguires. When Fermanagh was settled by English families in the seventeenth century, the natives of the southern part of the county were separated from the British planters by a lovely chain of lakes. As a result of this separation, Irish remained the mother tongue of the southern inhabitants until quite recently. It is not surprising, then, that the dialect of these people is noticeably different from that of the inhabitants of Tyrone, Fermanagh's neighboring county. In the southern part of County Tyrone, words and expressions current in Elizabethan England are often heard, and to such an extent that scholars familiar with this dialect have been able to make clearer certain passages of Shakespeare that were obscure in the past.

So wooded is County Tyrone that it is often described as "Tyrone among the bushes." Tyrone is very hilly and picturesque. Characteristic of the countryside are the low whitewashed farmhouses, which are usually sheltered by clusters of sycamore or beech trees. Often the doors of the outhouses — more properly called outoffices in Ireland — are painted a bright orange, and in certain districts the two-wheeled carts are also painted orange.

The town of Strabane on the River Mourne boasts of having been the birthplace of John Dunlap. In 1771 Dunlap founded the *Pennsylvania Packet,* the first daily newspaper in the United States. He also printed the Declaration of Independence. During the Revolutionary War, Dunlap subscribed £4,000 to supply Washington's army and later became a member of the general's bodyguard. Gray's printing press where John Dunlap served his apprenticeship still stands in Strabane. It was here that James Wilson, grandfather of President Woodrow Wilson, was employed before he emigrated to America in 1807.

A few miles west of Cookstown, birthplace of Bernadette Devlin, is Tullaghoge Fort where the inauguration of the O'Neills was once held. In 1602 the inauguration stone was destroyed by the Elizabethan general, Lord Mountjoy. O'Neill Castle stands high above the Blackwater at Benburb, looking out over the spot where Owen Roe O'Neill inflicted a crushing defeat on the Parliamentary army in 1646. Carved in a stone on the walls of the ruined castle is a man's head; the saying goes that when the stone head falls the race will be extinct.

Shane, son of Con O'Neill, waged his last war on the English and won a crushing victory in what became known as the Battle of the Redcoats. In 1567 his head was set on a pike on the northwest gate of Dublin. Shane's oldest son by his first wife, Owen Roe, fought Cromwell. Hugh O'Neill, who was Shane's eldest son by his third wife, succeeded to Shane's chieftainship. Hugh led the rebellion of 1595 in which the English who, up until that time, embraced a relatively small area of Ireland, were the victors. In 1607, twelve years after this rebellion, Hugh, along with other Irish leaders of Gaelic Ireland, fled to the European mainland. In doing so, they not only left Ireland leaderless, but unwittingly set the stage for what is happening in Ulster today.

"Kathleen ni Houlihan, your road's a thorny way."

This observation refers to the many troubles of Ireland, especially of the six separated counties, among them the fact that an ageless and spirited woman is being victimized by an unfair press. Since most journalists covering the violence in the six counties are guarded by the British police, they are somewhat hampered in their efforts to get at the truth. Furthermore, all news is strictly censored before being released to the American press. And while most editors attempt to be objective, there are times when the happenings in Ulster are reported in a confusing and misleading way.

This has only made it more difficult for the people of other nations to understand the reasons for the Irish dilemma. Unpleasant as may be the dredging up of old grievances, it is necessary if we are to even come close to understanding the tragic situation that exists in Ulster. To suggest that the conflict is simply a struggle between Roman Catholics and Protestants is as far from the truth as to say that all Irishmen living in the north are Orangemen, or even that all Protestants are Orangemen. Indeed, many of the great Irish leaders, including Emmet, Davis, Tone, and Mitchel, were Protestants. Both economic and political differences have played their part in the conflict.

The dispute over land rights began with the exodus of the Irish earls in 1607. No sooner had these men departed than Sir Arthur Chichester, Lord Deputy of Ireland, seized their estates and settled them with Protestants from Britain. Thus there rose a new class of landlords, all of them Protestants, the native Irish having been pushed into the hills or kept on as serfs by the new owners. Meanwhile, in south Antrim and Down, Montgomery and Hamilton, the two clever Scots who had taken Con O'Neill's lands, began to gain prominence. They had done an excellent job of colonizing, settling the area with other Scots, most of them Calvinists. Their ministers formed churches and eventually brought about the formation of the Presbyterian Church in Ireland. Oddly enough, the descendants of these settlers were to be the advocates of republican democracy two hundred years later. In fact, it was this group of Presbyterian Ulstermen who helped form the Society of the United Irishmen and fought alongside their Catholic neighbors for national independence.

What has happened since to cause these people to change their allegiance? Of course, numerous factors were involved. First of all, they were forced to stand by and watch their rebel leaders be hanged. Even three of their ministers were hanged, and many of their people were sent to prison or into exile or transported to penal settlements. Under the circumstances, it was natural they should ask themselves if the goal was worth the price, especially since it was not they who were affected by the Penal Laws, but the native Irish, especially those who professed the Roman Catholic faith.

But even though the Presbyterians gradually abandoned their revolutionary principles, Catholics and Protestants continued to live together in peace until as late as 1830. Indeed, there are many instances when the Protestants made generous contributions toward the building of Catholic places of worship. Conceivably, these men of different faiths might have gone on in such fashion had it not been for the activities of the Orange Societies.

The Society of the United Irishmen had always worked toward the unity of Catholics and Protestants on the basis of their common nationality. Not so with the Orange Society. Originating in 1795 in the Diamond, an area similar to a marketplace, located in County Armagh, the Orange Order was named after William III, Prince of Orange. The Orange Order, exclusively Protestant, enjoined its members to take the following oath:

I do solemnly swear of my own free will and accord, that I will, to the utmost of my power, support and defend the present King George III, and all the heirs of the Crown, so long as they support the Protestant ascendency, the constitution, and laws of these kingdoms: and I do further swear that I am not, nor ever will be, an United Irishman, and that I never took an oath of secrecy to that society . . . .

Although this society, which was to exert such a great influence on the destinies of Ulster, contained in its Book of Rules and Regulations phrases adjuring its members to be humane and compassionate and to refrain from persecuting anyone because of his religious opinions, there were Protestants, including the English Halls, who were forced to conclude that though in principle the order was charitable, it was in practice often otherwise.

It was an order that would no longer allow a Catholic to exist in County Armagh, one which forced masters to get

rid of Catholic servants, and landlords their Catholic tenants. In a frenzy of religious fervor the fanatical element
of this society assembled at night, burning Catholic chapels,
destroying houses, forcing families to seek shelter elsewhere. People were left homeless, many of them dying
along the roadside, while others, jailed as vagrants, were
later forced to serve in the British fleet. In fact, the Orangemen carried on in much the same manner as the Black-and-
Tans who terrorized the Irish during a later period.

Members of the Orange Lodge, incidentally, were not
descendants of the Scots but of the English settlers. In
time, the English became disturbed upon observing the
liberal attitudes of the dissenting Ulster Presbyterians. In
an attempt to counteract the influence of these Ulster Presbyterians, the Orange landlords embarked on a campaign
aimed at accomplishing a reversal of the Catholic Emancipation Act of 1829 and the Reform Act of 1832, which
extended the boundaries of democracy and hit at the
corrupt pocket boroughs by which the aristocracy had
dominated Parliament. Fanning the flames of anxiety,
Hugh Boulter, Protestant Bishop of Armagh, warned the
government in London that a union of dissenters and
Catholics could mean a farewell to English influence in
Ireland. Quite understandably, the landed nobility of Ulster
were only too happy to rally to the cause so that they
might protect their financial and political interests.

The Ulster Presbyterians were subjected to further conflicting philosophies when two of their leaders, Henry
Cooke, a man with pronounced anti-Catholic views, and
Henry Montgomery, a liberal, fell into dispute. Cooke,
often accused of being a framer of Sectarianism in the
politics of Ulster, held fast to his Tory principles. Before
he died in 1868 he had successfully scattered his seeds of
bigotry, seeds which were to be nourished by roaring Hugh

Hanna and Thomas Drew, and in more recent times, by
Ian Paisley. Playing on the anxieties of the poor and
ignorant, these able orators painted grim pictures of Papists,
regaling their trusting parishioners with stories of the Pope's
prisons and torture chambers, working them up to such a
hysterical pitch they would cheer lustily at the sound of
"William" and howl like a banshee when there was a mention of the Pope.

Although thousands of Protestants as well as Catholics
have been victims of Unionist misrule, many Protestants
now consider Northern Ireland a frontier defending the
Protestant faith against the Counter-Reformation. These
Protestants forget, or are perhaps ignorant of the fact, that
the Pope supported the Protestant William, not the Catholic
James. Ironically enough, children in Protestant schools
learn that William of Orange was Ulster's savior, while
Republican offspring look upon the Protestant Wolfe Tone
as a martyr.

Out of the present conflict have come many martyrs. In
the summer of 1969, violence was escalated throughout the
six counties, causing the death of several people in Belfast
and Armagh. The civil rights marches in that long, hot
summer caused a backlash on the part of what is considered to be a somewhat irresponsible faction of the Protestant majority. Led by the Royal Ulster Constabulary
which ought to have been neutral, this faction invaded the
Catholic area of Derry city. During the invasion, the
"Apprentice Boys," the old and very determined Unionists,
sang songs about King William.

Reports concerning the ensuing violations were for a
long time confusing, the accounts having been presented
in conflicting ways depending on the bias of the journalist.
But on that day in the summer of 1969 when not only
Derry was invaded but the Bogside area too, the scene lay

open like a deep and terrible wound for all the world to see.

Following the violation of Derry in which numerous Catholic homes were burned to the ground, Northern Ireland's Prime Minister, James D. Chichester-Clark, called for troops to keep order. Actually, it was because of the desperate appeal to the British government on the part of the Catholic Bishop of Belfast, who wished to prevent the massacre of hundreds of Catholics, that troops were finally rushed to Belfast. The new contingent of troops sent by Britain as a peace-keeping force, and welcomed by the Catholics, were neutral in the beginning. But alas, with the changing winds of politics, the Labor government in London was replaced by the Tory government. Almost immediately, British troops abandoned the Protestant enclave and began concentrating on the Catholic enclaves. Then in July of 1970, General Freeland ordered an invasion of Falls Road. His troops barged into Catholic homes and smashed furniture as they searched for arms.

Up until this time, no terrorist tactics had been employed by the I.R.A. Previous to the invasion they had been represented in comparatively small numbers, and had for the most part done nothing more than serve as stewards in the non-violent civil rights marches. As a matter of fact, when the British troops, aided by the irresponsible element of the Protestant majority, destroyed Falls Road, no more than five or six I.R.A. members were there to defend the helpless Catholics. So appalled were these Catholics to find that the I.R.A. did not offer support when it was needed that certain of the Irish dubbed them the "I Ran Away Army." An ironic aftermath of the Falls Road invasion came when a British helicopter began circling overhead, and a voice dropped from the heavens.

"Don't despair," was the message the voice sent to the Irish Catholics. "The British army are your friends."

The Catholics had been given little reason to place their trust in troops. Out of the Falls Road holocaust was born the provisional wing of the I.R.A. Breaking away from the official I.R.A. group, the provisionals go back to Wolfe Tone and the Republican Ideal of Ireland, expressing their philosophy in the creed, "We will defend; we will attack; we will call the state of Northern Ireland to be ungovernable."

That the provisional wing of the I.R.A. has shown the state of Northern Ireland to be ungovernable can hardly be denied. Much has been written about the needless bombing carried on by this group. On the other hand, few writers call attention to the fact that the first bomb exploded was set off by the Protestant Volunteer Forces back in 1969 in an attempt to bring down O'Neill's supposedly liberal form of government. Indeed, the diverse and sometimes merely incomplete accounts of the conflict have tended to create an impression that the I.R.A. is the only militant faction operating in the six counties. On the contrary, one of the most active units is the Ulster Volunteer Force. It was members of this force who looted and drove countless numbers of Catholics from their homes back in 1920 shortly after the six counties were separated from the rest of Ireland.

In 1966 the Ulster Volunteer Force declared war on the then inactive I.R.A., and after carrying out a series of murders, was outlawed as a sordid conspiracy of criminals by Terence O'Neill, then Prime Minister of the province. It is the U.V.F., so often sheltered under the wings of that familiar phrase, "other loyalist organizations," that the army and police believe responsible for the 1972 assassinations. Members of this organization are also thought to have been responsible for the assassination threats received by six leaders of the Social Democratic and Labor Party. The party's chief manager, Paddy Devlin, had an attempt made

on his life. Another leading member of the party whose
life was threatened is Ian Cooper. A Derry Protestant,
Cooper was so appalled at the lack of housing and at the
conditions of so many middle-aged Catholic men, some of
whom had never been able to get work in their entire lives,
that he forsook the Apprentice Boys and the Unionist Party
to become a civil rights leader.

While the background of the conflict is indeed of a
religious nature, anyone closely associated with the six
separated counties will hasten to point out that the conflict
has been ignited by the industrialists. Surprising as it may
seem, Britain has extracted a lot of poundage out of Ireland,
the revenue coming mainly from insurance and bricks, and,
of course, from the shipyards. Unfortunately, as Mr. John
Lynch, Prime Minister of the Republic of Ireland until
1973, has so often remarked, "The British government has
allowed itself to be dragged into a jungle of Unionist
politics where there is neither justice nor reason."

Justice is the key word, or more appropriately, injustice.
Let us take a look at some of the injustices that prevail
in this section of Ireland where a man's religion determines
his whole life and economic prospects.

First of all, in local elections one has no vote unless he
owns a house. Since Catholics, who comprise but one-third
of the population, find it all but impossible to acquire a
house — that is, unless they are loyal to the Unionist government — they are often forced to emigrate, thus enabling
the controlling forces to successfully maintain their two-
thirds majority. Since members belonging to the majority
group are usually landowners and householders, they are
often permitted some three or four votes to the Catholic's
none.

Other injustices visited on the Irish Catholics have to
do with employment. In many instances, particularly in the

factories, only the women, who can be hired at a much cheaper rate, are given employment. To make matters worse, there are certain employers who simply would not dream of hiring a Catholic. In fact, Mrs. O'Neill, whose husband was at one time Prime Minister of the six-county area, placed an advertisement in the newspapers some years ago that read: "Protestant girl required for housework."

"All the members of the minority groups are asking for is that they be allowed to live as others live," an Irishman said sadly, "and not have to live in constant fear they will be flung into prison to be subjected to torture and detained without trial."

An Irishwoman visiting the United States who had lived through several terrible years in the troubled counties was saddened to find out how little the people of other nations understood the problems of the Irish people living in Ulster. "Please do not judge the people involved from such a distance," she implored. "Instead of calling them hateful, jealous, greedy murders, try to remember it is not northern England that is occupied by Irish soldiers."

And what of the opposing faction? Surely there must be compassionate men among them. But they are afraid. Afraid of losing their present dominance in a state which is basically their own, and has been for fifty-one years. Afraid of bringing to an end a situation in which they are both judge and jury, one in which they have complete political power and a link with England, who subsidizes them to the tune of a hundred million pounds a year.

Just how a measure of peace will be accomplished is difficult to say. Mr. Lynch, who has long maintained that a divided Ireland will never be happy or at peace, expressed his desire for a United Ireland in these words:

The unity we seek is not something forced but a free and genuine union of those living in Ireland, based on a mutual respect and guaranteed by a form, or forms of Government authority in Ireland providing for progressive improvement of social, economic and cultural life in a just and peaceful environment.

Stressing the need for establishing a constitution for a United Ireland that should be as acceptable to the Protestant ethos as to the Catholic ethos, Mr. Lynch went on to suggest: "The Irish people as a whole should draw their constitutions and laws from Christian ethic, making certain the system does not infringe in any way on, or derogate from, the right of private conscience, personal belief and the free practice of religion."

There are Catholics and Protestants in Northern Ireland who are still managing to live together peaceably, and who weep with each other over the burning of a house or the death of a loved one. It is further important to call attention to the fact that most English people do not approve of their government's actions in Northern Ireland. But although it is heartening to note that certain British men of power are finally beginning to realize that the solution may lie in a United Ireland, the blood bath still goes on. In its wake, headlines spread the news about IRISH PROTESTANTS DEMANDING ARMS, PROTESTANTS BARRICADING AREAS TO BLOCK PEACE, CATHOLICS AND PROTESTANTS SHARING FEARS, IRISHWOMEN ASKING FOR PEACE.

The Roman Catholic people of the Bogside area, upon witnessing the arrival of the British military power, threw their hats in the air and danced with joy. Now, having endured the long baptism of blood during which time they were surrounded, as one Catholic housewife put it, "by the British Army, the Royal Ulster Force, the Territorial Army, the Ulster Defense Regiment, and the Ulster Defense Association," they can only hope devoutly that the various troops will pack up their guns and go home.

So appalling is the situation in the six sorrowful counties that even the poets find it hard to write so much as line about it. Gone are the Ethna Carberys who were once forced to refer to Ireland through figurative Gaelic expressions. But perhaps the oppressed ones, held down by a government that has for so long tried to strip them of the last shreds of dignity, have looked back down the years to reflect on a poem written by the blind poet Anthony Raftery:

> Look at me now,
> My face to the wall,
> Playing music
> To empty pockets.

CHAPTER 20

NEW LOOK ON THE LAND

Slow is the winding call
On the shades of Cormac sleeping westward.

ALTHOUGH THESE ARE lines taken from a poem composed
by an ancient Irish bard, they might very well have been
written in our own times. Slow indeed is the winding call
on the shades of Ireland. The progress of the civil rights
movement in Ireland is often discouraging — one is
tempted to say futile. But it is well to remember that when
it comes to change, Ireland has always moved at a relatively
slow pace.

Furthermore, the Irishman has always had an esteem
for moral law and authority, which allows him to submit
to governmental restrictions of a sort that would outrage
liberals in other Western democracies. The Constitution
of the Irish Republic, drawn up by Eamon de Valera in
1937, forbids divorce and provides for censorship that has
banned the books of a number of Irish writers, along with
the works of the Catholic novelist, Graham Greene. Defending its precepts, the former Jewish Lord Mayor of
Dublin, Robert Briscoe, once said, "But you must remember that this Constitution was drawn to suit the Irish people
who are very strict in the matter of morals."

There are a few who take issue with the severe requirements of the laws of the Irish Republic. Recently, a group

of Women's Liberation militants, protesting the fact that it is illegal for an Irish druggist to sell any sort of contraceptive devices, set off for Belfast. Flouting the law, the forty-three defiant women shopped diligently there for the forbidden paraphernalia and then marched to the train that would take them back to Dublin. Observing their activities with more than a passing degree of interest, a middle-aged porter simply could not resist calling out, "All aboard for the sex-thirty train!"

The Women's Liberation movement appears to have had little appeal to most Irishwomen. Perhaps many of them share this opinion, stated by an Irishwoman recently: "It is the man who needs to be liberated," she said. "And the best way for him to accomplish the liberation is to have a talented wife."

Of course, many of the Women's Liberation members are not militants. Indeed, a good many of their members are more interested in the type of revolution that leads to emotional, cultural, mental, and above all, spiritual growth. Other women's groups in Ireland have somewhat different interests. The Irish Countrywomen's Association, for example, has been relentless in its campaign to improve the quality of television, and it is interested in seeing more programs relating to homemaking. Another worthy undertaking is the "Bring and Buy Cake Sale" project in Dublin which makes it possible for a hundred or more old people to go on an outing during the summer months.

Women, Wives and Widows, a new magazine whose primary purpose is to establish communication between 127 thousand widows and their families, announced publication of its first issue in June of 1971. There are few rich widows in Ireland; consequently, the periodical furnishes information concerning pensions, pension increases, and legislation, and keeps the reader informed of her entitlements and extra benefits. Since the title of the magazine was selected in recognition of the fact that the widows had experienced the three phases of womanhood, the single state, the married state, and widowhood, its editors are hopeful that it will be of interest to all women.

Undoubtedly, it is to the credit of the women of Eire that there is very little juvenile delinquency in Ireland. Possibly the inroads of industrialization may change all this. At present there is no indication of such a change. The fact that the Irish child is brought up with a strong sense of family solidarity, and is not easily given to boredom, may prevent it from happening. Like their counterparts of the early part of the twentieth century, many of Ireland's young people are beginning to show a lively interest in their country's past.

Not long ago, seven teenagers in a northern Galway town launched a campaign to preserve hundreds of the country's "fairy forts." At one time the Irish farmers were reluctant to disturb them, but now that the myth of fairies is dying out, hundreds of these prehistoric settlements are being bulldozed to make way for crops, pasture lands, and roads. The teenagers are determined to prevent any more of the forts being destroyed until they are at least examined by experts. In their attempts to jog public conscience they have mounted an exhibition in the town of Tuam showing a homemade plaster-cast ring fort, along with the type of articles that can be found in the "fairy forts."

At this point, however, people seem less concerned with rescuing the inhabitants of the fairy forts than with digging their graves deeper. The Irish are sensitive about their leprechauns. They may believe in them, but they don't wish anyone to know they do. When the actor Donald O'Connor attempted to film a television documentary for a British firm in 1971, he came close to being run out of

Dublin by angry Irishmen who accused him of depicting them as a bunch of leprechauns.

But if the educated man of modern Ireland has been successful in clamping the lid on the "little people," he has had no success whatsoever explaining away such legendary healers as Biddy Early. Born in County Clare, Biddy not only acquired a reputation for being able to cure all sorts of diseases, but for acquiring four husbands during her lifetime. She married the last one, a man by the name of Pat O'Brien, when she was over eighty years old. Accused by some of being a witch, she used her magic bottle of colored water to foretell death, cure human beings and even farm animals, read minds, find lost objects, and predict the results of horse races. It was from the story of Biddy Early and her miraculous bottle that Lady Gregory gleaned much of the material for her book, *Visions and Beliefs in the West of Ireland.*

Although Biddy died in 1847, there has always been someone to take her place. The best-known healer in Ireland at present is Finbarr Nolan, a young man living in Aughnacliffe, County Longford. Young Nolan is the seventh son of a seventh son and therefore gifted with magical powers. When he first discovered his ability to heal, he began practicing on a restricted basis. But as time went on he found it necessary to expand, and with the aid of his six brothers he set up operations in a building in Arva, where constables are better equipped to handle the large crowds attracted by his healing powers. People come from all over Ireland and from America and Britain to be healed by Nolan. His method consists of the laying-on of hands along with a liberal sprinkling of holy water. At this point, the clergy is taking a somewhat jaundiced view of Nolan's operations, since he appears to be combining the ritual of the Church with the superstitions of the ancient Celts.

Even today the parish priest on a local level exerts a great deal of control and influence over the lives of the people. His image, however, has changed considerably. If he still concerns himself with the morals of the young — up until now the clergy have managed to scotch all attempts to build drive-in movies — he goes about it in an entirely different manner than he did during the period when the Irish considered the parish priest to be on a par with the Heavenly Father Himself.

Today's young people of Ireland, though respectful toward their pastors, have come to the conclusion that certain decisions ought to be left to themselves alone. When hot pants were the rage, they were so popular in such places as the seaside resort of Ballybunion that one was inclined to believe they were some sort of Girl Scout uniform. There are, of course, a few of the old parish priests who still measure virtue by the amount of clothes a girl leaves off. A certain conservative man of the cloth happened to be strolling along the beach one Sunday afternoon when he saw a bikini-clad girl who belonged to his parish. Enlisting the aid of another young parishioner, he sent her a note advising that she would do well to stick to the one-piece suit in the future. With the aid of pen and paper and that ever-useful weapon of the Irish called wit, the offender wrote back, "Father, which piece shall I leave off?"

Actually, today's parish priest has more to do than occupy himself with such childish pastimes as snooping about hedgerows to interrupt the overtures of some young swain courting his girl. The majority of the younger clergy have been educated along more progressive lines — Maynooth College supplies two-thirds of the present hierarchy — and are well aware that the Church cannot remain a purely religious institution, but that it must become more responsive to the pressing problems of our times.

There is Father Lennon, for example, the port chaplain who established a seaman's club called Anchor House near the Quays of Cork city when it was feared that the Irish girls were endangering their morals by consorting with foreign sailors. The club provides a bar and dance floor, where local girls supply the need for dancing partners. The club also has a room where the sailors may watch Irish television. Proselytizing is no part of the program whatsoever, and since the Reverend Mr. Kennedy of the Church of Ireland shares the supervisory duties of the club with Father Lennon, it would appear that this is a somewhat ecumenical project as well.

The Church's new concern for social welfare was again evident when Dr. Eamonn Casey was appointed Bishop of Kerry. Bishop Casey established a reputation in England for dealing with homesick and disoriented Irish Catholics. In 1963 he established the Catholic Housing Society in London. He is now attempting to find a practical approach to the problems of a section of Ireland in which agriculture and tourism are the economic mainstays. One of his primary concerns has to do with the effect of tourism on the character of the people and the possibility that it may bring about a corruption of the old values and destruction of the old simplicities.

"Should we let Killarney grow like Dublin or London?" he shouts, and then answering his own question, "Over my dead body!".

Another evil the Kerry Bishop is attempting to combat relates to the practice of letting children go to work in hotels at the age of thirteen or fourteen. Deploring the fact that these young people are being forced into making decisions that most people would ordinarily not have to make until the age of twenty-one, he reminds the Irish people that "These kids are at their most impressionable age," and then adds thoughtfully, "I want them to see only the best and nicest things — there are enough awful ones later in life."

Although not all of the hierarchy are in accord with the views of Bishop Casey, much credit is given Cardinal William Conway, Primate of all Ireland, Archbishop of Armagh, for having appointed him in the first place. Indeed, it would seem that the majority of the clergy are aware that some dissent is needed and that a more varied hierarchy will not only produce a more inspired people but may also keep the more individualistic priests from leaving the Church.

Evidence that numerous members of the clergy are concerning themselves with matters that go beyond the salvation of the soul can be found all over Ireland. In a remote corner of Donegal, Father James McDyer, dismayed because many young people were fleeing the countryside, brought about what has been referred to as the "Miracle of Glencolumbkille." He proved in the process that miracles are the by-product of faith, hope, and hard work. Father McDyer persuaded the people to organize a cooperative to find markets for their produce, urged them to get off the dole and obtain subsidies for their small holdings, and furthermore talked them into building a hall so the young people might have a place for recreation. Eventually, he was able to establish a canning factory in Glencolumbkille, and later on, after reviving interest in the traditional craft of weaving Donegal tweeds, he built a tweed-weaving factory.

Responding to a letter sent by Pope Paul to the Guardians of the great Marian Shrines in the world, telling them they must promote peace and save these holy places, another spirited man of the cloth, Father Gabriel Harty, National Director of the Rosary at Knock Shrine, cried out, "Great is the crime of those who destroy or ignore our material monuments and our natural human culture; greater still is the crime of those who, by their failure, destroy the heritage of a nation's soul!"

No destroyer of monuments is Father McDyer. In addition to saving souls and giving proper attention to the more mundane needs of man, he has also found time to involve himself with the preservation of Ireland's ancient landmarks. In an effort to interest more tourists in Glencolumbkille, an area rich in prehistoric and early Christian monuments, he commissioned a guidebook to the monuments. Published in 1971, the book, compiled by Dr. Michael Herrity of the Archaeology Department in University College, Dublin, contains references to the megalithic tombs in Malin More, which are said to be the most massive and spectacular group of portal dolmens in Ireland.

Ballintubber, located near Westport in County Mayo, also has been blessed with a savior of landmarks. Father Egan has known the joy of seeing the restoration of the thirteenth century Augustinian abbey carried out. "The abbey that refused to die" was founded in 1216 by King Cathal O'Connor of Connacht. Mass has been said within the abbey walls for over 750 years, despite Cromwellian efforts to destroy it. Through Father Egan's efforts, a commemorative stamp has been issued in honor of Ballintubber Abbey.

Considering the energetic activities of these priests, and their total dedication to so many aspects of Irish life, it is not surprising that Ireland is said to be more Catholic than the Pope. Here is an island where religion is dynamic, alive, a place where an Archbishop dares to reflect the attitudes of his flock by shouting, "In the past the congregation has been taught to be a congregation of Puritans. This will have to be changed and a bit of disturbance is the best thing that ever happened." Or where one might openly criticize the Pope for having spent money on building an auditorium for papal audiences instead of spending it on apartment dwellings for Rome's some 70 thousand shanty dwellers.

There was a time when Irish cardinals and bishops opposed any war of defense being waged by their oppressed flock. Some of them still do. But the flock — and even many of the clergy — are no longer willing to put up with such high-handed moral dictatorship. Those who have seen the brutal treatment accorded prisoners at Long Kesh and such places as the Armagh jail have no fear of speaking out. Father McManus said not long ago, "This State was conceived and born in violence, and by the gun it has been maintained. And those who created it and those who sustain it are the real men of violence."

Lest it be thought that the Catholics of Ireland restrict their religious practices to attending daily Mass, climbing up the rocky slope of Croagh Patrick, or making rounds at holy wells, it might be well to call attention to the highly developed lay apostolic movement that sprang into life during the last century. One of the strongest of these apostolic movements is the Legion of Mary, a volunteer force having an active membership of more than 100 thousand. Founded in Dublin in 1921, its members devote themselves to charitable works, including baby-sitting for working mothers, spending nights in the homes of lone elderly people, and offering guidelines to alcoholics.

Yet for all of their involvement in charitable works, and the efforts of countless members of the Catholic community to uplift the spirits of others, it would seem that one of the most pressing problems of Ireland is the need to rid itself of its theocratic image. And while it is true that until very recently the State acknowledged the special position of the Holy Catholic Church as the guardian of the Faith, under the Constitution, people of all faiths have always been guaranteed their liberty. It is unfortunate that the Protestants of Ulster who are opposed to a United Ireland have an exaggerated impression of the influence the Church has on affairs of State.

One way to dissipate such an erroneous impression is through educational reform, a subject that has been the main topic of conversation in Ireland for the past thirty years. As it is generally known, primary school education, compulsory for all children up to the age of fourteen or fifteen, is under the direct supervision of the Catholic and Protestant clergy. But even though Protestants in the Republic of Ireland are satisfied with the present system of school control, that is, in the sense that its financial operations are administered with complete impartiality, such a system is bound to create other problems. In Ballydehob, for example, there are two national schools, one under the jurisdiction of the parish priest, one managed by the Church of Ireland's minister, and still another school for the children of less than twenty families of other Protestant faiths. The attitude of tolerance is commendable, the advantages to be gained by combining the three schools, obvious.

It is generally agreed in Ireland that the present system of education needs to be modernized. Nevertheless, the government plan to create what has been referred to as the comprehensive or community school has caused a furor among the populace. Some feel these proposed larger schools, having the advantage of being able to cater to the aptitudes and ability of all people, can best answer the country's needs. But it has never been proven, at least to the satisfaction of most educators, that larger schools provide a better education than smaller schools. Neither are they convinced of the advantages of a wide curriculum. Indeed, the humanists fear that centralization, with its inevitable offspring, standardization, will in the end bring

about a loss of individuality, and, as Bishop Casey remarked, "the destruction of the old simplicities."

A number of ordinary, concerned citizens resent the
bulldozing of the small independent centers of culture and
are afraid that the withdrawal of religious teachers will
mean religion will no longer be relevant. These citizens
point out that forcing the small schools out of existence
is undemocratic, that it interferes with the rights of parents
and teachers.

"But it is happening everywhere," say the advocates.

"And why should Ireland join the crowd?" retort the
dissenters, who hasten to add, "Especially since they are
offering no new wine, only old wine in bigger bottles."

The final question in the minds of concerned citizens is
simply this: "What are they giving us with one hand and
what are they taking away with the other?"

Aware of the government's propensity for seeing only a
financial solution to a complex problem, the Irish are not
about to accept any "pig in the poke" attempts to bring
about educational reform. The choice open to them, if
indeed there is a choice, appears to be between an authentic
community school and a totalitarian state, so-called community school. Assessing what may be taken from them,
Desmond Fennel wrote in the *Irish Press*:

Between the 1920s and the early '60s the Irish
nation in the twenty-six counties built up a public
value-system which was also accepted, in its essentials,
by the nationalist people in the North. Its sacred cows
ranged from the two-teacher rural school to Dail
Eireann; from the Easter Rising, the Friday fast and
sexual purity to the politician with a national record,
the minister of religion, and loyalty to our people in
the North. It included the graves of dead heroes, the
quiet unintelligible Mass. High in honour stood the

Irish language, the idea of rural life, the inviolability
of marriage, the virgin (especially if consecrated to
God), national ballads and the Angelus on the national
radio, and Radio Eireann itself. This was the public
value-system which was restraining the latent violence
in our nation. How ironic that those who have shown
most zeal in wrecking it take the lead in parading
"abhorrence of violence in the North!"

Ultraconservative though Mr. Fennel's views may seem,
they reflect the thinking of many of his fellow countrymen.
In a nation where community life and community development have always been of prime importance, it is not surprising that a system of education geared toward urbaniza-
tion and industrialization, and even toward emigration,
should be viewed with dismay by a large segment of the
population.

Perhaps the greatest criticism of the Irish educational
system is that it is based on money and class. No matter
what his intelligence, or lack of it, the rich child receives
the best possible education available while the working-
class child, no matter what his talents, must leave school
in his middle teens.

But it must be remembered that from out of Irish schools
came men like John O'Donoghue, who began his life in a
two-room house in Kerry. In his boyhood days, seeing a
lonely place where ruins of old houses deserted after the
famine still stood, he used to say a verse made up by himself and his sisters. "Goodbye, goodbye to all of you,
wherever you may be, at home among the ruined walls or
scattered on the lea."

In the foreword to O'Donoghue's autobiographical novel
In a Quiet Land, Sean O'Faolain calls attention to the
author's awareness and his responsiveness to the presence
of traditions, and goes on to say, "Such customs and beliefs,

the very essence of folk culture and the stuff of poetry, precious at all times, are becoming rarer than gold."

Although there are still writers in Ireland who feel they must go abroad to be discovered — one literary columnist complained that "Irish literary blood is draining away into foreign gutters" — there are many who choose to remain. John B. Keane is one of the latter. Operating a pub in his hometown of Listowel, County Kerry, Keane began writing plays after he had closed up his pub for the night. While some of his works have been staged in Cork and Dublin, they have little chance of ever reaching an international audience. But for all of that, Keane, who writes of and for the Irish and in a somewhat melodramatic vein, is content to write for the rural theater, which he maintains is as international as Broadway or the West End because, as he puts it, "Yeats and Shakespeare were country boys."

Back in the early nineteenth century, the people in the ancient market town of Listowel were too poor to buy books. But the picture has changed: during the past fifty years alone, twenty-six writers from the area have been recognized as major talents. To celebrate this gift of the flowing pen, a Listowel Writers' Week was initiated in 1971.

Playing an important role in the activities of Writers' Week in Listowel are John B. Keane and Bryan Mac-Mahon, the local schoolmaster, who is internationally known as a short story writer and novelist. As a part of the program for Writers' Week, short story and theatre workshops are held, as well as literary competitions. The 1973 gathering in Listowel attracted many young writers from the United States. When one of the visitors asked a local woman how she liked meeting all these writers, she answered, "Sure I meet them every day of the week."

The theatre is experiencing a rebirth in the Irish countryside. There are eight hundred amateur dramatic societies

participating in the regional drama competitions, which
lead to an all-Ireland competition. Such has been the impact
of the small-town dramatic societies that a number of
country boys have taken to writing plays. John Keane,
writing in his autobiography, had this to say about the
development of rural theatre: "It is taking a strange shape,
but the stranger the better, and the more independent of
outside influence, the better."

Obviously, the adaptation of *Borstal Boy* and the success
of Brian Friel's *Philadelphia Here I Come* have both helped
stir the Abbey Theatre out of its apathy. No doubt the
famous theatre would have experienced a renaissance in
any case, after Tomas MacAnna was appointed a member
of its Board of Directors. In January of 1972, the amazing
Sinead de Valera had her story *The Enchanted Lake*
produced as a play in Gaelic in the Abbey. MacAnna himself has written a book about the Abbey Theatre which is
soon to be published. During the summer of '72 under the
auspices of the Irish American Cultural Institute, this
brilliant theatre director conducted a class at St. Thomas
College in St. Paul, Minnesota.

The Irish American Cultural Institute is continuing its
program of encouraging writers in the Gaelic language.
The third in a series of annual awards for literature were
made at a presentation ceremony at the Abbey Theatre in
the fall of 1971. The awards, the largest ever granted in
Ireland, were made possible by the generosity of Patrick
and Aimee Butler and Larry and Betty O'Shaughnessy.

Another Irish American organization, the Ancient Order
of Hibernians, is showing considerable interest in helping
bolster the country's economy. Only recently, six hundred
of its members met in Dublin to formulate plans and they
are already in the process of setting up various businesses
in Ireland.

The Irish themselves, that is, the affluent ones, are making an effort to start up new enterprises. The Guinness Brewery people invested in a company for developing cruises on the Shannon. They are also establishing a metallurgical plant in Waterford which expects to employ around a hundred people.

The new wave of export industry that began back in the sixties has brought about the introduction of products not previously manufactured in Ireland. Irish-manufactured electronic products, for example, have made their mark in some of the world's most sophisticated and demanding export markets. According to the Eire-Ireland Bulletin of the Department of Foreign Affairs, torsion balances from Ireland were use to weigh the first moondust obtained by the United States. The factory that produces them is the largest of its kind in Northern Europe.

Although the country has in the past been almost completely tied economically to England, it is interesting to note that Japanese and United States companies are investing in Ireland so as to find a back door to the United Kingdom and the Common Market. The greatest hope for Ireland's economy as a whole comes from the boost in the cattle trade which is expected from their entry into the Common Market. But despite the fact that the Irish people voted by an overwhelming majority in favor of Ireland's joining the Common Market on May 10, 1972 — a number of the Irish remain apprehensive about the outcome of entering what they refer to as a jungle. As one Irishman put it, "I fear the Market even when bearing gifts."

In some quarters, it is even hoped that entry into the Common Market may help create an atmosphere more congenial to the culmination of a United Ireland. "Give Ireland back to the Irish" was the cry of the Beatles on a record banned in Britain. And of course it is Britain who must make some sort of constructive move.

Meanwhile, in the Republic of Ireland, where over 90 percent of the inhabitants are Catholic, a new Irish Government took office on March 14, 1973. Following a victory of the National Coalition of Fine Gael and Labour in the general election held on February 28, Mr. Liam Cosgrave, whose father, William T. Cosgrave, was the first President of the Executive Council of the Irish Free State, was elected Prime Minister. In another recent election, the people of the Republic of Ireland — no doubt with the hope of encouraging Britain to bring peace to the six troubled counties — elected a London-born Protestant, Erskine Childers, as the Republic's next president. Childers took office in June of '73 when the ninety-one-year-old de Valera and his wife moved from the presidential mansion to a retirement home in the Dublin suburbs.

No longer will the Irish be able to call themselves "Ourselves Alone." Industrialization is already igniting the land, and like a candle held in a dead man's hand, can never be blown out. While this sort of progress is needed, it would be a pity if the rush of progress were to mean a loss of Irish individuality, a greater pity still if the "four green fields" were to be marred with the scars of pollution.

Perhaps a miracle will come about so that a country which has survived so many onslaughts will somehow be able to preserve her ancient charm and beauty. It may be that Ireland, whose story has the scope of an epic novel, a river that rushes down from such a high mountain it never reaches valley or sea, will be spared when the end of the world comes to pass. And if Kathleen ni Houhilan is spared, then she will be ready to deal out the proper number of currachs so that her people, hardy enough to survive in the deepest and most turbulent waters, can sail off to the land of Tir na nOg where "you get happiness for a penny." There, with Patrick guarding the one side and Bridget the other, the Irish people will remain young for all eternity.

SIGNIFICANT DATES IN IRISH HISTORY

B.C.	6000	Earliest known inhabitants in Ireland
	3000	Construction of earliest known megalithic tombs
	1500	Irish bronze and gold art objects being exported to the Continent
A.D.	432	Arrival of St. Patrick
	563	Colmcille's mission to Iona
	750	Approximate highpoint of Irish craftsmanship in art metalworking (Tara Brooch, Ardagh Chalice)
	795	Beginning of Norse raids
	1002	Brian Boru recognized as "Emperor of the Irish"
	1014	Battle of Clontarf: Brian Boru defeats the Danes, but is himself slain
	1169	Anglo-Norman invasion
	1315-18	The Bruces come to Ireland's aid
	1366-67	Statutes of Kilkenny
	1494	Poyning's Law: a measure to ensure English supremacy in Ireland
	1541	Henry VIII declared "King of Ireland"
	1562-67	Shane O'Neill's war against English supremacy, ending in his death
	1595-1603	Hugh O'Neill's rebellion
	1601	Irish-Spanish defeat at the Battle of Kinsale
	1607	Flight of the Earls

1649-50	Cromwell's campaign in Ireland; wholesale confiscation of Irish lands
1688-91	The war between the Irish supporters of King James II and William III, ending in the fall of Limerick and, shortly afterwards, the introduction of the penal laws
1783	English Parliament's Act of Renunciation renounces any claim to govern Ireland
1791	Formation of the United Irishmen (in Belfast) by Wolfe Tone
1798	United Irishmen rebel against increasing tyranny of British government
1800	Act of Union suppresses the Act of Renunciation
1803	Rising organized by Robert Emmett
1828	O'Connell wins the Clare Election
1829	Catholic Emancipation; minimal civil rights granted
1842	The periodical *The Nation* founded
1845-50	The Great Famine: 2 million dead or emigrated
1848	Young Ireland movement
1854	Catholic University of Ireland founded; J. H. Newman first rector
1867	Fenian rebellion
1870	Gladstone's first Land Act
	Home Rule movement launched in Ireland by Isaac Butt
1875	Charles Stewart Parnell elected to Parliament
1879	The Land League founded by Michael Davitt
1879-82	Gladstone's first Home Rule Bill (1880): the "land war"
1891	Death of Parnell
1893	Foundation of the Gaelic League
	Gladstone introduces second Home Rule bill which is defeated in the House of Lords

1899	Irish Literary Theatre founded, forerunner of the Abbey Theatre
1905	Sinn Fein established by Arthur Griffith
1913	Third Home Rule bill twice defeated in House of Lords Ulster Volunteers established Irish Citizen Army founded Irish Volunteers founded
1914	Home Rule bill passed; operation suspended until end of World War II
1916	Easter Rising begins, April 21
1918	General Election; 73 out of 104 candidates were Sinn Feiners
1919	Independent Irish parliament, Dail Eireann, meets in Dublin on January 21 to declare independence
1919-21	England suppresses this democratically elected government. The "troubles" follow, with the IRA defending the new Irish government
1920	The infamous Black-and-Tans arrive from England England legislates the partition of Ireland
1921	Truce between England and Ireland
1922	Irish Free State comes into being, ratifying partition Civil War begins
1927	New Fianna Fail party, with de Valera as head, enters the Dail
1932	de Valera becomes Taoiseach (Prime Minister)
1937	New constitution passed, changing the name Irish Free State to Eire Dr. Douglas Hyde elected first President of Eire
1949	Republic of Ireland officially declared
1959	de Valera becomes President

1969   Civil rights troubles break out in Northern
              Ireland, gradually escalating to guerrilla war
              between the IRA and the English army

1973   Vote by the people of the Irish Republic
              removes from its constitution a clause giving
              special status to Roman Catholic Church
              Liam Cosgrave elected Prime Minister
              Erskine Childers, a London-born Protestant,
              elected President of the Irish Republic

IRISH PROVERBS

Its own child is bright to the carrion crow.

Handsome is as handsome does.

A woman's tongue is a thing that does not rust.

A thorn in dung, the tooth of a hound, and the saying of a fool are the three sharpest things in existence.

The three things that run swiftest are a stream of fire, a stream of water, and a stream of falsehood.

The peacemaker does not go free.

A wise woman is better than a foolish doctor.

Don't spread your cloak any farther than you can cover it.

Bare is the companionless shoulder.

He who stares into the middle of the fire does be heavily in love.

While the cat is out the mouse will dance.

However long the road there comes a turning.

It is not the same to go to the king's house as to come from it.

What is gathered meanly, it goes badly.

Better the fighting than the loneliness.

Rattling silver, rattling sorrow.

The devil is good to his own in this world and bad to them in the next.

Pride goeth before a fall.

It is difficult to tame the proud.

What a person does not spend himself, his enemy spends it.

The old person is a child twice.

The mouth of the grave gives to the needy one.

Death puts its own appearance on everyone.

Death is the poor man's doctor.

Call no man a wise man till the worms have done with him.

If you want praise, die, if you want blame, marry.

There's hope from the ocean but none from the grave. *(An emigrant proverb.)*

In every land hardness is in the north of it, softness in the south, industry in the east, and fire and inspiration in the west.

IRISH BLESSINGS

God grant you to be happy as the flowers in May.

The Almighty shower down blessings on your head day and night.

God's fresh blessings be about you.

The blessings of God be with you ever and always.

That the Divine Infant will light the road before you every night and day.

That every hair on your head might turn into a candle to light your way to heaven.

May the smile of the Lord light you to glory.

May the light of Heaven shine on your grave.

May your bed be made in Heaven.

May God and His Holy Mother take the harm of the year away from you.

Health and long life to you.

That the doctor might never earn a pound out of you.

May you get the reward in heaven that's been denied you for your goodness on this earth.

That 'tis no plain priest you'll have to annoint you but a bishop at the very least.

That the devil mightn't hear of your death till you're safe inside Heaven.

That the ten toes of your feet might always steer you clear of misfortune.

That money may fly in the doors to you if it be for your soul's good.

That the dust of your carriage wheels may blind the eyes of your foes.

That the sons of your sons may smile up in your face.

That the frost might never afflict your spuds.

May the pitcher be filled with wine instead of water the next time you call to the house.

May the blessing of Light be on you —
light without and light within.
May the blessed sunlight shine on you
and warm your heart till it glows like
a great peat fire, so that the stranger
may come and warm himself at it, and
also a friend.
And may the light shine out of the two
eyes of you, like a candle set in two
windows of a house, bidding the wanderer
to come in out of the storm.

And may the blessing of the Rain be on you —
the soft sweet rain. May it fall upon your
spirit so that all the little flowers may
spring up, and shed their sweetness on the air.
And may the blessing of the Great Rains be on
you, may they beat upon your spirit and wash
it fair and clean, and leave there many a
shining pool where the blue of heaven shines,
and sometimes a star.

And may the blessing of the Earth be on you —
the great round earth; may you ever have a
kindly greeting for them you pass as you're
going along the roads.
May the earth be soft under you when you
rest upon it, tired at the end of the day, and may
it rest easy over you when, at the last, you lay
out under it;
May it rest so lightly over you, that your soul
may be out from under it quickly, and up, and
off, and on its way to God.

For a young man contemplating marriage:
That you might have nicer legs than your own under your
   table before the new spuds are up.
For a journey:
God spare you and those you meet until your journey is done.
That holy Saint Christopher might always be a passenger in
   your car.
At the end of a story:
Safe be your storyteller.

Wishing you always —
Walls for the wind
And a roof for the rain
And tea beside the fire.
Laughter to cheer you
And those you love near you,
And all that your heart might desire!

May the road rise to meet you.
May the wind be always at your back.
May the sun shine warm upon your face,
And the rains fall soft upon your fields.
And until we meet again
May God hold you in the palm of his hand.

FESTIVALS AND EVENTS IN IRELAND TODAY

There is almost always something lively and colorful going on in Ireland — music, theatre, films, local festivals, greyhound and horse racing, sailing regattas, angling, competitions, golf tournaments. The following is a list of the more important cultural and sporting events that take place annually.

February
International Rugby Football, Dublin
Exhibition of Irish Publishing, Ireland House, Dublin
March
Dublin Arts Festival
Dublin Theatre Festival
St. Patrick's Week. Main Centers: Dublin, Cork, Limerick, Galway, Wexford
Railway Cup Finals, Croke Park, Dublin: hurling and football
National Breeders' Produce Stakes at Clonmel, Tipperary: greyhound racing
April
Welcome Wales Week, Cork
Irish Grand National, Fairyhouse, Dublin
International Hockey Festival, Dublin
West of Ireland Amateur Open Championships, Co. Sligo: golf
All Ireland Amateur Drama Finals, Athlone
May
Cork International Choral and Folk Dance Festival
Dundalk Maytime Festival and Amateur Drama International
1,000 and 2,000 Guineas: Classic Race Meeting at the Curragh, Co. Kildare
Pan Celtic Week, Killarney
Howth Festival of the Sea, Dublin
Feis Ceoil, Dublin
Bundoran Lobster Festival, Co. Donegal
Ulster Fleadh Ceoil, Monaghan
Kilkenny Beer Festival

June

An Fleadh Nua, Dublin

East of Ireland Amateur Open Championships, Co. Louth:
  golf

Westport Horse Show on the grounds of Westport House,
  Co. Mayo

Festival in Great Irish Houses

Carroll's International Golf Tournament, Woodbrook, Co.
  Dublin

Irish Sweeps Derby, Curragh, Co. Kildare

Dublin Festival of Twentieth-Century Music

International 4-Day Walks, Castlebar

Wicklow Game Fair

Westport Sea Angling Festival

Listowel Writers' Week

Festival of Tipperary

Cork Summer Show, Showgrounds, Cork

July

Galway Horse and Connemara Pony Show

Strawberry Fair, Enniscorthy, Co. Wexford

Greyhound Racing, Carrolls Derby at Shelbourne Park, Dublin

Avoca Melody Fair

August

Greyhound Racing, Laurels at Cork

Birr Vintage Week

Letterkenny International Folk Festival

Fleadh Cheoil na hEireann

Yeats' Summer School

September

Greyhound Racing, Oaks at Harold's Cross, Dublin

Liffey Descent: marathon canoe race

Festival of Kerry

All-Ireland Hurling Final, Croke Park

Waterford International Festival of Light Opera

Cork International Film Festival

All-Ireland Football Final, Croke Park

Greyhound Racing, St. Leger at Limerick
Irish St. Leger, Curragh: one of the Classic Race Meetings
Feale Festival, Abbeyfeale, Co. Limerick: selection of Feale
    Baron, traditional entertainments
Munster Veteran Car and Motor Cycle Rallies (from Blarney)
Galway Oyster Festival
Listowel Harvest Festival
International Bowling Tournament, Dun Laoghaire
October
Ballinasloe October Fair
International Song Contest, Castlebar
West of Ireland Speed-Boat Championships, Oughterard, Co.
    Galway
Wexford Festival Opera
Oireachtas Festival

APPENDIX E

GENEALOGICAL SOURCES

If you have Irish blood you will almost certainly be proud of it — quite properly. You will also, with almost equal certainty, think of some day trying to find out a little more about your Irish ancestors.

The task of tracing one's ancestors can be difficult, especially if it happens that a grandfather or great-grandfather, for political or financial reasons, saw fit to change his name along with his religious affiliations. For instance, descendants of an O'Grady from County Clare may now bear the name of Brady. It is well to remember, too, that Ireland's records have inevitably suffered in the course of her troubled history. Much valuable material has been preserved, but not as much as the searcher would like. To make the task even more difficult, an Irish surname may be borne by a very large number of people; thus, identification becomes a serious problem.

One must therefore gather and verify as much as possible every scrap of information from sources available — family papers, the memories of elderly relatives, records of church and state in one's own country. A local genealogical or historical society may be able to help. It is important to find out the full name of the emigrant ancestor, the background of his family (whether they were rich or poor, merchants or farmers), and his religion. Above all you should try to find the name of the precise place from which the emigrant came. An Irish county can be quite a large area and a surname can be borne by perhaps thousands of people in the same county. Here, particularly, a family tradition preserving the name of a parish or townland can be of great assistance.

It is to be hoped that a survey of sources listed below will also prove helpful. The author is indebted to a booklet entitled *Ireland, Tracing Your Ancestors,* issued by Bord Failte Eireann (the Irish Tourist Board) for much of this information.

Public Records. Many of the important sources of genealogical information are centralized in the city of Dublin. At the Office of the Registrar-General in the Custom House one can find the registers of births, marriages, and deaths from the year 1864, when general civil registration began, to the present day. Marriages of non-Catholics are recorded from 1845. Certified copies of entries are supplied and searches are carried out by the officials or may be made in person by those who visit the Office. A small fee will be charged. The collections of the Public Record Office at the Four Courts suffered severely in 1922, but the Office nonetheless houses today a valuable body of material. Of particular interest are the Tithe Applotment Books, which give the names of those whose holdings were subject to tithes about the year 1825; and the Valuation Office records, relating also to the first half of the last century. Also preserved here are wills, administrations, and marriage license bonds no longer extant, and valuable collections relating to particular families. In Henrietta Street is the Registry of Deeds, a most useful source of genealogical information. Its records run from 1708 to the present day, and relate to all the usual transactions in property which involve the execution of a deed — leases, mortgages, settlements. Searches may be made in person, for a small fee.

Libraries. The National Library in Kildare Street, Dublin, has a splendid collection of books and manuscripts relating to Ireland. Among the printed works are many of obvious use to the genealogist — directories, family histories, journals of local antiquarian and historical societies, topographical works, and histories of particular areas. Important also are the series of newspapers, national and local, even though birth, marriage, and death announcements were not as numerous formerly as they are now. The manuscript collections include deeds, letters, rentals, and other papers relating to many Irish families. The library is preparing an immense card index that will facilitate the use of all this material, both printed and manuscript. The Genealogical Office, a part of the National Library, is situated in Dublin Castle and has its own collections of officially recorded pedigrees, registers of armorial bearings, will abstracts, printed family histories and pedigrees, and much other genealogical and heraldic material. The Office provides advice and general information — about surnames, for example — without charge. It also undertakes searches in its own records and in outside sources, such as those described above, for a fee.

Church Records. Church records are the best source for the primary genealogical facts in the period before general civil registration. A record of baptism is obviously a proof of birth. The parochial registers of the Catholic Church are in the custody of the parish priests all over Ireland. In urban areas they can be of considerable antiquity, covering two hundred years or more, but in rural areas they are generally found to begin about the second quarter of the last century. Many parochial registers of the Church of Ireland were destroyed in 1922 in the Public Record Office where they had been deposited, but some survived and many are still in the custody of the incumbents of parishes throughout the country. The registers often go back to the eighteenth century and even before. If your ancestors were Presbyterians, the Presbyterian Historical Society (Church House, Fisherwick Place, Belfast) may be able to offer valuable assistance. The Society itself holds some Presbyterian registers and can provide information about others in the custody of local ministers. Other religious groups, such as the Religious Society of Friends (6 Eustace St., Dublin), may be able to help you.

Sources in Northern Ireland. If your emigrant ancestor or his forebears came from the northern counties of Ireland, the Public Record Office of Northern Ireland (Law Courts Building, May Street, Belfast) will have much to offer. Since this office was founded in 1924 it has built up a fine collection of records relating to the six counties of Northern Ireland — Antrim, Down, Armagh, Tyrone, Fermanagh, and Derry. The Tithe Applotment Books and other such records for these counties are in this office. In other parts of Ireland, local public libraries may have information to offer. All over the country there are cemeteries and tombstone inscriptions providing details of name and date which might not be available from any other source. These, combined with local knowledge and tradition, would be of particular interest to a genealogically-minded visitor.

Obviously there can be no guarantee that your search will be successful. But Ireland's archives are constantly growing as more sources come to light, and cataloging and indexing make them steadily more useful for your purpose. And even though the search may not be easy or fruitful, it will in most cases be well worth the effort. Indeed, a journey into the past through the pages of faded manuscripts and dusty deeds can often be quite as fascinating as the trip to Ireland itself.

NATIONAL ANTHEM

A SOLDIER'S SONG

Words by : PEADAR KEARNEY.   Music by : PADDY HEANEY

WE'LL sing a song, a soldier's song
With cheering, rousing chorus
As round our blazing fires we throng,
The starry heavens o'er us ;
Impatient for the coming fight,
And as we wait the morning's light
Here in the silence of the night
We'll chant a soldier's song.

REFRAIN :

Soldiers are we, whose lives are pledged to Ireland,
Some have come from a land beyond the wave.
Sworn to be free, no more our ancient sireland
Shall shelter the despot or the slave ;
Tonight we man the bearna baoghal
In Erin's cause, come woe or weal ;
'Mid cannon's roar and rifle's peal
We'll chant a soldier's song.

Amrán na bFiann

Seo díb a cáirde duan Oglaig
Caitréimeac, bríogmar, ceolmar,
Ár dteinte cnáim go buacac táid,
'S an spéir go mín réaltógac.
Is fionnmar faobrac sinn cum gleo
'S go tiúnmar glé roim tigeact do'n ló,
Fa ciúnas caom na h-oidce ar seol,
Seo líb, canaid Amrán na bFiann.

CURFÁ :

Sinne Fianna Fáil atá fá geall ag Éirinn,
Buidean dár sluag tar túinn do ráinig cugainn :
Fámóid beit saor, sean-tír ár sinnsear feasta
Ní fágfar fá'n tiorán ná fá'n tráil ;
Anoct a teigeam sa bearna baogail,
Le gean ar Gaedil cum báis nó saogail,
Le gunna sgréac ; fá lamac na piléar,
Seo líb canaid Amrán na bFiann.

SELECTED BIBLIOGRAPHY

Bord Failte (Irish Tourist Board). *Ireland.* An illustrated Guide to the Counties of Ireland. Dublin.

Bord Failte (Irish Tourist Board). *Ireland of the Welcomes.* Dublin.

Bulfin, William. *Rambles in Eirinn.* Dublin: M. H. Gill & Son, 1907.

Butler, Anthony. *The Book of Blarney.* London: Wolfe Publishing, 1969.

Corkery, Daniel. *The Fortunes of the Irish Language.* Cork: The Mercier Press, 1954.

Danaher, Kevin. *In Ireland Long Ago.* Cork: The Mercier Press, 1962.

Danaher, Kevin. *The Pleasant Land of Ireland.* Cork: The Mercier Press, 1970.

Dowling, P. J. *The Hedge Schools of Ireland.* Dublin: The Talbot Press, 1935.

Edgeworth, Maria. *Castle Rackrent.* London: Thomas Nelson & Sons, 1953.

Encyclopaedia of Ireland. Dublin: Allen Figgis, 1968.

Evans, E. Estyn. *Irish Folk Ways.* London: Routledge & Kegan Paul, 1957.

Garrity, Devin, ed. *The Mentor Book of Irish Poetry.* New York: The New American Library of World Literature, 1965.

Hall, Mr. & Mrs. S. C. *Ireland, its Scenery and Character.* Vol. 1-3. London: Jeremiah How, 1843.

Hyde, Douglas. *A Literary History of Ireland.* London, 1899.

Kelley, Thomas P. *The Black Donnellys.* Winnipeg, Canada: Harlequin Books, 1954.

McKiernan, Eoin, O'Shaughnessy, Lawrence, and McMahon, Sean, eds. *Eire-Ireland.* A Journal of Irish Studies. St. Paul, Minn.

MacLysaght, William. *The Tragic Story of the Colleen Bawn.* Tralee: The Kerryman, 1953.

MacMahon, Bryan. *Children of the Rainbow*. New York: Dutton, 1952.

MacManus, Seumas. *The Story of the Irish Race*. Rev. ed. New York: Devin Adair, 1972.

Macken, Walter. *The Silent People*. New York: Macmillan, 1962.

Maguire, John F. *The Irish in America*. London: Longmans, Green, 1868.

Moody, T. W., and Martin, F. X., eds. *The Course of Irish History*. Cork: The Mercier Press, 1967.

Muirhead, L. Russell, and Rossiter, Stuart, eds. *Ireland*. London: Ernest Benn, 1962.

Neeson, Eoin. *The First Book of Irish Myths and Legends*. Cork: The Mercier Press, 1965.

O'Casey, Sean. *Drums under the Window*. New York: Macmillan, 1945.

O'Casey, Sean. *Purple Dust*. London: Macmillan, 1965.

O'Connor, Frank, ed. *A Book of Ireland*. London: William Collins Sons, 1959.

O'Connor, Richard. *Portrait of a People*. New York: G. P. Putnam's Sons, 1971.

O'Donoghue, John. *In a Quiet Land*. New York: Coward-McCann, 1958.

O'Leary, Peter. *My Story*. Translated by Cyril T. O'Ceirin. Cork: The Mercier Press, 1970.

O'Mahony, Jeremiah. *West Cork and its Story*. Edited by C. B. O'Donoghue. Tralee: The Kerryman.

Orpen, Goddard H. *Ireland under the Normans*. Vol. 1. London: Oxford University Press, 1892.

O'Sullivan, Donal, ed. *Irish Folk Music*. Cork: The Mercier Press, 1969.

O'Sullivan, Maurice. *Twenty Years A-Growing*. London: Oxford University Press, 1933.

Raftery, Joseph, ed. *The Celts*. Cork: The Mercier Press, 1964.

Reynolds, James. *Ghosts in Irish Houses*. New York: Farrar, Straus and Giroux, 1947.

Roche, Richard. *The Norman Invasion of Ireland*. Tralee: Anvill Books, 1970.

Russell, Diarmuid, ed. *The Irish Reader*. New York: Viking Press, 1946.

Sayers, Peig. *An Old Woman's Reflections*. London: Oxford University Press, 1962.

Smith, Cecil Woodham. *The Great Hunger*. London: Hamish Hamilton, 1962.

Synge, John Millington. *Riders to the Sea*. London: George Allen & Unwin, 1962.

Weiner, Margery. *Matters of Felony*. New York: Atheneum, 1967.

Woodgate, M. V. *The Abbé Edgeworth*. New York: Longmans, Green, 1946.

Yeats, William Butler, ed. *Irish Folk Stories and Fairy Tales*. New York: Grosset & Dunlap.

INDEX

351